This study offers a new and original analysis of the problem of religious language. Taking as its starting point Karl Barth's doctrine of analogy, it places this doctrine within the context of German *Sprache* and *Rede* philosophies and reveals the historical links between them and the work of the philosophers Emmanuel Levinas and Jacques Derrida. Drawing out the parallels between this work and Barth's insights into the language of theology, it concludes that Barth's doctrine of analogy is a theological reading of Derrida's economy of *différance*.

This important contemporary interpretation of Karl Barth reveals his closeness to postmodern thinking and underlines his relevance to current debates on the language of theology. It will be of interest to those studying both general questions of theology and language and the particular relationship between theology and postmodernism.

BARTH, DERRIDA AND THE
LANGUAGE OF THEOLOGY

BARTH, DERRIDA AND THE LANGUAGE OF THEOLOGY

GRAHAM WARD

Peterhouse, Cambridge

CAMBRIDGE
UNIVERSITY PRESS

Published by the Press Syndicate of the University of Cambridge
The Pitt Building, Trumpington Street, Cambridge CB2 1RP
40 West 20th Street, New York, NY 10011–4211, USA
10 Stamford Road, Oakleigh, Melbourne 3166, Australia

© Cambridge University Press 1995

First published 1995

Printed in Great Britain at the University Press, Cambridge

A catalogue record for this book is available from the British Library

Library of Congress cataloguing in publication data

Ward, Graham.
Barth, Derrida and the language of theology / Graham Ward.
p. cm.
Includes index.
ISBN 0 521 47290 3 (hardback)
1. Barth, Karl, 1886–1968. 2. Derrida, Jacques.
3. Language and languages – Religious aspects –
Christianity. 4. Postmodernism – Religious aspects –
Christianity. I. Title
BR115.L25W37 1995
230′.014–dc20 94–12744 CIP

ISBN 0521 47290 3 hardback

For
Mary, Rachel and David

We walk by the sea-shore
holding firmly in our hands
the two ends of an antique dialogue
— do you love me?
— I love you.

Zbigniew Herbert

Contents

Acknowledgements

I could not now complete this book without saying something about those without whom this project would never have been realized. Three people stood alongside me – Professor Nicholas Lash, Fergus Kerr O.P. and Bishop Rowan Williams. They inspired, they encouraged, they commented and they gave generously of time they did not have. One diocese, one parish, one church and its congregation fed, housed, nurtured and nourished me throughout. Without the support of the Bishop of Bristol, Barry Rogerson, the clergy and the people of St Mary, Redcliffe (both parishioners and congregation) this book would still be gestating.

An earlier version of chapter 7 appeared in *Modern Theology*, vol. 9, no. 2, April 1993. I would like to thank Gregory and Stephen, the editors, for their patience and encouragement.

Abbreviations

Wherever it is deemed necessary, or where my study of a text is detailed, the page reference to the English translation is followed by the page reference to standard editions of the text in the original language. Where texts have not yet been translated I refer to the title in its original language. Similarly, where the titles of texts are untranslatable, then I have kept to the original. Following what has now become a custom in translating Levinas's terms *Autrui* and *Autre*, Other with a capital is used for the former, with other in the lower case for the latter.

K. BARTH

1R	*Der Römerbrief: Erste Fassung*, Gesamtausgabe Bd. 16 (Zurich: Theologischer Verlag, 1985)
2R	*The Epistle to the Romans*, tr. Edwyn C. Hoskyns (Oxford: Oxford University Press, 1933). *Der Römerbrief: Zweiter Fassung* (Munich, 1926)
WW	*The Word of God and the Words of Men*, tr. D. Horton (London, 1928). *Das Wort Gottes und die Theologie* (Munich, 1924)
GD	*The Göttingen Dogmatics: Instruction in the Christian Religion*, vol. 1, tr. Geoffrey W. Bromiley (Eerdmans: Michigan, 1990). *Unterricht in der christlichen Religion* Gesamtausgabe, Bd. 17 (Zurich: Theologischer Verlag, 1990)
A	*Anselm: Fides Quaerens Intellectum* (London: SCM, 1960)
CDE	*Die christliche Dogmatik im Entwurf*, Gesamtausgabe, Bd. 14 (Zurich: Theologischer Verlag, 1982)
I.1, I.2, II.1, III.2	*Church Dogmatics* (Edinburgh: T. & T. Clark), volumes I.1 (1936, revd edn 1975), I.2 (1956), II.1 (1957) and III.2 (1961). *Die Kirchliche Dogmatik*, I.1 (Evangelischer Verlag A. G. Zurich: Zollikon, 1952), I.2 (1948), II.1 (1948) and II.2 (1948)

M. BUBER

L   *Logos* (Heidelberg, 1960)
KM   *The Knowledge of Man*, tr., Maurice Friedman (New York: Harper Torchbooks, 1960)
D   'Dialogue' in *Between Man and Man*, tr. Ronald Gregor Smith (London: Fontana, 1961)
IT   *I and Thou*, tr. Ronald Gregor Smith (New York: Scribner's, 1958). *Dialogisches Leben* (Zurich: Gregor Muller, 1947)

E. CASSIRER

EM   *An Essay on Man* (New Haven: Yale University Press, 1944)
PSF   *Philosophy of Symbolic Forms*, in three volumes, tr. R. Manheim (New Haven: Yale University Press, 1953)
LM   *Language and Myth*, tr. S. K. Langer (New York: Dover Publc., 1953)

J. DERRIDA

SP   *Speech and Phenomena*, ed. and tr. David B. Allison (Evanston: Northwestern University Press, 1973). *La Voix et le phénomène* (Paris: Presses Universitaires de France, 1967)
WD   *Writing and Difference*, tr. Alan Bass (Chicago: Chicago University Press, 1978). *L'écriture et la différence* (Paris: Editions de Minuit, 1967)
OG   *Of Grammatology*, tr. Gayatri Spivak (Baltimore: Johns Hopkins University Press, 1976). *De la grammatologie* (Paris: Editions de Minuit, 1967)
D   *Dissemination*, tr. Barbara Johnson (Chicago: Chicago University Press, 1981). *La dissémination* (Paris: Editions du Seuil, 1972)
MP   *Margins of Philosophy*, tr. Alan Bass (Chicago: Chicago University Press, 1982). *Marges de la philosophie* (Paris: Editions de Minuit, 1972)
Pos.   *Positions*, tr. Alan Bass (Chicago: Chicago University Press, 1981). *Positions* (Paris: Editions de Minuit, 1972)
LI   *Limited Inc*, tr. Samuel Weber, ed. Gerald Graff (Evanston: Northwestern University Press, 1988).

	French edition (Paris: Galilée, 1990). First published in *Glyph* 2, 1977
Sp.	*Spurs: Nietzsche's Styles* (bilingual edition) tr. Barbara Harlow (Chicago: Chicago University Press, 1979)
EO	*Ear of the Other*, tr. Peggy Kamuf and Avital Ronell (Lincoln: University of Nebraska Press, 1988)
TA	'Of an Apocalyptic Tone Recently Adopted in Philosophy', tr. John P. Leavey, Jr. *The Oxford Literary Review*, vol. 6, no. 2 (1984). *D'un ton apocalyptique adopté naguère en philosophie* (Paris: Editions Galilée, 1983)
Alt.	*Altérités*, with Pierre-Jean Labarrière (Paris, Osiris, 1986)
OS	*Of Spirit: Heidegger and the Question*, tr. Geoffrey Bennington and Rachel Bowlby (Chicago: Chicago University Press, 1989). *De l'esprit: Heidegger et la question* (Paris: Editions Galilée, 1987)
P	*Psyché: Inventions de l'autre* (Paris: Editions Galilée, 1987)
DR	*Derrida Reader: Between the Blinds*, ed. Peggy Kamuf (Hemel Hempstead: Harvester Wheatsheaf, 1991)
MPM	*Memoires for Paul de Man*, tr. Cecile Lindsay, Jonathan Culler, Eduardo Cadava and Peggy Kamuf (New York: Columbia University Press, 1989). French edition (Paris: Editions Galilée, 1988)

F. EBNER

S	*Schriften*, Bd. 1 (Munich, 1963)

J. G. HAMANN

Nadler	*Sämtliche Werke*, ed. Josef Nadler, Bd. 1–6 (Wien, 1949–57)
Ziesemer	*Briefwechsel*, ed. Ziesemer and Henkel (Leipzig, 1949)

M. HEIDEGGER

BT	*Being and Time*, tr. J. Macquarrie and E. Robinson (Oxford: Blackwell, 1962)
OWL	*On the Way to Language*, tr. Peter Hertz and Joan Stambaugh (New York: Harper and Row, 1971). *Unterwegs zur Sprache* (Pfullingen: Gunter Neske, 1959)

PLT   *Poetry, Language, Thought*, tr. Albert Hofstadter (New York: Harper and Row, 1971)

DT   *Discourse on Thinking*, tr. John M. Anderson and E. Hans Freund (New York: Harper and Row, 1966)

EGT   *Early Greek Thinking*, tr. David Farrell Krell and Frank A. Capuzzi (New York: Harper and Row, 1975)

ID   *Identity and Difference* (Bilingual edition), tr. Joan Stambaugh (New York: Doubleday, 1962)

MFL   *The Metaphysical Foundations of Logic*, tr. Michael Heim (Bloomington: Indiana University Press, 1984)

WP   *What is Philosophy?*, tr. W. Kluback and J. T. Wilde (New York: Twayne, 1958)

TB   *On Time and Being*, tr. Joan Stambaugh (New York: Harper and Row, 1972)

J. G. HERDER

OL   *On the Origin of Language*, tr. Alexander Gode (Chicago: University of Chicago Press, 1966)

Suphan   *Sämtliche Werke*, ed. Bernhard Suphan, Bd. 1–33 (Hildeshiem, 1967)

W. HUMBOLDT

DHS   *On Language: The Diversity of Human-Language Structure and its Influence on the Mental Development of Mankind*, tr. Peter Heath (Cambridge: Cambridge University Press, 1988)

E. HUSSERL

CM   *Cartesian Meditations*, tr. Dorion Cairns (Le Hague: Nijhoff, 1960)

E. LEVINAS

To.In.   *Totality and Infinity*, tr. A. Lingis (Le Hague: Nijhoff, 1969). *Totalité et infini* (Le Haye: Nijhoff, 1961)

EDE   *En découvrant l'existence avec Husserl et Heidegger* (Paris: Vrin, 1967)

NP   *Noms Propres* (Montpellier: Fata Morgana, 1976)

OB   *Otherwise than Being or Beyond Essence*, tr. A. Lingis (Le

Hague: Nijhoff, 1981). *Autrement quêtre ou au-delà de l'essence* (Le Haye: Nijhoff, 1974)

DVI *Le Dieu qui vient a l'idée* (Paris: Vrin, 1982)

TI *Transcendance et intelligibilité* (Geneva: Labor et Fides, 1984)

CP *Collected Philosophical Papers*, ed. and tr. A. Lingis (Le Hague: Nijhoff, 1987)

TO *Time and the Other*, tr. Richard A. Cohen (Pittsburgh: Duquesne, 1987)

LR *Levinas Reader*, ed. Sean Hand (Oxford: Blackwell, 1989)

E. ROSENSTOCK-HUESSY

JC *Judaism Despite Christianity: Letters between Rosenstock and Rosenzweig* (University of Alabama Press, 1969)

CF *The Christian Future* (London: SCM, 1960)

F. ROSENZWEIG

SR *The Star of Redemption*, tr. William W. Hallo (Notre Dame: Notre Dame Press, 1970)

B *Briefe* (Berlin: 1935)

KS *Kleinere Schriften* (Berlin: 1937)

F. SAUSSURE

CGL *Course in General Linguistics*, trans. Roy Harris (London: Duckworth, 1983)

Introduction

In the Lent term, when damp winds blew in across Cambridge from the North Sea, Professor Nicholas Lash would conduct his eight-week course in the Faculty of Divinity on analogy. And in as far as any action has a definitive origin, then this book took fire and spread from the flow of molten ideas that kept each student in those classes fanning the air for breath. Why is language so important for Christian theology? Why is Christian theology forced to examine the way it speaks, writes and represents? Why must Christian theology pursue the question of, the grounds for, the character of analogy? It is from questions like these and others inchoate that this book arose.

Its argument might have started in many places, in varied times. I might have chosen to begin with the fine awareness of a correspondence between the incarnate Word and the Gospel witness in Mark and in John.[1] Another possibility for a starting point presents itself with Augustine's sophisticated understanding of the relation between *res* (or what is independent of ourselves), *signum* (or the means we use to represent what is there) and desire (the economy of love and delight).[2] A *point de départ* might have been located in the skein of potential reference which Aquinas discerns between certain creaturely *modi signifi-*

---

[1] I have examined this perspective in an essay 'Christology and Mimesis in Mark's Gospel', *Literature and Theology*, 8.1 (1994).

[2] See here R. A. Markus's pioneering 'Saint Augustine on Signs', *Phronesis*, 2 (1957); 'Language, Reality and Desire in Augustine's *De Doctrina*', by Rowan Williams and 'Augustine on Language', by Andrew Louth in *Literature and Theology*, 3.2 (1989); and chapter 2 of Caroline Harrison's *Beauty and Revelation in the Thought of Saint Augustine* (Oxford: Oxford University Press, 1992).

candi (like 'good' and 'wise') and their divine *res significata*.[3] Or I might have wandered through the tortured labyrinths of those seventeenth-century divines who struggled to find an interpretative legitimation for Scripture by equating literalism with the voice of God.[4] In fact, there are a plethora of points from which a study into the association between theology and language might have been launched. The choosing of one's beginning is, then, to some extent pragmatic. I chose to start with a reading of Karl Barth's explication of the relationship between the Word and words in *Church Dogmatics* (II.1, chapter 5). And my reasons for doing so might be distinguished as philosophical, theological and historical.

Philosophically, Barth's work was executed within the context of a major philosophical reorientation towards the problem of language. George Steiner describes the 'profound crisis of confidence in language brought on by the ruin of classic humanist values after 1914'.[5] But the crisis of and in language or, more precisely, representation had been gathering pace for many decades. The rise of empirical science, the 'discovery' of verifiable laws of nature, created a dominant belief in the early eighteenth century in the rationally determined stability of Nature. Those Shakespearean doubts about the inviolability of natural law voiced by Ulysses in *Troilus and Cressida* had been exorcised by the work of Newton, Hooke and Boyle. Alexander Pope could confidently reinstate the great chain of being and proclaim 'Unerring Nature, still divinely bright,/One clear, unchanged, and universal light' (*Essay on Criticism*, 1711). But in the post-Kantian universe any correspondences between a word and an object 'out there' were increasingly viewed as a projection of our own transcendental reasoning. Words were histori-

---

[3] Extensive work has been done in this field by: Henri Bouillard, *The Knowledge of God* (London, 1969); Richard Swinburne, *The Coherence of Theism* (Oxford: Clarendon Press, 1977); Roger White, 'Notes on Analogical Predication and Speaking about God', *The Philosophical Frontiers of Christian Theology*, eds. Brian Hebblethwaite and Stewart Sutherland (Cambridge: Cambridge University Press, 1982); David Burrell, *Knowing the Unknowable God* (Notre Dame: University of Notre Dame, 1986); and Nicholas Lash, *Theology on the Way to Emmaus* (London: SCM, 1986).

[4] See my article 'To be a Pilgrim: John Bunyan and the Language of Scripture', *Literature and Theology*, 4.1 (1990).

[5] *Extra-Territorial* (London: Faber and Faber, 1975), p. 136.

cally, culturally and even psychologically contingent. And language, which was believed to picture transparently the natural order, gradually became more opaque and problematical. If, earlier, words had been considered by some as arbitrary and conventional constructions the truth of the world, Nature, had arbitrated. Nature had been the touchstone for 'the facts of the case'. But now, in the post-Kantian universe, for words unhinged from any natural correspondence with reality there was no means of arbitration – for our models of Nature too were understood as historically and culturally conditioned. There was no access to things in themselves. All we have, to use Wittgenstein's word, is a *Weltbeschreibung*, a description of the world.

Hence the crisis of representation, which George Steiner alludes to, was twofold. First, it was a crisis concerning the *what* of representation – what was the 'natural and objective reality to which language referred?' And secondly, it was a crisis concerning the *how* of representation – how could language ever, adequately, mirror (*re*-present) what was there? The crisis was expressed in a new appeal to a nihilistic (or ambivalent) silence – the closing lines of Wittgenstein's *Tractatus*, the parables of Hugo von Hofmannsthal, the frozen heights and amnesia of Thomas Mann's sanatorium on the Magic mountain, Malévitch's *Blanc sur fond blanc*. Walter Benjamin asks 'What does language communicate? ... Language communicates the linguistic being of things. The clearest manifestation of this being, however, is language itself. The answer to the question "What does language communicate?" is therefore "All language communicates itself."'[6] The essay from which this comes, 'On Language as Such and on the Language of Man', is probably contemporary with Barth's massive unveiling of his theology of the Word in the opening volume of *Church Dogmatics*.

Barth stood biographically amid a growing concern with and for the character of language. Before him, the foundations had been laid for a philosophy of meaning and representation (*Sprachphilosophie*) through the work of Hamann (1730–88),

---

[6] Included in *One-Way Street and Other Writings*, trans. Edmund Jephcott and Kingsley Shorter (London: Verso, 1985), p. 109.

Herder (1744–1803), Humboldt (1767–1835) and the Czech
priest Bolzano (1781–1848). Surrounding him was the continuation and modification of that tradition – with Cassirer and
Saussure on one side, Carnap and Wittgenstein on another,
Benjamin and Heidegger on yet another and the philosophers of
dialogue, or *Rede* (Ebner, Rosenzweig, Buber and Rosenstock-
Huessy) on a fourth. There were others whose work still mined
the rich seams of German philology, such as Karl Vossler, whose
book *The Spirit of Language in Civilization* (1925) summed up a
whole idealistic tradition. I am not arguing that Barth was
familiar with the extent of the debate and the details of various
philosophies of language; I simply wish to point out that this was
the context within which he was situated when he came to
consider the relationship between the Word and words and the
consequences of that relationship for theology. Furthermore,
there is some evidence that he did have contact with certain
aspects of this debate.

To examine Barth's theology of language and its association
with his Christology in the context of this crisis of representation
is, therefore, not only important for understanding Barth. It is
also important for examining the relationship between Logos
and language at quite a dramatic point in the history of
theological and philosophical thought.

Furthermore, those philosophical debates about language in
the earlier part of this century have not waned in significance.
Rather, they have stirred up great dust-clouds among the ruins
of Babel. The work of Saussure (and then Benveniste), the
Moscow (and then the Prague) linguistic circles, Heidegger and
Wittgenstein, provided the joists for postmodern models of
discourse. Emmanuel Levinas, Jacques Derrida, Jacques Lacan
and Julia Kristeva inherited the legacy of those whose work
formed the context for Karl Barth's. In beginning with Barth,
then, I am concerned not simply with positioning him within an
historical and philosophical context – I am attempting to
analyse a problematic that remains a relevant problematic for
theologies and Christologies of today. For a reaction against
idealism's espousal of an absolute meaning able to stabilize and
guarantee all reference, characterizes postmodern models of
discourse. Derrida terms this immediate access through lan-

guage to the defined and meaningful 'logocentrism'.[7] Logocentric philosophers of language regard words as referring to people, objects and circumstances in the world. Words represent stable truths or facts. Derrida *et al.* criticize the metaphysical assumptions, even the ideologies, in such a view of language. Indeed, they criticize the metaphysics of language itself, which continually deceives us into believing that words are merely windows on the world. It is Barth's insight into the dialectical necessity of assuming that words name while also countering such an assumption that draws his theological work into the orbit of the postmodern debates.

Theologically, running parallel to the crisis of the representative sign was the crisis of Christology. In the wake of Enlightenment thinking theology was collapsing into philosophy and concern with the transcendent was yielding to a new immanentism. The reality of God had no need to be established upon His revelation of Himself in Jesus Christ.[8] In the post-Newtonian

---

[7] Derrida did not coin the word 'logocentrism', he is merely the first to use it extensively and systematically. Its early uses are very general. *Le Robert* defines it as only recorded in academic contexts where it is understood as '*Attitude philosophique conférant au langage la place centrale dans toute métaphysique*'. Its history in the French language goes back to 1942. The *Oxford English Dictionary* offers a more terse definition, 'Centred on reason'. It records, rather interestingly, that the first use of the word in English was by the theologian V. A. Demant in 1939. The German *Logozentrisch* is found earlier, in the vast *Der Geist als Widersacher der Seele* written by Ludwig Klages, the philosopher and psychologist, between 1929 and 1932. It is defined by *Brockhaus* as '*die den Geist als logisch-metaphysisch ordendes Prinzip in den Mittelpunkt stellen. Gegensatz – biozentrisch*'.

Earlier this century, it appears, 'logocentrism' concerned the character of ordered representation and reference, and, by extension, the philosophical debates on the relationship of mind to reality, body to soul. Derrida, in *Of Grammatology* and *Speech and Phenomena*, unearths from the word significant theological connotations. As his translator, Gayatri Spivak, observes, logocentrism comes to mean 'the belief that the first and the last things are the Logos, the Word, the Divine Mind, the infinite understanding of God, an infinitely creative subjectivity, and, closer to our time, the self-presence of full consciousness', 'Translator's Preface', *Of Grammatology*, p. lxviii. Spivak's definition draws together Derrida's analysis of logocentrism in Plato and Husserl, but something yet remains lest we forget. And too easily it is forgotten. Certainly Spivak's single sentence elides a very important distinction. The distinction, that is, between logocentrism as relating language and metaphysics to the Divine Mind of God, to the Word of God, and logocentrism as relating language and metaphysics to a transcendental subjectivity. These two forms of logocentrism play an important role, as we shall see, in both Barth's work and any appreciation of Derrida's.

[8] See here Michael J. Buckley, *At the Origins of Modern Atheism* (Yale: Yale University Press, 1987); and John Macquarrie, *Jesus Christ in Modern Thought* (London: SCM, 1990), chapter 11.

universe, arguments for the existence of God discussed Jesus Christ in relation to miracles and prophecy.[9] And with the rise of positivism in the nineteenth century, the concern with the historical Jesus focussed upon his ethical relevance, not his metaphysical claims.

It is not simply that with Barth we return to a theology that wished to reconceive Jesus of Nazareth as the Logos. Barth's predecessors (Ritschl, Herrmann and Harnack), despite their historical and ethical emphases, still wished to understand Jesus as the Son of God. But by primarily regarding the historical facts and the ethical implications as evidence for or expression of the Christological, these theologians opened themselves, in different degrees, to two problems. The first was a hermeneutical problem: the relationship between the contingent first-century events of Jesus' life and our twentieth- or nineteenth-century interpretation of them. This was a problem not adequately tackled until Heidegger developed his notion of the hermeneutical circle and Gadamer his model of dialectical horizons. Significantly, both thinkers recognized language as the hub of the hermeneutical problem. Dilthey, aware of the centrality of hermeneutics for the construction of historical worlds, nevertheless saw today and yesterday related organically, part to whole. Discovering the patterns of existence which linked the past to the present hindered the recognition of historical difference. The wholly other of the incarnation, the divinity of Christ, was eclipsed by the universal and the human. The second problem Barth's predecessors ran into, related to the first, was strictly theological. Does history not provide other figures whose lives express an ethical excellence? Why is Jesus in particular the Christ? And so the anthropological bias with which these theologians examined the life of Christ continued the dissolution of Christology. Christ was thrown into the winds of relativism.

With Barth's work a new Christological note is sounded. An historical *and* suprahistorical particularism is argued for. A new direction for theology was initiated. Barth stands, then, at the confluence of a new emphasis upon Christology and mediation,

---

[9] See here A. E. McGrath, *The Making of Modern German Christology* (Oxford: Blackwell, 1986).

and the crisis of representation. His work, this book argues, is dominated by a concern to relate these two themes and reveal their intimate association.

Historically, Barth's theology is situated at a cultural juncture that profoundly influences us today. Fritz K. Ringer, in his classic study of the German educated middle classes between 1890 and 1933, writes: 'By the early 1920s, they were deeply convinced that they were living through a profound crisis, a "crisis of culture", of "learning", of "values", or of the "spirit".'[10] The crisis of representation which we charted above was part of a wider crisis of legitimation and confidence in Western European civilization. (There appears to be a correspondence between semiotic, political and theological forms of representation.) It was a crisis intimately linked with the decline of idealism, the rise of positivism, the imperialism of technology and the mushrooming of what Adorno and Horkheimer called 'the culture industry'.[11]

The word *Krisis* echoed through Prussian and Austrian literature from the 1880s and infected the German *Zeitgeist* well into the 1930s when the phenomenologist Edmund Husserl, racing against a terminal illness, was attempting (ultimately in vain) to complete his monumental study *The Crisis of European Sciences*. Concurrently, another word was making its impact on the German language, the word 'Modern'. Towards the end of the nineteenth century German culture became preoccupied with the notion of modernism.[12] This reached fever-pitch in the early Weimar period[13] as the work of Musil, Rilke, Mann, the Futurists and Dadaists triggered an aesthetic revolution. Briefly, modernism's programme was to 'make it new'. It courted the unconventional and nonconformist in a conscious effort to overthrow the traditional perspective and stock expectations. Its dynamism was aggressive, disruptive and even apocalyptic.

---

[10] Fritz K. Ringer, *The Decline of the German Mandarins: the German Academic Community, 1890–1933* (Harvard: Harvard University Press, 1969), p. 3.

[11] See *Dialectic of Enlightenment* (London: Verso, 1973), pp. 120–67.

[12] See 'The Name and Nature of Modernism' by Malcolm Bradbury and James McFarland in *Modernism*, ed. Malcolm Bradbury and James McFarland (London: Penguin, 1976).

[13] See Ringer, *The Decline of the German Mandarins*, p. 276.

Hostility to the First World War fed its anger against the *status quo* and its desire for a creativity that would be transcultural, transclass and transfrontier.

The extent to which today's 'postmodernism' is a 'post-modernism' (as someone like Rosalind Krauss would argue[14]), or ironically a pre-modernism (as Lyotard argues[15]) or is in fact a late development within modernism itself,[16] remains a highly contentious issue, and one which I will not broach in this study. But Barth was born and raised among the cultural mandarins and his theology of the Word within our words was produced in the context of a modernism fuelled by *Krisis*. The radicalism, the iconoclasm and the prophetic tones of his second edition of *Romans* cannot be separated from, but rather augments our appreciation of, German culture at that time.[17] And to the extent that we are the cultural heirs of modernism, and arguably are still caught up in its problems and paradoxes, then Barth's work is part of that legacy. Barth's work is an expression of the modernist dilemma, a dilemma closely associated with the crisis of representation – a crisis dominating postmodern thought. As Lyotard has recently said: 'Postmodernity is not a new age, it is the rewriting of some features modernity had tried or pretended to gain ... such a rewriting, as has already been said, was for a long time active in modernity itself.'[18]

For those philosophical, theological and historical reasons, then, this book begins with the way Karl Barth attempts to bring together a theology of the Word as Christ, the revelation of God, with a philosophy of language.

The book is divided into three sections. The first section treats

---

[14] See her essay, 'The Originality of the Avant-Garde' in *Zeitgeist in Babel: The Post-Modernist Controversy*, ed. Ingeborg Hoesterey (Bloomington: Indiana University Press, 1991), pp. 66–79. See also *Weimar Culture: The Outsider as Insider*, Peter Gay (London: Penguin, 1969).

[15] Jean-François Lyotard, *The Postmodern Condition*, trans. Geoffery Bennington (Manchester: Manchester University Press, 1986).

[16] See C. Barry Chabot's essay in *Zeitgeist in Babel*, pp. 22–41.

[17] See here Stephen Webb's *Re-figuring Theology: The Rhetoric of Karl Barth* (Albany: State University of New York Press, 1991) – chapter one; Richard Roberts' 'Barth and the Eschatology of Weimar: A Theology on its Way?' in *Theology on the Way?* (Edinburgh: T. & T. Clark, 1992); and Walter Lowe's *Theology and Difference: The Wound of Reason* (Bloomington: Indiana University Press, 1993).

[18] 'Rewriting Modernity', *SubStance*, 54 (1987), p. 8.

the development of Karl Barth's doctrine of the *analogia fidei*, placing his treatment of it in the context of *Sprachphilosophie* and *Redephilosophie*. It concludes by pointing out Barth's evident difficulty in defining the nature of a transcendental Word that is nevertheless immanently apprehensible in the language we speak and read. He is struggling to define the operation of a Logos beyond the embrace of any language system, that is, beyond logocentrism. The second section examines Barth's problematic as it is handled in the later work of his contemporary Heidegger, who is seen as making an important step towards a coherent and consistent account of Barth's problematic. But Heidegger's work, I will argue (as Heidegger himself argued), is not theological. It is the French philosopher, Emmanuel Levinas, who, starting from Heidegger, presents a theological account of a transcendental Logos (*un logos de l'infini*) disrupting, while also providing the condition for, the logocentric (*un logos du fini*). Levinas's philosophy of Saying can then be directly compared with Barth's theology of the Word. The comparison reveals why Barth, as a theologian, cannot avoid the metaphysics of language, and, similarly, why Levinas, as a philosopher of language, cannot avoid being theological. But the comparison also reveals how much more penetrating is Barth's examination of the Otherness of God and the manner in which this Otherness both offers itself to and withholds itself from the language whereby we represent our knowledge of the divine. The final section looks at the model for discourse propounded by Jacques Derrida in dialogue with the work of Emmanuel Levinas. It analyses a relationship between Derrida's economy of *différance* and Barth's understanding of the *analogia fidei*. The conclusion argues that Barth's theology of the Word in relation to words – his *analogia fidei*, his Christology and incarnational theology – are theological readings of a law of textuality, a law of performance and repetition described by Derrida as the economy of *différance*. Or, looked at the other way around, I suggest that language is always and ineradicably theological.[19]

---

[19] Barth's contemporary, Karl Vossler, in his book *The Spirit of Language and Civilization*, trans. Oscar Oesar (London: Kegan Paul, 1932), recognized exactly this point: 'in every language a peculiar upward urge manifests itself, which, in its ultimate orientation, is religious ... religious in the widest sense of the spiritual', p. 50.

The burden of this book is, therefore, threefold. First, it is a new reading of Barth's work on the Word, a reading which attempts to show not simply his relevance but his centrality for theology in the midst of today's postmodern debates on rhetoric. Secondly, it is a reading of the theological significance of Derrida's work, particularly the operation in discourse of *différance*. It sets out to chart the relationship between Barth's theology of the Word and Derrida's analysis of discourse, both diachronically (in terms of the historical connections) and synchronically (in terms of the structural and thematic parallels). Thirdly, it argues for theology's necessarily intimate association with philosophies of language and representation. To return to those multiplying questions in Professor Lash's seminars, what I am arguing here is that theology's primary concern is with its own possibility, its own relationship as a discourse to the original *Deus dixit*. Hence theology always requires investigations into the nature of discourse and the character of its relationship with the Word of God. Because this is theology's fundamental concern, it has always been critical and suspicious of representation and so it is uniquely able to find a place in postmodern thinking. If my thesis and analysis suggest anything, they suggest that the time is ripe for a new theology of the Word, arising from a re-reading of Barth's.

Part I
Logocentrism

CHAPTER I

Karl Barth's two models for the nature of language

'The Church', Barth writes, in the opening paragraphs of *Church Dogmatics*, 'produces theology ... by subjecting itself to self-examination' (1.1, p. 4/2). And the task of dogmatics, he adds a little later, 'is the self-examination of the Christian Church in respect of the content of its distinctive talk about God [*Rede von Gott*]' (1.1, p. 11/10). The content and concern of theology is, therefore, 'talk about God' [*Rede von Gott*]. This 'talk' is the distinctive possession of the Church. There are two questions which arise here. Who talks? And whence comes such talk? And there are two possible answers to both questions: human beings or God. The whole content and concern of theology lies between the stakes of these two questions. This is why theology for Barth is a theology of the Word and why understanding the nature of language is fundamental to theology's examination of the Church's 'talk about [*von*] God'.

In the first chapter of *Church Dogmatics*, Barth maps out a grid for his subsequent analysis of the Word. Section 4 examines its form [*Gestalt*]; section 5 its nature [*Wesen*]; section 6 its episteme [*Erkennbarkeit*]. The contents and structure of sections 5 and 6 parallel each other in so far as they each begin with a question concerning the object under discussion (the nature or the episteme of God's Word, respectively) and each conclude on what remains hidden and unable to be presented (on the mystery of God in section 5 and the need for faith in section 6). What can be affirmed and understood of the nature and episteme of God's Word must then always become questionable. Section 5 makes the two facets of God's Word plain: its imme-diacy, as a physical occurrence [*physisches Geschehen*] which implies that a 'naturalism is not to be banished from theological utterance [*Sprache*]' (1.1, p. 136/141), and its mediation, since in theological utterance we have to be clear about what it means to employ naturalistic terms (1.1, p. 136/140). The grid Barth maps out in the opening volume, then, is composed of two antithetical axes. The first is the form, nature and epistemology of language as they are revealed directly by God. The second is the relationship between Word [*Wort*], talk [*Rede*] and utterance [*Sprache*] which mediate, for the Church, this immediacy. The axes are examined in dialectic relationship to each other and within the context of an enshrouding agnosticism, a pervasive sense of the mystery of God and the need for faith.

The grid will inform the whole of the *Church Dogmatics*, to the extent that the doctrine of the Word of God provides the dogmatic basis for the three-fold doctrine of God as seen in Creation, Reconciliation and Redemption. Fundamental to the coherence of this structure, and to the coherence of the immediacy of the Word in the mediation of words, is chapter 5, in which Barth develops his notion of the *analogia fidei*. This is the theological *and* linguistic hub around which the whole of the *Church Dogmatics* circulates. It is with chapter 5 that our analysis of Barth's theology of language must begin.

Our words are not our own property [*Eigentum*], but His . . . We use our words improperly [*uneigentlich*] and pictorially – as we can now say, looking back from God's revelation – when we apply them within the confines of what is appropriate to us as creatures. When we apply them to God they are not alienated from their original object and therefore from their truth, but, on the contrary, restored to it . . . Now it certainly does not lie in our power to return our words to their proper use . . . In His revelation God controls His property. (II.1, pp. 229–30/259–60)

We are presented here, *in nuce*, with Barth's doctrine of *analogia fidei*. Barth, who is repeatedly concerned with bringing flights of theological abstraction down to the concrete and contingent, has already illustrated his position as follows:

We possess no analogy on the basis of which the nature and being of God as the Lord can be accessible to us . . . No idea [*Vorstellung*] that we can have of 'lord', of 'lordship', will ever lead us to this idea, even though we extend it infinitely. Outside the ideas that we can have, there is a lordship over our soul, a lordship even over our being in death, a genuine effective lordship. Only as we know God's lordship will our own ideas [*möglichen Vorstellungen*] of lordship have content, and, within their limits, existence. (II.1, pp. 75–6/82)

There are potential representations [*moglichen Vorstellungen*] of lordship and then there is genuine, effective [*wirklich vollzogene*] lordship. The measure of that effectiveness lies in the adequation of the word with its 'original object' *and* our recognition of that adequation. The move from potential to realization lies with the event of revelation. This transforms our perceptions, enabling us to recognize the object that our word names. Without this revelation human beings can only use words 'pictorially' or equivocally. Their meaning (Barth's 'content'), without revelation, is either a distortion or an illusion – depending upon how Barth (who does not elaborate further) understands the association between the pictures or image-words and the original object they are referring to. It is only when God's Word (Christ as Logos) takes on human form (as both Jesus of Nazareth and the phonetic/graphic flesh of discourse) that we have genuine knowledge. Revelation (which can only be appropriated retrospectively, as a memory, a 'looking back') enables us to recognize that our language is analogical. The analogical character of language is substantiated by God alone and, as that character appears, so we, as recipients, believe. We read this language by faith, through faith, to faith; we read the language as analogous by revelation, through revealedness to the revealer. Our reading by faith, therefore, is a participation in the Trinity as Barth describes its operation in chapter 2 of the *Church Dogmatics* – the Father as Revealer, the Spirit as Revealedness and the Son as the Revelation. The doctrine of *analogia fidei* is inseparable from a more general theology of reading which Barth is developing.

A hermeneutic circle is being described which moves within and understands the divine intra-dialogue, and faith is the condition for entry. But Barth insists we recognize that there are two radically different forms of hermeneutical activity in operation. On the one hand, there is a human being's continuous attempt 'to answer the riddle of his own existence . . . to strike a balance between himself and his world' (II.1, p. 85/93). The question provoking the hermeneutical activity here is an existential one. The meaningfulness of life for a human being lies in being able to master himself and the world and regard the goal and origin of this endeavour as his god (II.1, p. 86/93–4). Human beings are, then, *natürlich, homo hermeneuma*. Our knowledge of ourselves and our world is conditioned by transcendental *a priori* which govern and constitute what we perceive and how we understand that perception. Our knowledge is mediated. Barth's *natürlich Mensch* is founded upon a Kantian anthropology. On the other hand, by faith, human beings participate in a second hermeneutic activity, that of the Trinity, in which God speaks and human beings are brought to understand the meaning of that Word. In this hermeneutic activity, where there is an equation of word with object and the communication is direct, God speaks and interprets God by God (Jesus Christ) through God (the Holy Spirit) to God. No synthesis is possible between these two activities, the one anthropological and the other theological; the latter reveals the former to be an idol, or, in terms of linguistics, the endless play of signifiers.

A dialectic remains, evident in the structure of the sections composing chapter 5, for each of its three sections are subdivided into two parts, the first part viewing the matter from God's perspective and the second viewing it from the human perspective. Furthermore, what is called 'The Fulfilment of the Knowledge of God' in section 25 is both balanced and radically qualified by 'The Limits of the Knowledge of God' in section 27. Dialectical thinking structures Barth's discussion of the Word in words, the *analogia fidei*, but it is a dialectic without synthesis. The dialectic is a paralogical journey towards the horizon of an eschatological dawn.

There are many questions raised by this doctrine of the *analogia fidei* which several other theologians have attempted to tease out and answer,[1] questions which branch into the far

---

[1] The coherence of Karl Barth's doctrine of *analogia fidei* has preoccupied the following studies: from *Antwort: Karl Barth* (Zollikon-Zurich: Evanglische Verlag, 1956), Gottlieb Sotingen's '*Analogia Entis in Analogia Fidei*', pp. 266–71 and Walter Kreck's '*Analogia Fidei oder Analogia Entis?*', pp. 272–86; John McIntyre's 'Analogy', *Scottish Journal of Theology*, 12 (1959); H. G. Pohlmann's *Analogia Entis oder Fidei?* (Göttingen, 1965); Henri Bouillard's *The Knowledge of God* (London, 1969), pp. 97–126; W.

reaches of Barth's theology. We will be unable to understand the operation of *analogia fidei* without examining Barth's doctrines of time and history, election and providence. Eventually we will need to enter the *analogia entis/analogia fidei* debate and discuss the extent to which one doctrine requires the other. We will need to examine what appears to be the punctiliar intrusion of what Barth describes as the self-evidencing Word-event and discuss the extent to which he is aware of the potential for self-deception and solipsism. We will also need to examine the relation between description and reality in his work – the relationship between rhetoric and truth. These questions, and the analyses they demand, will shape the material of Part I of this book.

For the moment, in this first chapter, we must examine more particularly the nature of language as Barth conceives it; we must excavate the presuppositions about language that he is working with in describing this doctrine of *analogia fidei*. For God as both language's absolute Signifier and the enforcer of an *a priori* univocity necessarily robs language of any human value. And where semantics are consumed in theophany, from whence comes the phenomenon of language? To what extent can it be God's property paralleling the created order itself? Is language God-given (Adam being taught by revelation how to name), or a human response to the divine (Adam being allowed to name the world for himself), or a postlapsarian product having nothing to do with God Himself and everything to do with human conventions, processes of socialization and civilization? What is, then, the economy of signification for Barth? If, on the one hand, language is divine in origin, then, as the Word presses in upon human words, language becomes sacramental. If it is sacramental, then its sacramental character needs explication (is it sacramental in a transubstantial or a consubstantial sense?)

Pannenberg's 'Analogy and Doxology' in *Basic Questions*, vol. 1 (London: SCM, 1970); Roger White, 'Notes on Analogical Predication and Speaking About God', *The Philosophical Frontiers of Christian Theology*, ed. B. Hebblethwaite and S. Sutherland (Cambridge: Cambridge University Press, 1982); Henry Chavannes's *The Analogy between God and the World in St Thomas Aquinas and Karl Barth* (New York: Vantage Press, 1992). I have learnt much from these penetrating studies, although my own approach offers different answers because it approaches the question of the doctrine's coherence from a very different point of view.

especially if Barth is to avoid allowing language to become the basis for a natural theology. Where phonetic codes are viewed as 'containing' meaning or ideas (whether these ideas belong to God or human beings) language presents the possibility of being a *tertium quid*, a necessary mediator between God and human beings. Barth's rejection of (his version of) the Catholic doctrine of *analogia entis* is precisely because it provides a contact point between the divine and the creaturely. He embraces the Reformed notion that only revelation itself establishes the contact point between the divine and the human; that without this revelation human sin entails the loss of 'all benefits of divine grace by which he [man] could have been led back into the way of life', to quote Calvin.[2] So then what role does language informed by God have in the economy of salvation?

On the other hand, if language is a human construct, defining, even constituting, human realities, can Barth's God really speak to human beings at all without compromising His nature? And how are we to identify such speaking? Since there is evidently communication between human beings, what is the economy of this signification and how does it differ from or relate to *analogia fidei*? Suggestions that language 'contains' ideas smacks of some notion of a correspondence-theory of language. What model of the operation of 'ordinary' language, then, is Barth presupposing throughout chapter 5?

These are the questions that will concern us in this chapter. They are necessarily at the root of those deeper questions informing the whole of this book: why theology requires a philosophy of language and how a theology of language or the Word relates to the Incarnation, Jesus Christ as the Incarnate Logos. Barth, like Augustine and Aquinas before him, cannot and does not leave these questions unanswered. To leave these philosophical (and what has been more recently termed semiotic) questions unanswered or untackled is seriously to undermine the coherence of his theological project: the description of the relationship between human knowledge and the operation of the Trinity.

---

[2] *Institutes of Christian Religion: 1536 edition* (London: Collins, 1986), p. 16.

THE UNFOLDING OF CHAPTER 5

Barth's theology of language develops dramatically as his ideas unfold over the three sections of chapter 5. He begins by drawing attention to specific words: 'the accessibility of the nature and being of God as Lord, Creator, Reconciler and Redeemer' (II.1, p. 79/86). As such, he appears not to be outlining a theology of language *tout court*, but rather, like Denys and Aquinas, a theology of predication or divine names. Aquinas developed a doctrine of analogy of attribution in which certain limit-concepts (words like 'good', 'pure' and 'wise') can only refer properly to God and improperly to the created order. All other predications are deemed metaphorical.[3] To a certain extent Barth is wishing to do something similar. Much later in the chapter (in section 27 on 'The Veracity of Man's Knowledge of God') he examines the notion of '*analogia attributionis*, a similarity of two objects which consists in the fact that what is common to them exists first and properly in the one, and then, because a second is dependent upon it, a second' (II.1, p. 238/268). He examines this notion in relation to the work of the seventeenth-century Reformed theologian Quenstedt and states plainly that '[w]e, too, have sought and found the analogy in an *attributio*, the relationship of an *analogans* with an *analogatum*' (II.1, p. 238/269). He develops his ideas through a critique of what Quenstedt termed *attributionis intrinsece*, where the 'analogy will belong to God, but also to the creature, "inwardly", *proprie . . . per habitudinem*' (ibid.). Barth returns to the Lutheran emphasis upon justification by faith alone, 'that which converts the creature into an analogue of God does not lie in itself and its nature . . . [but] lies only in the veracity of the object known analogously in the knowledge of God' (II.1, p. 239/270). Therefore, he concludes that the creature possesses the analogy '*extrinsece* in the form of *apprehensio*' (ibid.). This is an epistemological or intuitive possession, not an ontological one.

Barth accepts, then, what might be termed *analogia attributionis extrinsece*. But two questions arise. The first we will trace the

---

[3] *Summa Theologiae I. Q.13*, ed. H. McCabe (London: Blackfriars, 1964).

answer to as we continue – that is, what range of terms can be understood as such analogies and what status does the rest of language have in relation to this range of terms? The second is much more complex and will reoccur throughout our analysis of chapter 5 – that is, is *analogia attributionis extrinsece* possible at all? Is Barth's reasoning at all coherent ? Proceeding, as he does, from a neo-Kantian appreciation of the intentional activity of the human mind, *can* something be possessed *apprehensio* that is not also *intrinsece*? To what extent can there be knowledge at all of what is absolutely *extrinsece*? That, as we shall see, is the one question running throughout this book. How can anything be known without it also being recognized? How can there be a wholly other who addresses us? For the moment we must let this second question, and the questions consequent upon it, hang and draw, while we examine the first question concerning the relation of analogical predicates to non-analogical language.

The list of predicates Barth brings to our attention – 'Lord', 'Creator', 'Reconciler' and 'Redeemer' – are all Trinitarian titles issuing from Scripture. One might expect then that this list would be supported by a doctrine of Scripture in which the Bible is understood as opening up for us a transfigured world. In this world the meaning of such titles is dependent upon their context, their employment in the testimonies to the advent of God's Word, the incarnation of Jesus Christ. And to a certain extent this is what Barth does. We are told that the contents of the Bible constitute a single witness (II.1, p. 108/120), because even though 'in the form (*Form*) of human thoughts, it points above all human thoughts to the event (*Ereignis*) of the encounter of God with man in Jesus Christ, and therefore to the occurrence (*Ereignis*) of the truth in which there is no Yes and No' (II.1, p. 105/116). But such an account seems to suggest that it is not simply that certain titles can be attributed properly to God, but that every word in the Bible 'points' to the 'occurrence of the truth'. In Barth's analysis of the relationship between the Word and words in Scripture, then, we quickly move from nouns to statements, predicates to sentences, analogies to narratives.

This transition, from an attempt to outline a doctrine of analogy to a theology of Scriptural discourse, is fundamental, and the inability to perceive this transition and the resulting confusion of the two tasks have been the source of much misreading of chapter 5. It is important to see what questions arise because of this transition and how Barth fails to answer them because his ultimate concern is to move on from a theology of Scriptural discourse to a theology of discourse itself. For there is a traditional strand of conservative theology which has always held that Scripture *en face* gives access to the truth about God and that the language of Scripture somehow differs from other forms of language. In the seventeenth-century this literalist view of Scripture is evident in the work of John Owen and A. Quenstedt. The basis for the views of these Reformers was a doctrine of verbal inspiration that led, as a corollary, to a doctrine of the inerrancy of Scripture. 'The Holy Spirit not only inspired in the prophets and apostles the content and the sense contained in the Scripture, or the meaning of the words, so that they might of their own free will clothe and furnish these thoughts with their own style and words, but the Holy Spirit actually supplied, inspired and dictated the very words and each and every term individually', Quenstedt wrote.[4] But Barth provides no such account of biblical inspiration (in fact his *Göttingen Dogmatics* often inveigh against such an idea). Neither does he endorse a doctrine of the inerrancy of Scripture. So we are given, at this point, no insight into how the Word takes possession of human words and thoughts; we are merely told that it does so. There is no account of human cognition, reasoning or imagination.[5] Nevertheless an account is necessary as a consequence of the shift from analysing divine names towards a more general theology of language. For the doctrine of analogy does not require a doctrine of inspiration, in that it takes as its basis for explanation a God-given correlation between human logic, the order of creation and divine reasoning. A doctrine of analogy does not demand a doctrine of punctiliar

---

[4] Quoted by R. Preus in *The Theology of Post-Reformation Lutheranism* (Saint Louis: Concordia, 1970), vol. 1 p. 281.

[5] In the next chapter we will recognize the same problem as it occurs in Hamann's work. Paul Ricoeur has also drawn attention to the absence of any account of human cognition, of how the Word is recognized within words, in Bultmann's doctrine of the Word (see chapter 3).

revelation which bypasses human cognition, for a doctrine of analogical correspondence *is* a doctrine of general revelation.

Barth's reluctance to expound a doctrine of biblical inspiration is explicable when we understand that he does not wish to reduce the operation of the Word simply to Scripture. He takes another step beyond a concern with analogical predication – God as Lord, Creator, Reconciler and Redeemer – towards a concern for a theology of discourse generally, when he analyses the concept 'man'. Again the word is associated with a Christological title, 'Son of Man', and a Christological property, but the implications of what Barth has to say, as he himself realizes, are far wider than an understanding of the language of Scripture. It 'is not man as such, and not even Christian man, but Jesus Christ, the incarnate Son of the Father, revealed in his cross and resurrection, who is the truth and life of man – the real (*wirkliche*) man, to whom we have to keep if we do not want to speak meaninglessly and futilely, but with final substance and content of man' (II.1, p. 153/171). There is, then, the real 'man', Jesus Christ, and there is what he later terms in the *Church Dogmatics* the 'phantom man' (*der Schattenmensch*).[6]

The rhetoric of *wirkliche* has strong positivist overtones and points to what Barth now requires with this new turn in his argument. It is not simply a doctrine of the inspiration of Scripture that is needed, but a theological epistemology which clarifies the relationship between knowledge of the Word and our own language. He needs to outline this epistemology not simply in order to describe how the Word is apprehensible in words, and so how it is we have any knowledge at all; he needs to do it in order to legitimate what he himself is doing, in order to legitimate his own language-use, his theological exposition of the Word. And although he is aware that it is a theological epistemology rather than a 'general theory of human knowledge' (II.1, p. 183/205) that is required, he still needs to outline the relationship between a theological epistemology and 'a general theory of human knowledge'.

Barth's account of the 'general theory of human knowledge',

---

[6] See III.2 and section 44 on 'The Phenomena of the Human'.

as detailed in chapter 5, is Kantian to the extent that it endorses the constitutive nature of the subjective consciousness. He accepts that 'We are masters of what we can apprehend. Viewing and conceiving certainly mean encompassing, and we are superior to, and spiritually masters of, what we can encompass' (II.1, p. 188/211). He accepts the neo-Kantian anthropology, as Wilhelm Herrmann (his teacher) did before him: the 'original and proper unity between the possessor and the possessed ... is recollected [*Wiedererinnerung*] in the act of the knowledge of the world by man, and conversely, as the bolder philosophers have always seen and said, the world achieves self-awareness in man and his knowledge' (II.1, p. 189/212). Our knowledge is always a recollection [*Wiedererinnerung*]. There is always a temporal gap between perception and conception. So our knowledge is never a complete knowledge of what is, of the 'thing in itself', only of what is constituted in recollection.

It is within this 'general theory of human knowledge' that Barth articulates his theological epistemology.

In the act of the knowledge of God, as in any other cognitive act, we are definitely active as the receivers of images [*von Bildern*] and creators of counter-images [*von Gegenbildern*] ... Our viewing as such is certainly capable of receiving images of the divine [*Götterbilder*]. And our conceiving as such is certainly capable of creating idolatrous pictures [*Götzenbilder*] ... [And so] when we are occupied with God's revelation ... we are still not capable ourselves of having fellowship with God, and therefore viewing and conceiving Him, and therefore realising [*vollziehen*] our knowledge of God. (II.1, p. 182/204)

The dichotomy between impressions received and impressions created by our inevitable involvement in what is received and how, is unbridgeable. Barth offers us no synthesis, no mediation. In fact, there is a parallel drawn between the impressions received as God-images and the idol-images we create in responding to what is received. The gap between object and representation is not only unbridgeable, it is complex and nuanced. For there is God, the image of God and the counter-image of God. Furthermore, into this baseless 'knowledge' language has not yet been brought to play – although the notion of our creating counter-images can be translated as our creating counter-metaphors. There is, then, not just one gap but several – object, image, counter-image and language – issuing fundamentally from the Kantian divide between the noumenal and the phenomenal. So despite, again, the positivist language of 'real viewing' and 'real conceiving', there is, in fact, no positive, empirical communication at all. But for Barth that does not mean there is no knowledge: 'knowing God, we necessarily know His hiddenness' (II.1, p. 184/206). What we 'know' (and what legitimacy does this word 'know' have when it is really a not-knowing?) is an absence. More specifically, this absence becomes a positive property of God. The absence refers to, points to, is an index for, God. 'At this very point [*Gerade*] the truth breaks [*aufleuchten*] imperiously and decisively before us' (II.1, p. 183/205). The revelation, the truth, which is again described in a rhetoric connoting immediate and direct communication, is that God is absent, but it is an absence that Barth presents in positivist metaphors and reads theologically as the *incomprehensibilitas Dei*. What we know – and that only indirectly, through recollection and counter-image – is a rupture-in-continuity that cannot be 'dialectically encompass[ed]' (II.1, p. 188/211). It is a rupture of meaning that places everything in question simply by being other than meaning (though not necessarily meaningless). This rupture is read theologically as the judgement under which God places all human knowledge.

The question arises, then, as to why Barth combines a positivist rhetoric and a transcendental epistemology for an apophatic end. The answer (and Barth's brilliance becomes evident in his sheer anticipation of all the questions) lies in the fact that this negative moment becomes a positive one. For 'on the basis of revelation ... [our] views and concepts ... can and will participate in the truth' and provide us with 'an approximation (*proseggisis*), i.e., a movement in the direction of the being and essence of God, and it does not therefore lack the ability ... to attain a reflection [*Abbild*] of what it intends and seeks' (II.1, p. 202/226–7). The reflection is founded upon God laying claim to our 'views and concepts'. By revelation a relationship is forged between our viewing-image [*Bild*], our conceiving counter-image [*Gegenbild*] and a reflection [*Abbild*] of the Godhead. It is thus that revelation becomes both a radically negative and a radically positive moment in human cognition. This *Abbild* is the focussed site for a torsion between that which is immediate, direct, imperial, empirical and concrete and that which is mediate, indirect, subservient, synthetic and representational.

As yet there has been no analysis of language, only of 'views and concepts', which, as we have seen, constitute a dialectical tension within a Kantian epistemology. It is a notorious fact that Kant himself paid too little attention to language – as both Hamann and Herder, and later Bolzano, made plain. Kant built upon a semantic swamp.[7] Barth, on the other hand, began by examining a small group of Trinitarian terms – his concern throughout lies with the capacity of language to communicate the Word. It is at this point in chapter 5 that he adds to viewing and conceiving the act of speaking. He writes that it 'is well to establish explicitly that all this is true of any word which man can express on the ground of his viewing and perceiving [*Begreifen* – a misprint or mistranslation here, for on all other occasions *Begreifen* is translated as "conceiving"]. It is not only of the attempt of scientific theology to speak of God in strict concepts' (II.1, p. 195/218–19). Barth now develops his argument for the inadequacy and 'inner limitation of all human language' (ibid.). But how does the three-fold *Bild–Gegenbild– Abbild* of human cognition relate to words and propositions? Put another way – what is happening to the word 'image' (*Bild*) when Barth informs us that 'our images of perception [*Wahrneh- mungsbilder*], thought [*Denkbilder*] and words [*Wortbilder*] neither are nor can be images of God [*Bilder Gottes*]' (ibid.)?

It is in part 2 of section 27, 'The Veracity of Man's Knowledge of God', that Barth proceeds to explain:

> Our thinking, which is executed [*sich vollziehendes*] in views and concepts, is our responsibility to ourselves. Our speech [*Rede*] is our responsibility to others. In this two-fold responsibility . . . we are verily claimed by [revelation] . . . We have to tell ourselves what is told us, and we have also to tell it to others. (II.1, p. 211/237)

[7] See J. Alberto Coffa, *The Semantic Tradition from Kant to Carnap* (Cambridge: Cambridge University Press, 1991), p. 21.

Thought is an internal telling ourselves. Speech is the external telling it to others. Revelation is a telling that is both internal and external to the self. There is no revelation without *both* the passivity of reception (as revelation 'claims' us) *and* the twofold activity of telling ourselves and others. Only on the basis of this both/and, the dialectic, is there knowledge of God's revelation. But what is suggested by this distinction in 'our speech' is the existence of two languages, each foreign to the other, each maintaining its own integrity, each involved in the dialectic: human speech and God's Word. Since there is communication and something is 'told' then there must be a means of translation. But what is the economy of this translation? 'God's true revelation comes from out of itself to meet what we can say with our human words and makes a selection from among them to which we have then to attach ourselves in obedience' (II.1, p. 227/256). It appears that the omniscient God acts as translator, choosing particular words from the field of human language to act as vehicles for the transposition of meaning. He can do this because the words have been 'alienated from their proper and original sense and usage' and so 'He takes to Himself something that already belongs originally and properly to Him ... Creatures who are the suitable [*angemessene*] object of our human views, concepts and words are actually His creation. But our thought and language in their appropriateness [*Angemessenheit*] to this object are also His creation' (II.1, p. 228/257).

In the move, then, from analysing the act of revelation upon human cognition to analysing the act of revelation upon human language two observations are made. First, that human cognition and human language are separate activities. Repeated throughout the early part of chapter 5 is the dyad 'viewing and conceiving', to which is later added the triad 'viewing, conceiving, speaking' or 'views, concepts, words'. The continual employment of these formulas to discuss the relationship between perception of the world and human discourse can be no accident. Given the movement also from examining human cognition to examining language, it would seem evident that Barth understands these three 'viewing, conceiving, speaking' as successive stages by which intuition becomes expression. Perception gives rise to concepts which are subsequently robed in phonetic flesh. We find a similar economy outlined by Schleiermacher.[8] Thinking is distinct from language. Words are designatory; they are representations of ideas and truth is measured by the adequacy of the correspondence between these ideas and their verbal representations to objects in the world. God's revelation perfects that correspondence, restores the appropriateness [*Angemessenheit*] or the adequate proportion between views, concepts and words. In the act of revelation, then, God redeems human beings from that Kantian transcendental consciousness which divorced objects out there from one's perceptions and conceptions of them. The true correspondence or analogy is restored.

Secondly, in this move from the analysis of human cognition to human discourse, we have returned to an emphasis upon individual words as vehicles for meaning rather than sentences. God makes a selection. How this selection is made, upon what basis and whether the language of Scripture represents the scope of such a selection – these questions are not answered.

These two observations – the separation of thought from language and the return, via revelation, to a nomenclatural understanding of words and their objects – stand in a certain tension. The nomenclatural theory of language has always aspired to the ideal of a perfect correspondence between language and the world, to a universal and philosophical language.[9] If there is a strict equation between concept and word, then what is thought, what is said and what is remain objectively stable. If this were the nature of ordinary human discourse then there could be no act of revelation as Barth conceives it, for

---

[8] See Barth's *Anselm: Fides Quaerens Intellectum* where one finds again this connection between language and object: 'For the truth of thinking or speaking stands or falls by the relations of its sign language to what exists independently of its signs' (*A*, p. 164). Barth believes that the original Adamic language consisted of direct correspondences between three elements – thinking, words and objects. Within sinful human nature the three elements cannot be distinguished – thinking is words and words and thinking constitute objects which cannot now be said to exist 'independently of [their] signs'.

[9] Hans Aarslef's Introduction to Peter Heath's translation of Humboldt's *On Language: The Diversity of Human Language Structure and its Influence on the Mental Development of Mankind* (Cambridge: Cambridge University Press, 1988), p. xxxix.

revelation could not change the concept–word equation already established. But by insisting upon the disassociation of concept and word in ordinary human discourse, the act of revelation can change the 'content' without changing the word, thus restoring the word to its original meaning. Thus Barth adopts a nomenclatural or passive-copy theory of language as the model for the correspondence between perception, conception and language in the act of revelation whilst simultaneously rejecting such a theory of language as a description of discourse outside the act of revelation. It is the very possibility of a correspondence theory of language in revelation that legitimates Barth's positivist rhetoric.

What, then, is this language which is 'His creation', this language of perfect correspondence? Is it some *Ursprache*? Barth seems to write as if God spoke an idealized German – a German sounding and appearing the same to both God and human beings, but which each employs, reads and understands differently. He writes as if German was in some way related to a primary *Ursprache* – an idea not without considerable support from the Reformation to the work of Borinski, Barth's contemporary (see chapter 2). What remains certain is that Barth's distinction between human language and God's *Ursprache* is described in terms of two antithetical models of language, and he is attempting to forge a way between them. God's language is a direct and immediate transferral of meaning from object to word, the proper adequation of signifier and signified. His words are transparent vehicles for divine meaning. The model of language here, developed upon a nomenclatural theory of language, is of the ideal speech act: a pure communication without ambivalence or excess of meaning. The phonetic form of the words is absorbed into immediate significance, like the waves of sound which disappear following the moment of their utterance. Human language, on the other hand, is caught up in the transcendental subjectivity of perception and conception. Our use of them is 'improper [*uneigentlicher*] and merely pictorial [*bildlicher*]' (II.1, p. 229/259). It is improper because they are not our property. We have usurped the right to use them, without the ability adequately to relate them to the objects perceived.

And so we have no true knowledge. It is pictorial because, as we saw, the process of human cognition operates only with and upon various forms of images (*Bild–Gegenbild–Abbild* and *Wahrnehmungsbilder–Denkbilder–Wortbilder*). Without revelation there can only be semantic agnosticism – for all acts of signification make arbitrary connection between words and what is. Our 'knowledge' becomes groundless; it is placed within inverted commas.

Thus 'words of such simple content as "arm" and "mouth" – which to us are [*freilich* – certainly] as such incomprehensible – declare their truth only in the place where the reference is to the arm and mouth of God, His deeds and words' (II.1, p. 230/259).[10] 'Arm' and 'mouth' are arbitrary signs (as Saussure understands the word 'arbitrary' to mean that there is no natural association between the word and its object). Their true reference is appreciated only when they are taken metonymically and refer to God's deeds and words. Without revelation we occupy a world of circulating semiotics. By revelation God 'truly justifies human thinking and speaking' (II.1, p. 214/240). Outside that revelation divine meaning and human 'meaning' are antithetical. In revelation what is revealed is that very antithesis of human to divine meaning; how human meaning is illusory.

In these two models for the operation of language – which at this point we can term the communication model and the semiotic model – something yet remains to be clarified. That is, the difference between the particular and the general. For with 'arm' and 'mouth' and the act of communicating their import we are dealing with specific words and their relation to specific, identifiable, objects, but the semiotic model for the operation of language handles all language – it is a general principle for the nature of language, not a particular language event. Barth adopts both models and the principle of 'selection' moves between them. 'All kinds of things might be analogous of God ... It is exposition [*Auslegung*] of the revelation of God when it keeps

---

[10] At this point, Barth does seem to have, as certain Reformers before him had, some idea of a correlation between the *Ursprache* and ancient Hebrew, a scriptural language. For in Hebrew nouns do function metonymically and 'arm' and 'mouth' can mean 'deeds' and 'words', 'power' and 'speech'.

to the human words which are placed at our disposal as we are confronted by God's revelation, and which are therefore designated as serviceable for this employment' (II.1, pp. 232–3/ 261–2). Thus the selection and serviceability of particular words stand alongside statements that 'God is the first and last truth of *all* our words' (ibid., my emphasis). This tension is part of the paradox running throughout chapter 5, where words (the same words, apparently) owned by God, on the one hand, are human words on the other. It is, for Barth, a tension integral to the Christian faith, a tension testifying to the ontological and epistemological aporia opened by human sin and a tension evident within Jesus Christ Himself. So the story of language, according to Karl Barth, appears to be that in the beginning God gave Adam words as part of His creation, but post-lapsarian Adam, while retaining the words, could no longer appropriately name the world about him, nor his experience of it. Hence language is *both* divine (God-given, God-referring) and socially constructed (by human beings in association and agreement with each other, but now separated from God). But this suggests that the bridge between God and human beings is language, for the words *qua* words remain shared, even though what is understood by them differs radically.

Language is a potential *tertium quid* only actualized by revelation. But while language has only the potential to be meaningful, each model for the operation of that language contradicts the possibility of the other. The communication model (where words adequately represent and communicate their objects) cannot be accommodated within a model of language which understands words as constructing the reality of objects. Similarly, the semiotic model of language (which emphasizes the ineradicable mediation of a 'meaning' which forever lies beyond it) cannot accommodate the possibility of unmediated, direct disclosure. Knowledge of God, then, becomes either impossible or contradictory, for each model is the other's radical alternative.

There is no resolution of the paradox of language in chapter 5 – even though that must place in doubt all that Barth has constructed for us theologically. There is no coherent account of the Word in words. In attempting to unravel the logic of divine communication, Barth is aware that the logic is beyond him and he is unable to reconstruct its economy. The divine logic becomes a human paralogic. 'The confirmation our systematic needs cannot itself be systematic' (II.1, p. 249/282). There is an irreducible incompleteness to Barth's thinking which is reaffirmed while he constantly moves towards such a completeness. Early in the chapter Barth states that 'all openness ... is originally and properly His openness' (II.1, p. 68/73). He reads that openness in terms of a theological paradox – God's freedom for us as it is manifested in the paradox of Jesus Christ. In the closing pages of chapter 5, the paradox of language issues into a Christological discussion. In the aporia between two antithetical models for the operation of language Barth places Jesus Christ, the Word made human. At the deepest point of contradiction stands 'Jesus Christ to whom we must refer [*schlicht* – unceremonious(ly)] in conclusion' (II.1, p. 250/283).

It is Barth's Christology that bears the weight of any possible explanation or synthesis: the eternal Son of God made this particular man, Jesus of Nazareth (II.1, p. 252/286). But the question remains, can his Christology bear the weight he puts upon it? A keystone analogy holds up the edifice of Barth's theology, the *analogia Christi*: the Word is to Jesus of Nazareth as the Word is to the words of human beings. 'The Word was made flesh: this is the first, original and controlling sign of all signs' (II.1, p. 199/223). Put briefly, the incarnation is the meaning of and the hermeneutic for understanding all language. The analogy is necessary for there to be any knowledge at all. What is common to both parts of the analogy is an incarnation, but the two forms of incarnation are not the same – in fact, they are radically opposed. The incarnation of Christ is an historically particular event, and throughout the *Church Dogmatics* Barth emphasizes a Christological particularism, but the incarnation of the Word in words is not a particular event – it is the condition of language when language is viewed from its proper and original perspective. There is a difference between revelation as the actual manifestation of the Word and revelation as the condition for the meaning of words *in toto*. There is also a difference between incarnation as an historical event and incarnation as a metaphor to describe the immanent presence in language of transcendent meaning. These differences point once more to an ambiguous relationship between the particular and the general.

In fact, incarnation is the core problem in Barth's attempt to bring together a Christology and a theology of language; to locate in Christology a coherence for his theology of language. For the two models for the nature of language create, by analogy, the two models for the nature of Christ. In the communication model, Christ would be the full and immediate revelation of God as words unambiguously disclose their objects. But the greater the clarity of the disclosure the less emphasis there is upon the means whereby that disclosure has taken place. The signifier dissolves into its direct relationship to the signified. By analogy, the human and historical contingency of Jesus is only then significant in so far as it effaces itself. The Christology analogous to this would be a docetic one in which incarnation is not taken seriously at all. The creaturely in both sides of the analogy, Christ's and language's, is dissolved into the revelation of the divine. Where the human and semiotic body is taken seriously, as in the second model of language, then exactly the opposite occurs and the divine and transcendent is dissolved into the creaturely and immanent. To hold both models in paradoxical tension – language and the nature of Christ, the nature of Christ as analogous to the nature of language – is a linguistic form of Nestorianism.[11]

Christology alone cannot provide a synthesis for the paradoxical foundations of Barth's theology of language. Christology, as a theology of the Word, itself demands a coherent theology of language if it too is not to split irredeemably the divine from the human. If there is to be knowledge of God at all, if the economy

---

[11] Henri Bouillard raises this idea in *Karl Barth: Parole de Dieu et Existence Humaine*, volume 1 (Aubier: Editions Montaigne, 1957), p. 122. Regin Prenter systematically develops it in '*Karl Barths Umbildung der traditionellen Zweinaturlehre in lutherischer Beleuchtung*', *Studia Theologica*, 11 (1957), pp. 1–88. See Charles T. Waldrop's *Karl Barth's Christology* (New York: Mouton, 1984) for a different perspective and the argument that Barth's Christology is more Alexandrine than Antiochene.

of salvation is to be effected, there has to be found some ground for a theological realism. There has to be some coherent form of analogy between Jesus Christ as the Word of God and a theology of language, and both parts of the analogy require the support of the other. Barth needs to provide a coherent account of such an analogy and that means a coherent account of the interplay between two antithetical models for the nature of language. One offers a direct correspondence between signifier and signified, word and Word, but constitutes a natural theology and dissolves the distinction between the creaturely and the divine, the human and God as Wholly Other. The other denies the possibility of moving beyond mediation and, therefore, the possibility of any true knowledge of God as Wholly Other. The writing of chapter 5 is not simply an analysis but an attempt to overcome the aporia between the necessary immediacy of revelation and the inescapable mediation of human language. Has Barth then failed, as others have suggested? Is the task impossible? Is his Christology at odds with his theology of language so that no theology of language (even though his theological epistemology demands it) is possible without either weakening and compromising his Christology or presenting an incoherent account of the nature and operation of language? If he has failed, is the project redeemable should an alternative model of language be found which is able to account for the interplay between the two antithetical models in Barth's analysis? Can a coherent theology of language be uncovered which can both support and be accounted for by a theology of the Word made flesh?

In attempting to answer these questions we need to appreciate that Barth was not working in a theoretical vacuum, but at a time when the nature of language was coming to dominate philosophical thinking. We need to evaluate Barth's problematic in the context of such thinking, to see how it compares, to see how it parallels and to discover how distinctive it was. How far Barth was acquainted with such philosophical thinking is not an easy question to answer, but to assess how far he was part of a tradition and a dominant German intellectual *Geist* does not require the same degree of particularized guesswork. My argu-

ment in this book is that while Barth was struggling to read the
paradoxical nature of language theologically, contemporaries
like Buber and Heidegger were engaged in similar projects.
Their projects, treating the same double nature of language, are
subsequently taken up and developed by the French philosophers of discourse, Emmanuel Levinas and Jacques Derrida.
Finally, it is with Derrida's work on the economy of discourse
that we are presented with a key for understanding and reappre-
ciating what Barth is doing in chapter 5 of *Church Dogmatics*.
With Derrida's notion of *différance*, the coherence of Barth's
theology of language is clarified. And that has Christological
implications.

CHAPTER 2

Sprachphilosophie *from Hamann to Humboldt*

Barth may have been provoked into examining the divine origin of language when he embarked upon a study of Heinrich Heppe's *Reformed Dogmatics*, as we shall see, but the idea that language is divine in origin has a long history in Jewish and Christian thinking. Dante sums up the Christian tradition in his treatise *De Vulgaria Eloquentia*. 'A certain form of speech was created by God along with the first soul . . . In this form of speech Adam spoke; in this form of speech all his posterity spoke, down to the building of the Tower of Babel, by interpretation the Tower of Confusion; this form of speech the sons of Heber, who are called the Hebrews, inherited. After the confusion it continued with them alone, in order that our Redeemer, who in his humanity sprang from them, should use, not the language of confusion, but that of grace.'[1] The divine inception of language occurred when God first spoke and what he said became reality. Later Adam, in naming creation, reflects God's initial act and, in doing so, demonstrates that he was created in the image of God. The Hebrew language maintained its divine access to the meaningful. Even amid the ruins of Babel this language of grace continued, albeit buried beneath the babbling of so many other tongues. Hebrew too declined. Adam informs Dante that 'The tongue I spoke was all extinct before Nimrod's race gave their mind to the accomplished task.'[2] But in *Paradiso* Dante finds Adam in a place where the soul is perceived to move and speak with the transparency of breath. And this was the conception of that *Ursprache* – words as bodiless as breath, as lozenges of light,

---

[1] I, 6.33–6.
[2] Canto XXVI, 125–8, Sinclair's translation (Oxford: Oxford University Press, 1961).

in which meaning was immediate. As the Word made flesh, the Redeemer spoke again this language of grace.

Dante is not the last to accept this tradition. In the seventeenth century, when attention to Massoretic pointing challenged those who wished to believe God had dictated His Scripture down to the final consonant, others still maintained that Hebrew came closest to the Adamic tongue. There is ample evidence of this in the writings of Paracelsus, Boehme, Fludd, Comenius and, into the eighteenth century, in the work of Leibniz, Hamann and Herder. There were philosophers, poets and philologists who observed parallels between ancient Hebrew and German. Walter Benjamin, in his study of sixteenth-century tragedy, *Der Ursprung des deutschen Trauerspiels* (1928), points out that German's immediate [*unmittelbare*] descent from Hebrew was a widespread belief associated with the links being drawn between German and the classical languages (Greek and Latin). Benjamin quotes from Borinski's study *Die Antike in Poetik und Kunsttheorie* (Leipzig, 1914), in which Borinski lends contemporary support for the notion that ' "the origin of the whole world, therefore also classical antiquity, may be German" '.[3] More recently, George Steiner, in his panoptic study of translation, *After Babel*, has drawn attention to certain of Luther's versions of the Psalms and Holderin's recasting of Pindar's Third Pythian Ode, in which there is a strange 'evocatory inference to the reality of an *Ur-Sprache* in which German and Hebrew or German and ancient Greek are somehow fused'.[4] We move here through those sinister kingdoms of Nietzsche's *übermensch* and Hitler's *Völksdeutsch*. But we also move here into the context within which Karl Barth wrote chapter 5 of his *Church Dogmatics*.

J.C. HAMANN

It is Hamann's ghost who haunts this modern concern to place the origin of language firmly in the hands of God. It is Hamann to whom we shall return as we trace the development of German

[3] *Gesammelte Schriften*, 1.1 (Suhrkamp Verlag, 1974), p. 378.
[4] *After Babel* (Oxford: Oxford University Press, 1975), p. 64.

philosophy of language in the twentieth century. It is Hamann who writes the final word (until the twentieth century) advocating the divine origin of language in the midst of Enlightenment rationalism and secular morphologies. At the roots of modern philosophies of language lies the debate in which Hamann was engaged, here also lies the unresolved paradox of language which Barth inherits. The paradox is evident in Prussia in the late 1760s and early 1770s, while Hamann was writing. In 1766, the Prussian Academy awarded Süssmilch the celebrated essay prize for an essay entitled 'Proof that the Origin of Human Language is Divine'. In 1771, the Prussian Academy awarded Herder (Hamann's pupil) the same prize for an essay on the topic 'Supposing that human beings were left to their natural faculties, are they in a position to invent language and by what means?' In his essay, Herder crystallizes the paradox: 'Down one way, language appears to be so superhuman that God had to invent it; down the other, it is so inhuman that every animal could invent it if it were to take the trouble' (*OL*, p. 127).

The debate here stands upon well-trodden philosophical ground. While some maintained the belief in an Adamic tongue, an inquiry was being conducted into the possibility of a scientific language in which characters should 'signify things and not words [so] we should, by learning the character and names of things, be instructed likewise in their natures'.[5] The Royal Society, in particular Wilkins, Sprat and Locke, argued that language was a conventional and social phenomenon. Hence, by creating a new set of signs one could create a new and perspicacious language. The Abbé Condillac, in his 'Essay on the Origin of Human Knowledge' (1746), developed this materialist thesis by describing the move from human outcries of emotion to the formation of words which, by gradual consensus, are taken to name the objects the human cries are responses to. Three years later, Rousseau, in his 'Essay on the Origin of Language', reiterated that language was human in origin. He argued that it was not simply a development attributable to human physical and emotional responses. The moral need for

---

[5] Bishop Wilkins, *Essay Towards the Real Character and a Philosophical Language* (London, 1668), p. 21.

people to relate to each other, and express emotion, was a greater force in the creation of the social conventions whereby communication was established and meaning determined.

In the seventeenth and eighteenth centuries, then, the question of whether the origin of language was divine or social was a matter of intense philosophical concern. For Hamann,[6] language was not a social construct but intimately related to the revelation of God. Hamann was not concerned so much with the origin of language (a concern he associated with the Enlightenment's idolization of Reason); he was rather concerned with language as a process: *poeisis*, a divine and spirit-provoked creativity evident in speech. To be immersed in the creativity of language was to be immersed in the creativity of the Word. The meaning and value of words were not determined with reference to objects, 'words ... and their concepts are mutable in their definitions and relations according to time and place' (Nadler, II, p. 71). Meaning was not denotation, but participation in a dynamic creativity. 'Everything that man heard in the beginning, saw with his eye, contemplated and touched with his hands, was a living word; for God was the Word. With this word in his mouth and in his heart, the origin of language was natural' (Nadler, III, p. 32). By faith, human beings participate in a divine authorship made accessible by Christ the incarnate Word and the movement of the Holy Spirit. As a human speaks, quintessentially as s/he writes poetically, s/he is drawn up into the divine and redemptive economy of the Godhead. The mimetic function of a text mirrors the dynamics of speaking, which in turn mirrors lived experience and the breath of God circulating within creation (Nadler, III, p. 237). Thus Hamann

---

[6] Little of Hamann's work is available in translation. The authoritative edition of his *Sämtliche Werke, Historische-Kritische Ausgabe*, is edited by Josef Nadler, Bd. 1–6 (Wien, 1949–57). Hamann's *Briefwechsel* is edited by Ziesemer and Henkel (Leipzig, 1949). Of the studies of Hamann's work in English, besides biographies (by Walter Lowrie and Ronald Smith), the following are important and drawn upon in my work: J. C. O'Flaherty, *Unity and Language: A Study of the Philosophy of J. G. Hamann* (North Carolina: Chapel Hill, 1952); W. M. Alexander, *Johann Georg Hamann: Philosophy and Faith* (Le Hague: Martinus Nijhoff, 1966) – still probably the best, though largely ignored, study; Harold Stahmer, *Speak that I May See Thee: The Religious Significance of Language* (New York: Macmillan, 1968); and Terence J. German, *Hamann on Language and Religion* (Oxford: Oxford University Press, 1981).

defined himself as a philologist – a lover of the Word in words, a lover too of interpretation and the reading of God's semiotics. Language wove human beings into a threefold, perichoretic activity – speaking, interpreting and reading. 'Speech [*Reden*] is translation – from angel-language into human language, that is thoughts into words, – things into names, – images into signs.'[7] The speaker as poet is the interpreter and translator, transmitting the breath of God in his own act of breathing.

At first glance, this summary appears to place Hamann's thinking solidly within the *analogia entis* tradition. He seems to recognize the cosmic operation of an analogy of proportion in which speech–time–history–Holy Spirit runs like a golden thread between Creator and Creation. There are moments when he seems to be describing a network of correspondences between the divine and the human; moments when the *imago dei* is understood as a contact point, an unalientated ground, for a direct relation with God (Nadler, I, p. 78; II, pp. 206–7). His emphasis upon interdependence of speech, hearing, the event, revelation and the *nunc* of God, suggests he is advocating a cult of the immanent and immediate, the sensuous, even the Dionysiac (Nadler, III, p. 384). Hamann scholars are deeply divided on this issue.[8]

For there is another, countering, emphasis in Hamann's thinking. There are passages where he expressly portrays revelation as concealed and oblique and views language as an all too human form of mediation. The revelation of God through speech is then understood in terms of a divine kenosis. And so, in a letter to Gottlob Lindner, dated 9 August 1759, we find him writing about how humbling it is that thoughts can only become visible 'in the coarse clothing of arbitrary signs; and what proof of divine omnipotence – and humility – that He is able and willing to breathe the depths of his mysteries . . . into the concepts of human tongues, marked as they are by such gibber-

---

[7] Quoted by German, *Hamann on Language and Religion*, p. 36.
[8] For German, Hamann 'aims to put God-language in human form . . . God is met in God-language verging upon and becoming human language' (p. 97). For Alexander, there is a much deeper vein of scepticism in Hamann and emphasis is given to Hamann's admiration for Luther and Hume.

ish and confusion' (Ziesemer, I, pp. 393–4). Here is a post-lapsarian view of language which denies the possibility of analogy. Here is Hamann's Reformed acceptance of the 'infinite incongruity between man and God' (Nadler, III, p. 312) and 'between man and man' (ibid., p. 313). There are hints here that it is faith alone, and no *tertium quid*, which spans the gap between 'He who . . . alone can speak the true and certain words' and all 'our stuttering and copying [which] is nonsense' (letter to Jacobi, 23 August 1786, Ziesemer, VI, p. 529). There is no unity found here between creation and revelation.

On the one hand, then, Hamann advocates an onto-mimetology – that is, mimesis as presencing the divine Being.[9] As such, the threefold mirroring of language, nature and revelation provides the basis for a natural theology. On the other hand, Hamann proposes exactly the opposite, that there is no analogy only equivocation: 'people of the same tongue often misunderstand each other and associate entirely disparate concepts to the same outer signs or sounds of the word . . . this is the reason we can express a single image of the soul with entirely different signs' (Nadler, I, p. 220). Here, only by an act of faith is the secret meaning of all phenomena interpreted correctly as a sign of God (Nadler, I, p. 308).

Hamann was certainly aware of the contradictory positions he held and consistently refused to create a system in which the tensions were resolved. He read the paradox Christologically as the paradox of incarnation itself – the universal adhering to the historically contingent. He saw it as another example of Cusa's coincidence of opposites; a coincidence he once described as 'KOINONIA without transubstantiation' (letter to Herder, 19 December 1780, Ziesemer, IV, p. 254). All 'philosophical contradiction and the entire historical riddle of our existence . . . are solved by the document of the flesh-becoming Word' (Nadler I, p. 200).

But the refusal to be systematic only seemed to encourage a reluctance to explain the translation of angel-language into

---

[9] On onto-mimetology see Philip Lacoue-Labarthe's *Typography: Mimesis, Philosophy, Politics* (Cambridge Mass.: Harvard University Press, 1989).

human-language. Hamann never questioned and never examined the human reception of revelation.[10] Faith alone accepts that language constitutes an analogy between God and human beings. As one recent Hamann scholar has observed: 'There is no guaranteed "holy" language. The condescension of God in human language means that any word may be holy – and also profane ... Thus theological language becomes a constant task.'[11]

The complexity of Hamann's understanding of language finds significant echoes in Barth's analysis of language in chapter 5. The tensions each struggle with are very similar. But Hamann's reluctance to be more systematic and to provide more adequate accounts of the economy of his two languages, the angelic and the human, had its effect upon the history of *Sprachwissenschaft*. The paradox would be resolved, rather than worked with and examined. It would be resolved at a cost – as the direction of Herder's work shows.

HERDER

Herder's approach is governed by the desire for synthesis, a synthesis achieved through immanent development. The divine origin of language was not forgotten by Herder.[12] He alludes to it in an early essay 'On Diligence' [*'Über den Fleiss in mehreren gelehrten Sprachen'*], written in 1764: 'according to the simple, sublime word of Scripture, all the world was one language and one speech' (Suphan, I, p. 1). But by the time he came to write

---

[10] See Alexander, *Johann Georg Hamann*, p. 176.   [11] See Ibid., p. 194.
[12] Herder's essay 'On the Origin of Human Language' has been translated by Alexander Gode (Chicago: Chicago University Press, 1966). Other essays referred to are found in the massive *Sämtliche Werke*, ed. Bernhard Suphan, Bd. 33 (Hildesheim, 1967). Appreciation and interpretation of Herder's work in English is mainly biographical in emphasis – Alexander Gillies, *Herder* (Oxford: Blackwell, 1945) and Robert T. Clark, *Herder: His Life and Thought* (Berkeley: University of California Press, 1955). The best discussion of Herder remains Isaiah Berlin's *Vico and Herder: Two Studies in the History of Ideas* (London: Hogarth Press, 1976). More recently, there has been a collection of papers edited by W. Koepke, *Johann Gottfried Herder: Innovator through the Ages* (Verlag Herbert Grundmann, Bonn, 1982). Particularly enlightening for this study was Koepke's own contribution and an essay by Heinrich C. Seeba. Michael Morton's *Herder and the Poetics of Thought* (Pennsylvania: State University Press, 1989) concentrates on Herder's brief essay 'On Diligence'.

his essay 'On the Origin of Language', written in critical dialogue with Süssmilch's earlier essay for the Prussian Academy, he sites the development of language in an anthropological topos. He concludes that language is not at all superhuman and, contrary to Rousseau, he does not develop from the sounds of emotion (*OL*, pp. 99–101). The origin of language arises from humankind's distinctive ability to reflect upon creation, and such reflection necessitates words. To demonstrate his thesis, he describes an encounter between a primitive human being and a sheep, and how, as a consequence of this encounter, the sheep is named. First the creature manifests itself to the human being's senses. It bleats. When the animal is encountered again there is a recognition and, hence, reflection: 'He recognised the sheep by its bleating: This was a conceived sign (*Merkmal*) through which the soul clearly remembered an idea – and what is that other than a word' (*OL*, p. 117). Sensation gives rise to conceptual sign; thinking and language are concomitant. '[N]ot even the first and most primitive application of reason was possible without language' (*OL*, p. 120).

Herder dissolves one of the tensions of correspondence theories of language – the tension between mental conception and verbal expression. Language is a human invention, but it is not quite the human convention described by Locke, Condillac and Rousseau. Furthermore, for Herder it was an invention which had to differ from one human being to another, for it arose out of particular physical, geographical and historical contexts.

God is not forgotten by Herder, but once it is conceived that the 'invention of language is therefore as natural to man as it is to him that he is man' (*OL*, p. 115), then the role the divine plays in the development and character of language is minimal. Dialects, languages, nationalities all arise naturally the moment human beings become reflective and begin to adapt themselves to their environments. No pre-Babel, Adamic state is necessary for such an origin or development. Theology need have no toe-hold here. And yet Herder cannot quite come to terms with such an atheism. 'What we human beings know, we know only on the basis of analogy – from creature to us and from us to Creator' (Suphan, VIII, p. 170). In 'Another Philosophy of History', we are told that 'the Creator alone ... conceives the entire unity of one and all the nations, in all their multiplicity, without thereby losing sight of their unity' (Suphan, v, p. 505). God is the *All-Erhalter*, the Great Sustainer, and human beings are *Mittelges*, mediators, who translate God's Oneness into human categories through language. Despite, then, Herder's avowed anti-Kantian position,[13] there is a parallel between his reception of the revelation of God as Creator and the work of the faculty of the imagination in Kant upon things in themselves. For Kant, experience of the world was filtered through the categories of human understanding. For Herder, the human being's ability to understand at all is locked into the development of language which represents the world to us. Language is not then, for Herder (as it was for Hamann), a potential symbol of the divine; it is always a veil through which the world appears. God becomes aesthetically necessary as the point at which the manifold is synthesized. God presents the oneness and therefore the harmony towards which human beings and creation are returning. But such a pre-established harmony is not logically necessary. The Tower of Babel and God's confusion of tongues is a convenient catalyst for the multiplicity which Herder believes is returning (in a radically historicist form of redemption) to its original unity. The Tower of Babel is Herder's Big-Bang theory, enabling him to put questions concerning the relativism of myriad languages into a mythological deep-freeze. But there is no intrinsic reason why the development of human languages should be characterized by the Neoplatonic circle of procession and return. Why can the development not be seen as a line or even a million different lines?

Herder's appeal to God is pragmatic rather than necessary, and that is why it makes so little appeal to theological reasoning. Unlike Hamann, for example, he does not relate his understanding of language and historical development to the work of the Holy Spirit and the operation of the Trinity. Similarly, although he wishes to integrate all language in the one Word, 'a Word, in whose fullness one could conceive everything' (Suphan, v, p.

---

[13] This position is most evident in his 1799 attack 'Metacritique' – although a substantial body of Herder's work pre-dates *The Critique of Pure Reason* (1781).

502), this Word is not read Christologically. Human beings, not Jesus Christ, are the translators of God's revelation. Human beings, not Christ, mediate between the plenitude of creation and the unity of the Creator. Herder advises us to 'feel yourselves into everything – only then will you be on the right path to understanding the Word' (ibid.). Rather than faith in Christ, a proto-Coleridgean 'empathy' is called for in order to participate in the redemption of language. At best, then, there is only room for an Enlightenment Deism in Herder's *Sprachphilosophie*. Once the biologicalism of nature and history is understood to function immanently then there is no need to look beyond the evolutionary development of the organism itself for transcendental explanations. In synthesizing Hamann's double perspective – language as God-given and language as human invention – Herder collapsed the tension into an anthropological and organic entelechy.

For Hamann, language like the world, when read by faith, becomes iconic. A sign [*Zeichen* or *Symbol*] has immanent power to reveal the Godhead when it is understood by faith to be participating in God's own breath. For Herder, language is materialistic – the sign [*Merkmal*] arises out of reflection upon what is perceived by the senses, and so, signs change from country to country and climate to climate. Herder is the first to use the term *semiotik* to describe this,[14] and these emphases upon semiotics and linguistic relativism are his bequest to *Sprachwissenschaft*. These emphases distinguish *Sprachphilosophie* from Hamann's emphasis upon the immediate meaningfulness of divine address, or what might be termed *Redephilosophie*. With Herder God becomes an optional extra, and the secularization of discourse is no longer a matter for debate. The title of Hamann's response to Herder's essay for the Prussian Academy illustrates how he considers himself a crusading knight (even a Don Quixote) from a bygone era: 'The Last Will and Testament of the Rose Cross Knight Regarding the Divine and Human Origin of Language'.

As Hans Urs von Balthasar has astutely pointed out, Hamann

---

[14] See Morton, *Herder and the Poetics of Thought*, pp. 134–6.

espouses what Paul called the *analogia fidei*.[15] He quotes from a letter Hamann sent to Herder warning him not to let the imagination be given too free a rein 'so that obedience, the analogy of faith, is thereby denied'.[16] This, as von Balthasar also points out, is the evangelical doctrine of faith – a precursor to Barth's own doctrine of analogy.

Herder, on the other hand, epouses a form of logocentrism, where the One and the Many are correlated through the synthesizing power of language and reasoning, language *as* reasoning. A theory of knowledge would have to become a theory of language, for Herder, on the basis of his belief that 'language determines the entire scope and limits of human knowledge' (Suphan, ii, p. 17). Revelation, if it is at all possible in Herder's system, arises from becoming part of the historical movement of experience (history) towards the grand synthesis. Barth observes this in his own essay on Herder.[17] For Barth this sails too close to a natural theology.

Barth tends to read Herder through Herder's influence on Schleiermacher, the Erlangen group and Troeltsch. He emphasizes Herder's Romantic appeal to feelings and intuition. But in terms of Herder's *Sprachphilosophie*, as we saw, the sensuous is the moment displaced by the 'veil of language' and the material nature of the sign. It is the materiality of language that grounds Herder's radical historicism and becomes the principal force behind change. It is a materiality which Herder believes roots us in the process of reality and its historical teleology. Furthermore, it is the German language above all which is considered to be the language *par excellence* of synthesis.[18]

The materiality of the sign, the *Semiotik*, rather than the transcendence of the symbol, dominates *Sprachphilosophie*. And paralleling this emphasis is the development of hermeneutics and philology. Since language constitutes reality and reality is constantly evolving, then human beings must forever ask what is being meant by the words employed. Hermeneutic's search for

---

[15] *The Glory of the Lord: A Theological Aesthetics*, iii (Edinburgh: T. & T. Clark, 1986), p. 274.   [16] Ibid., p. 275.
[17] *Protestant Theology in the Nineteenth Century* (London: SCM, 1972), p. 275.
[18] See Morton, pp. 115–19.

truth in and through the mediation of language and its wager upon a truth that forever eludes it starts here.

HUMBOLDT

German philosophy of language continued to develop the analogy between art and the organic and correlate historical, logical and biological determinism. Humboldt's thinking may have been indebted to the earlier French school of Condillac,[19] but in terms of German *Sprachphilosophie*, his work endorses and advances Herder's. The character of that endorsement and advancement can be seen in Humboldt's *Introduction* to his massive study of the Kawi language (published in 1836). The book itself retells the story (told by Herder, and Condillac before him) of the formation of language from its autogenesis, its development as an 'intellectually creative power' (*DHS*, p. 24) and its movement towards perfection. Perfection was understood to have been realized in Sanscrit, a language which 'presents the true nature of the verb, the pure synthesis of being and concept' (*DHS*, p. 83). This standard of perfection was related to Kawi, a Malayan language which combined Indo-European Sanscrit vocabulary with a far Eastern form. Kawi was thus a synthesis of East and West – the very basis for the study of comparative linguistics.[20] Language is again an organism and the expression of a nationalism. But there are several points of innovation in Humboldt's work: a developed interest in ethnography, a concern to see the study of language and comparative linguistics as a science with a scientific methodology, and a deeper commitment to the examination of language as anthropology. These innovations are summed up in Humboldt's own statement of intention:

---

[19] See Aarsleff's 'Introduction' to *On Language*. Aarsleff argues against the traditional view that Humboldt was following in the steps of Hamann and Herder. On Humboldt's *Sprachphilosophie* see Ernst Cassirer, *Philosophy of Symbolic Forms*, three volumes (New Haven: Yale University Press, 1965). More recently: R. L. Brown's *Wilhelm Humboldt's Conception of Linguistic Relativity* (Le Hague: Mouton, 1967) and R. Miller's *The Linguistic Relativity Principle and Humboldtian Ethnolinguistics* (Le Hague: Mouton, 1968).   [20] Aarsleff, 'Introduction' to *On Language*, p. xii.

The division of mankind into people and races, and the diversity of their language and dialects, are indeed directly linked to each other, but are also connected with, and dependent upon, a third and higher phenomenon, the *growth of man's mental powers* into ever new and often more elevated forms ... This revelation of man's mental powers, diverse in its degree and nature, over the course of millennia and throughout the world, is the highest aim of all spiritual endeavour, the ultimate idea which world history must strive to bring forth more clearly from itself. (*DHS*, p. 21)

Gone is the notion of a pre-Babel unity. Neither Sanscrit nor Kawi is understood as an *Ursprache*, and Hebrew is distinctly inferior to Sanscrit. In fact the origin of language is regarded as an unscientific question since it cannot be dealt with by empirical research (*DHS*, pp. 42–3). Scientific methodology obviates theological questions. The universal focus is the 'unity of human nature' (*DHS*, p. 57) which guarantees that there is a 'congruence of all human tongues' (*DHS*, p. 59). The congruence is evident in the inner-form of a language and Humboldt's research is governed by discovering these forms and relating them one to another. The diversity of tongues does not, therefore, lead to relativism but to idealism. There are three arterial directions of the thesis.

First, there is a qualified Kantianism. Language rather than the categories of transcendental reasoning governs the relations between subjective being and objective existence. For 'language never represents the objects, but always the concepts that the mind spontaneously formed from them in producing language' (*DHS*, p. 84). There is only mediation, then; language constructs our worlds. But in this constructive process nature remains the constant stimulus for language, and 'language is able to depict it. For in passing, by means of it, into the world of sounds, we do not abandon the world that actually surrounds us'. So language brings us close to 'an understanding of the formal impress of nature' (*DHS*, p. 61). Language is the *tertium quid*. It is the means of synthesis not because it produces a copy, but because it is itself an expression of the natural life-principle. Meaning is a matter of sentences and utterances, not nomenclature, because it is the verbs, not the nouns, which most closely imitate the spirit of life.

Secondly, Sanscrit, Greek and Latin become the models for the evaluation of all languages.[21] Sanscrit was the most perspicuous because its sounds are so closely related to its concepts. Sanscrit therefore achieves a superior clarity and economy. As a yardstick, it is a form of linguistic absolutism.

Thirdly, there is an insistence upon an analogical correspondence between the individual and the corporate, so that 'in language the *individualization* within a *general conformity* is so wonderful, that we may say with equal correctness that the whole of mankind has but one language, and that every man has his own' (*DHS*, p. 53). What Noam Chomsky later termed the 'deep structure' of a language corresponds to Humboldt's anthropological constant. It is the unity of the human *Geist* which prevents linguistic variety and diversity from dissolving into relativism, even solipsism.

A more thorough-going relativism stood in history's wings, emphasizing the role of the arbitrary much more than Humboldt allowed himself to do. Humboldt presupposed the unity of nature and the organic (though synthetic) relationship between sense impression, sound-form and concept. Each language created its own world-view, but nevertheless there was a common world-view, just as there was a common anthropology and the congruence of all languages. Humboldt remained committed, then, if not to an *Ursprache* then certainly to a meta-structure and a metanarrative.[22]

Even so, Humboldt was aware of certain arbitrary elements about the sign. A pervasive humanism kept the signifier under the power of the signified, and in this way semantics were privileged above semiotics. But for Humboldt, language began in a moment of articulation when a sound-form was produced in response to 'the impress of nature'. And while this sound-form designated the sensed object, Humboldt recognized it was only

---

[21] This led to criticism of his imperialism and Eurocentrism. See Aarsleff, 'Introduction' to *On Language*, pp. lxi–lxiv.

[22] Metanarrative is used here in the sense of Jean-François Lyotard's concept of 'grand narrative' – a narrative which locates and legitimizes all other narratives. It places all other discourses within a mastering design or story, which grounds their meaningfulness. See *The Postmodern Condition* (Manchester: Manchester University Press, 1984).

one of many possible sounds designating only one of many possible perceptions of an object (*DHS*, pp. 81 and 84). Furthermore, in this moment of articulation 'the whole genesis of language also occurs' (*DHS*, p. 69), which makes it the most significant moment in the formation and destiny of that language and all that it will be able to attain culturally. Yet this moment 'primarily comes down to a fortunate organization of the *ear* and *vocal organs*' (*DHS*, p. 68).

We find arbitrariness again when it comes to the relation between the combination of several sounds to form 'a dual unity, of sound and concept' (*DHS*, p. 70). In the formation of these early words 'there is naturally an element of chance' (*DHS*, p. 71). And though three reasons are given why certain sounds are linked to certain concepts (*DHS*, p. 73), there is a confession that 'we cannot eliminate even a high degree of arbitrariness from explanation of this type' (*DHS*, p. 74). This leads Humboldt to recognize the moment within all language of private meaning: 'Nobody means by a word precisely and exactly what his neighbour does' (*DHS*, p. 63). In the admission of private meaning lies a disquieting note of agnosticism.

The recognition of a degree of linguistic relativity and semiotic arbitrariness may be kept at bay by a belief in 'the larger spiritual economy of mankind' (*DHS*, p. 87), but they fuel a more fundamental tension in Humboldt's work. The future of German *Sprachphilosophie* lies in the struggles between various camps positioned around this tension. On the one hand, there is Humboldt's idealism. Language, reasoning, history and nature chase each other in the spiral of immanent meaning and organic development towards a synthesis. The synthesis is a moment of pure and immediate referentiality. Language moves towards a paradise in which the community live in transparent meaning. The redemption of language and the gathering of all peoples occurs through the explicit congruence of all words in the one Word. But though we might term this logocentric, the Word here is not Christ; it is not theologically coloured at all. At best the goal is a fully secularized humanism. On the other hand, there is Humboldt's materialism. By turning philology into comparative linguistics, attention is moved from meaning to form. By emphasizing that sound-form determines the character of language, then 'the physical, with its shape already actual . . . must necessarily gain an easy ascendency over the idea' (*DHS*, p. 77). Emphasis here is upon the semiotic and phonetic. When this is coupled with an insistence that there is no stepping outside language (*DHS*, p. 60), then we are one step from Nietzsche (and Derrida): 'What, then, is truth? A mobile army of metaphors, metonyms and anthropomorphisms . . . truths are illusions about which we have forgotten that this is what they are.'[23] Either way, questions about language which had once been raised on the wings of angels have now become thoroughly secularized. And pinned now to the scientific study of language, the questions have also become institutionalized.

THE SEMANTIC TRADITION

The fundamental tension of Humboldt's work is a characteristically neo-Kantian one, in which a synthesis was sought between idealism and empiricism, mediation and intuition. His thinking is situated within what might be termed the hermeneutical tradition.[24] The concern with understanding and the act of speaking, evident in Schleiermacher's hermeneutics, is developed by Humboldt as a 'linguistic turn'.[25] There was another tradition in the philosophy of language which led through the work of the scientist and philosopher Hermann von Helmholtz and the logician and mathematician Gottlob Frege to the establishment of the Vienna School and the work of Carnap and Wittgenstein. This has recently been termed the 'semantic tradition', where the 'logic' of Frege, Russell, Wittgenstein and

---

[23] 'On Truth and Lie in the Extra-Moral Sense', *The Portable Nietzsche*, ed. W. Kaufmann (London: Penguin, 1980), pp. 46–7.

[24] In *The Hermeneutics Reader* (Oxford: Blackwell, 1986), Kurt Mueller-Vollmer places Humboldt's thinking at the foundations of modern hermeneutics.

[25] The phrase is Rorty's, in his description of the move from epistemology to the study of language in twentieth-century philosophy. See *The Linguistic Turn: Recent Essays in Philosophical Method* (Chicago: Chicago University Press, 1967) and chapters 6 and 7 in *Philosophy and the Mirror of Nature* (Oxford: Blackwell, 1980).

Husserl 'was our semantics, a doctrine of content, its nature and structure'.[26]

The exponents of the semantic tradition developed an analysis of language upon scientific and mathematical methods, whose fundamental concern was to clarify the possibilities for *a priori* knowledge. Hence their work discusses the nature of number and geometry and their question concerned 'the semantic pineal gland that links the world of universals and forms with merely human epistemology'.[27] Humboldt is not a thousand miles from this concern, but the main body of work within the semantic tradition concerns logical form, its relation to syntax, the presupposition that a transparent and complete transferral of information is available and the correlation of propositions to the facts of the case. Closely related to this work is the possibility of an objectivity that could avoid all subjectivism or psychologism or intentionality. It is precisely the need to evaluate intentionality – national, local, personal – that ties epistemology ineluctably to language for the hermeneutical tradition.

The semantic tradition and the hermeneutic tradition in *Sprachphilosophie* both issue from Kant and the Enlightenment project. Richard Rorty calls the former the 'pure' philosophy of language, and the latter the 'impure' philosophy of language.[28] What both traditions share is a logocentric ideal – purely logical and perspicacious form, on the one hand, and the 'larger spiritual economy of mankind' operating through the medium of language, on the other. Both traditions are rooted in various shades of neo-Kantianism. The semantic tradition, as it developed towards logical positivism, issued from one of the dominant forms of neo-Kantianism, the scientific neo-Kantianism associated with Helmholtz; Moritz Schlick and Hans Reichenbach were both neo-Kantian apostates. The hermeneutical tradition as it developed in the work of Cohen, Natorp and Cassirer arose from the Marburg school of neo-Kantianism which emphasized the immanence of all objects of knowledge,

---

[26] J. Alberto Coffa, *From Kant to Carnap*, p. 64.   [27] Ibid., p. 126.
[28] *Philosophy and the Mirror of Nature*, p. 257.

their intentional inexistence. Both traditions were fundamentally split. The semantic tradition had its positivist feet in both a pre-Kantian correspondence theory of knowledge and its representation and a neo-Kantian emphasis upon the mediation and construction of knowledge, while Dilthey, who represents another strand of the hermeneutical tradition and who was heavily indebted to Humboldt, wished to emphasize lived experience [*Erlebnis*] in a way which distinguished him from neo-Kantian idealism.[29]

It is in this rich and complex philosophical *milieu* that Barth and the German contemporaries who shared his concern with the relationship between knowledge and language are to be placed. From 1906 Barth wanted to go to Marburg.[30] At first, his father, strongly against Marburg's theological liberalism, forbade it. He wanted Barth to go to Halle or Greifwald, both with more reformed schools of theology. In the end Barth went to Berlin – once the home of Schleiermacher and Humboldt and now the home of Dilthey – where he became the pupil of Wilhelm Herrmann. Then, in 1908, his father allowed him to go to Marburg. Here he came to know Bultmann. He left to become an assistant pastor in Geneva in 1909. But Marburg remained Bultmann's academic home and, particularly after Barth's second edition of *Romans* (and Bultmann's review of it), their lifelong correspondence began. To Marburg, fourteen years after Barth's departure, Martin Heidegger came to teach (who had himself been the pupil of the neo-Kantian Heinrich Rickert). In 1925, when Barth was teaching at Göttingen (and composing his first systematics), Bultmann paid him a visit and 'read aloud for hours from lectures by Martin Heidegger which he had heard and written down in Marburg'.[31]

---

[29] See *Dilthey: Selected Writings*, ed., trans., and introduced by H. P. Rickman (Cambridge: Cambridge University Press, 1976); and 'Dilthey: Hermeneutics as a Foundation for *Geisteswissenschaften*' in Richard E. Palmer's *Hermeneutics* (Evanston: Northwestern University Press, 1969).

[30] Eberhard Busch, *Karl Barth: His Life from Letters and Autobiographical Texts* (Philadelphia: Fortress Press, 1976), p. 38.

[31] Ibid., p. 161.

CHAPTER 3

Forms of logocentrism among Barth's contemporaries

With the work of Ernst Cassirer and Martin Heidegger the hermeneutic tradition divides.[1] The infamous *mise-en-scène* for that division was a conference held in Davos in 1929 when Cassirer faced Heidegger and each argued for his own interpretation of Kant. In brief, for much could be said here on the comparative methodologies of neo-Kantism and phenomenology, each describes a different form of logocentrism. Human beings interpret the world, they can do no other, but each philosopher begins with a different understanding of the nature of human beings, or a human being's relationship to the *Ding an sich*, and this anthropological difference leads to radically different perspectives on the nature of language.

CASSIRER

For Cassirer,[2] all human knowledge lies in the formation of symbols. The Kantian moment of synthesis is paramount. There

---

[1] It might seem perverse that among these contemporaries I have not examined the work of one of the century's renowned philosophers of language: Wittgenstein. Wittgenstein is mentioned throughout the book, but there is no specific section on his work. The reason is mainly historical. Wittgenstein pursued a highly individual way. Influenced in his early work by the semantic tradition (cf. Coffa, *From Kant to Carnap*) of Frege and Russell, his later work certainly has parallels with both Barth's and Derrida's. See here Ernstpeter Haurer's '*Biblisches Reden von Gott – ein Sprachspiel?*' *Evangelisches Theologie*, 50, 1 and H. Straten's ground-breaking work *Wittgenstein and Derrida* (Lincoln: University of Nebraska Press, 1983). Nevertheless, Wittgenstein is not part of the trajectory I am examining in this book, which concerns the trace of a transcendent alterity as it inheres to language.

[2] There are two important essays on Cassirer and language both in *The Philosophy of Ernst Cassirer*, ed. P. A. Schilpp (Illinois: La Salle, 1949). The first is by Susanne K. Langer, entitled 'On Cassirer's Theory of Language and Myth'. The second is by

is no immediate intuition of the sensible, no access to a naive perception of the world. 'What immediately is, is thrust into the background by what it accomplishes with its mediation, by what it "means"' (*PSF*, I, p. 94). There is a shift 'to a realm of pure meaning ... [that] results in the subordination of the notion of truth to that of meaning' (*PSF*, III, p. 6). Human beings are therefore by necessity *homo hermeneuma*, interpreters of signs. Language, *par excellence*, illustrates the grammar of signs within which we are caught. 'The function of language is not to copy reality but to symbolise it' (*PSF*, I, p. 132).

It is important to distinguish the form of hermeneutics that Cassirer's work implies here. There is no pursuit of extra-mental truth, no word–object relationship, only a relationship of symbols. To relate this symbolizing operation with what is 'out there', to hold the opinion that this reasoning process is not solipsistic, one has to believe that the structures of thinking relate to the structures of reality itself. This is what we find in Hermann Cohen's work, where the structures of thinking correspond to a form of pre-existing Torah: 'Law is reality, which means reality is to be conceived of as an abstract thought'.[3] The return of the Messiah is conceived by Cohen in terms of a Messianic Age in which there will be a fulfilment of man's moral ideals. His is a return to Stoicism. Although there are mystical aspirations or at least the employment of mystical language in Cassirer's work, he seems to shy away from an explicitly theological *ens realissimum* – he views religions as forms of mythical thinking which over time become clarified and depend more on abstract concepts. Monotheism is a step along the trajectory of such a development and eventually 'belief in the one and only God makes man aware of his own inner unity' (*LM*, p. 83). The 'incarnation of God must no longer be taken as a mythical or historical fact, but rather as a process which operates continuously in human consciousness' (*PSF*, II, p. 249). For Cassirer human nature is at

---

Wilbur M. Urban, entitled 'Cassirer's Philosophy of Language'. Fritz Kaufmann's essay, 'Cassirer, Neo-Kantianism and Phenomenology', in the same volume is well worth reading. More recently, Sigbjørn Stensland has published his *Ritus, Mythos and Symbol in Religion* (Uppsala: Uppsala University Press, 1986), which draws on Cassirer's work.

[3] *Kants Begrundung der Ethik* (Berlin: Bruno Cassirer, 1910), p. 12.

the centre of all knowledge, and when pressed by Moritz Schlick to clarify his understanding of where the ultimate synthetic *a priori* principles lay, he explained that they 'really consist only in the idea of the "unity of nature", that is, the law-abiding character of experience in general'.[4] A deontologized form of Leibniz's monadology arises in which there is a plurality of symbolic codes each with a functional correspondence with the others. The harmony between the symbols is not pre-established, as in Leibniz, but there are laws of transformation and therefore structural links between each monadic code.

This brings Cassirer one step closer to collapsing epistemology into semiotics; only the belief in a teleological evolvement of symbolic codes guarantees a meaning which is not simply arbitrary. The paradigm for this process is language: 'all the concepts of theoretical knowledge constitute merely an upper stratum of logic which is founded upon a lower stratum, that of the logic of language' (*LM*, p. 28). All thinking moves towards 'unity of the Word, the unity of the God-idea' (*LM*, p. 73). Cassirer was aware that this emphasis upon '[t]he fundamental structural unity of language' (*EM*, p. 122) brought his work into close parallel with Saussure's distinction between synchronical and diachronical linguistics, between *la langue* (which is the universal structure) and *la parole* (which is the temporal and changeable process). He was also aware that his thinking orbited that of the linguistic circles of Moscow and Prague, the work of Jakobson and Trubetzkoy, and early structuralism.

Language, while being paradigmatic for Cassirer, is also one of three main forms of the symbolizing process. It is the most advanced of these forms, but it too is evolving towards a greater degree of abstraction. First there is the mimetic gesture, the dance, the song, which imitates what is perceived by a similar means of sensuous expression. Then comes language, speech, writing and mythic thinking. This is the analogical stage, the move 'from a more subjective state to an objective state ... [in] a process of progressive objectification' (*EM*, pp. 131–2). This is the act of denomination where 'we select, out of the multiplicity

---

[4] Quoted in Coffa, *From Kant to Carnap*, p. 200.

and diffusion of our sense data, certain fixed centres of perception' (*EM* p. 134). This is also text book Humboldtian
linguistics. But it is in the next step, a typical neo-Kantian step,
that Cassirer spells out the consequences of Humboldt's position.
Names 'are not designed to refer to substantial things, independent entities which exist by themselves. They are determined
rather by human interests and human purposes' (*EM*, p. 134).
Language operates at a borderline between the objectification of
a mode of experience (a mode of experience unintelligible
without that objectification) and the world of concepts, the
world of reasoning. There is then 'a complete lack of any clear
division between mere "imagining" and "real" perception'
(*PSF*, II, p. 48), while the symbolic and syntactic nature of
language lead towards discursive thought. Here the symbolization of things gives place to the symbolization of relations. The
final stage of this immanent dialectic is the symbolic representations of the world in science and mathematics. 'The ascent to
categories appears, therefore, to be very slow in the development
of human speech; but each new advance in this direction leads to
a more comprehensive survey, to a better orientation and
organisation of our perceptual world' (*EM*, p. 136). There is an
aspiration, therefore, towards pure notation, a quasi-mystical
and silent transparency (Cassirer quotes Eckhart and Tauler)
which is not necessarily theological. This is an important
distinction between Cassirer's and Heidegger's forms of logocentrism. Cassirer's schema remains profoundly anthropological;
Heidegger's is almost anti-humanistic. For Cassirer, God can
only be an absolute of human consciousness, because neo-
Kantian idealism negates the *Ding an sich*.

Cassirer's logocentrism – knowledge governed by both the
formation of linguistic signs and the operation of transcendental
reasoning, by the Logos principle within human beings – is
'monadological'. Words are part of symbolic codes each of
which relates to the fundamental structure of the real. As this
fundamental structure becomes more manifest so the relationship between these codes moves, dialectically, towards more
abstract forms of symbolism and finally towards unmediated
understanding. But each symbolic code encodes the totality and
therefore functions synecdochically. Cassirer seems agnostic

about whether the unity aspired to is 'out there' in terms of nature, especially in his later work *An Essay on Man* (see p. 112 where he argues for natural connections between the symbol and its object). Generally, and more in keeping with neo-Kantianism, he conceives symbolic representation as concerning a transcendental object which is immanent throughout and which resides initially as a projection that the representation objectifies. The representation is itself a stage for further objectification in an historical move towards the pure realization of the object. The logocentrism never moves beyond the anthropological and in its deification of man it is, in a sense, anti-metaphysical. Its proximity to nihilism (in which solipsistic human beings are spun from a web of floating signifers) will become more apparent when the historicism, the idea of teleological development, and the humanism are called into question. The post-structural work of Roland Barthes and Jean-François Lyotard stands waiting in the wings of Cassirer's thinking. The final *mise-en-scène* of German liberalism stands poised on the edge of postmodernism. When 'history' collapses into *histoire* or '[hi]story' then all symbolic codes become relative and no overall, embracing principle collects them into the fold of the meaningful. And historicism was under radical attack while Cassirer was writing. Futurism and Dadaism were radically anti-historicist art movements.[5] Dialectical theologians, like Gogarten and Barth, were calling historicism into question, warning that it 'leads to total relativism'[6] and speaking of the '*end* of history' (*2R*, p. 77). Cassirer's logocentrism, the zenith of modernity (the zenith of Enlightenment thinking) was being constructed at a time of sea-change – a sea-change that was ushering in a post-modernity.[7]

---

[5] Gianni Vattimo, *The End of Modernity* (Cambridge: Polity, 1988), p. 100.

[6] Gogarten, 'Historicism', in *The Beginnings of Dialectical Theology*, ed. James M. Robinson (Louisville: John Knox Press, 1968), p. 343. See also Paul Mendes-Flohr's essay 'Rosenzweig and the Crisis of Historicism' in *The Philosophy of Franz Rosenzweig*, ed. Paul Mendes-Flohr (Hanover and London: University Press of New England for Brandeis University Press, 1988), pp. 138–61.

[7] 'The post-modern cannot be confined to a specific historical era *after* the end of modernity; it is rather an experience of the end of metaphysics and the end of history with accompanies the most advanced stages of modernity itself', Jon R. Snyder, 'Translator's Introduction', to Vattimo, p. xlviii.

Cassirer's work placed ontology in suspension, focussing its attention for validity upon a waning belief in historicism. One of the great pillars of Western metaphysics, Being, was weakened. Cut off from any ontological roots, language becomes merely rhetorical gesturing; the power to persuade substitutes for the conviction of truth; hermeneutics can slide into semiotics. The unity of man and history holds Cassirer's thought together. When both humanism and historicism are undermined then the transcendental ego (detached from its body and sensibility) floats in a vacuum. Either God can be introduced to guarantee that the laws of reality perceived are indeed universal laws (as with Descartes), or God can be forgotten. Either way the dawn of a radical scepticism already flickers on the horizon. For Wilhelm Herrmann, the teacher of both Barth and Bultmann, this human condition has to become the platform for faith; faith as an alternative epistemology. Barth, as we shall continue to see, works within this neo-Kantian framework with its 'monadological' logocentrism.

Other critics like W. M. Urban and Fritz Kaufmann have spoken about the spectres of solipsism and relativism in Cassirer's work. What is important for this study of Barth and the language of theology is to make explicit the form of logocentric thought in neo-Kantianism and point to how, once its foundationalism was undermined, it could feed directly into postmodern thinking. Barth's work can be read both as neo-Kantian and part of 'the dissolutive tendencies already apparent in the great early twentieth-century avant-garde movements ... key event[s] for the definition of post-modern'.[8]

HEIDEGGER

In his monograph *Heidegger*, George Steiner writes that 'the Johannine formula, "In the beginning was the Word", is obviously present in [Heidegger's] whole paradigm of being and saying'.[9] Logocentrism is the very core of Heidegger's thinking. But it is a logocentrism which changes (see chapter 6, in which

---

[8] See Vattimo, *The End of Modernity*, p. 106.
[9] London: Fontana Press, 1978, p. 54.

we examine more closely Heidegger's later work) and which differs radically from that of Cassirer. The main thrust of Heidegger's difference lies in the way he questions idealism's subjective centre and reopens an ontological investigation. The investigation 'keep[s] within the horizon of the Kantian problematic' (*BT*, p. 54), but effects a critique of the way 'Kant demands any proof at all for the "Dasein of Things outside of me"' because this 'shows already that he takes the subject – the "in me" – as the starting-point for this problematic' (*BT*, p. 248). Heidegger's starting-point lies elsewhere, in a phenomenological analysis of the stucture of Dasein. He starts here because his argument is that '[i]f Dasein is understood correctly, it defies such proofs, because, in its Being, it already *is* what subsequent proofs deem necessary to demonstrate for it' (*BT*, p. 249).

It is, then, Cassirer's unity of human nature that Heidegger's *Being and Time* counters. Heidegger rejects the priority of the thinking subject – the Cartesian Ego which haunts both Kant and Cassirer's neo-Kantianism. Understanding is grounded in a subject's 'being-in-the-world' and it is the task of a phenomenological method, working within a hermeneutical circle, to uncover the existential structure of Dasein. 'Communication is never anything like a conveying of experiences, such as opinions or wishes, from the interior of one subject into the interior of another. Dasein-with is already essentially manifest in a co-state-of-mind and a co-understanding' (*BT*, p. 205). There is in human beings a primordial, existential understanding of what constitutes being-in-the-world. So that in 'discourse Being-with becomes "explicitly" *shared*' (*BT*, p. 205). Human beings are still essentially *zōon lógon echōn*, but logos is not understood here as *the power of reason*. Reason 'covers up the phenomenal basis for this definition of "Dasein"'. But human beings reveal themselves as those who talk (*BT*, p. 208). *Logos* is 'discourse' [*Rede*], and *Rede* makes 'manifest what one is "talking about" in one's discourse' (*BT*, p. 56). Logos here relates both to *legein* and to *phōnē metà phantasías* – a 'letting something be seen' (*BT*, p. 56). But because 'language already hides in itself a developed way of conceiving' (*BT*, p. 199) and *logos* is assertion and all assertion is interpretation, human beings are necessarily *homo hermeneuma*.

Heidegger works, then, within the Kantian framework of a Humboldtian model of language, but his ontological programme is concerned to emphasize that signification is rooted in the ontology of Dasein (*BT*, p. 209). That possibility of an ontological programme within the horizon of the Kantian problematic was the hotly debated focus for the Cassirer–Heidegger encounter at Davos. For both thinkers a circle of interpretation remains – we interpret an understanding that is already interpreted, so that there is no understanding without pre-understanding. 'In dealing with what is environmentally ready-to-hand by interpreting it circumspectly, we "see" it *as* a table, a door, a carriage, or a bridge' (*BT*, p. 189). There is never naive, immediate perception. But Heidegger would wish to distinguish between the 'primordial "as" of an interpretation . . . which understands circumspectly [which] we call the existential-*hermeneutical* "as"' . . . [and] the '*apophantical* "as"' of the assertion' (*BT*, p. 201). This '*apophantical* "as"' allows 'an entity [to] be seen from itself' (*BT*, p. 196). So that even 'if this entity is not close enough to be grasped and "seen", the pointing-out has in view the entity itself and not, let us say, a mere "representation" [*Vorstellung*]', (*BT*, p. 196). Language is a deictic for the presence, the 'peculiar phenomenon of Being' (*BT*, p. 203). So that although there is not a pre-linguistic moment and language is not simply an objectification of Dasein, language is a response to [*Entsprechung*], as a participation within, Being. Heidegger relates the apophantic quality of discourse specifically to 'the primordial meaning of *logos* as *apophansis*' (*BT*, p. 196) and it is this which characterizes his own logocentrism. *Logos* and language are not identical for Heidegger, that is the important point. *Logos* as *apophansis* occurs within language as an articulation of Being, particularly in poetry (*BT*, p. 205), but is not identical with language. As distinct from Cassirer (and Humboldt), the logos is that which transcends the teleological immanence of speech and reasoning. For Heidegger, '[i]f the phenomenon of the "as" remains covered up, and, above all, if its existential source in the hermeneutical "as" is veiled, then Aristotle's phenomenological approach to the analysis of the *logos* collapses into a superficial "theory of judgement"' (*BT*, p.

202). In other words, in Cassirer's 'monadological' logocentrism 'the *logos* has been interpreted in a way which is ontologically inadequate' (*BT*, p. 203).

Upon this basis, Heidegger distinguishes between authentic and inauthentic talk. In the former, the '*logos* gets experienced as something present-at-hand' (*BT*, p. 203); the discourse makes something manifest. Without this manifestation, the discourse is 'idle talk' [*Gerede*]. Heidegger returns us, therefore, to a classical logocentric model that is circular in design. Discourse both represents and is an index for Being-in-the-world. An articulation of Being is both what discourse emerges from and what discourse returns us to. But it is important for Heidegger that '[t]he primary relationship-of-Being towards the entity talked about is not "imparted" by communication; but Being-with-one-another takes place in talking with one another and in concern with what is said-in-the-talk' (*BT*, p. 212). Logos is always *logos tinos*; it remains embodied and immanent. The relationship-to-Being cannot be 'appropriated in a primordial manner, but communicates rather by following the route of *gossiping* and *passing the word along* [i.e. idle talk]' (ibid.). *Rede* and *Gerede* are not then distinct in the everydayness of Dasein, but idle talk discloses to Dasein its groundlessness, its state of being fallen or inauthentic. A phenomenological analysis of anxiety, arising from this inauthenticity, discloses that anxiety 'brings Dasein face to face with its *Being-free for* . . . the authenticity of its Being' (*BT*, p. 232). *Gerede* opens the possibility for *Rede*, or authentic discourse which manifests our Being-in-the-world as care [*Sorge*]-for. It is Dasein's care-for or concern-for which ruptures the self-containment of the Cartesian subject and discloses the possibility for a self-transcendence characterized by an ineluctable openness. Thus, in the rupturing of the subject through the disclosure of the authentic discourses in the inauthentic, Dasein's experiences its own mortality.

Since the '*logos* of the phenomenology of Dasein has the character of a *hermeneuein*, through which the authentic meaning of Being . . . [is] *made known* to Dasein's understanding of Being' (*BT*, p. 62), we can term this form of logocentrism 'hermeneutical'. A more detailed analysis of the relationship between *logos*,

Being and saying, of language speaking in and through language, will preoccupy Heidegger's later thinking. His further thinking develops a notion of the Event of the disclosure. We will be examining that thinking in chapter 6. For the moment it is significant that Heidegger's logocentric thinking remains concerned primarily with Dasein's capacity for self-transcendence – a transcendence, that is, as being-towards-death. Heidegger's logocentric thinking is not concerned with the transcendent itself; it is anthropology and philosophy as '*the* science of Being, the ontological science' (*MFL*, p. 16). Being is not God, despite the theological colouring of some of Heidegger's language: 'The existentiell involvement of fundamental ontology brings within the semblance of an extremely individualistic, radical atheism' (ibid. p. 140). Heidegger's hermeneutical ontology attempts to disclose a common state, the question of Being, into which we are all individually thrown.

It is Bultmann, of course, who attempts a Christological reading of Heidegger's phenomenological analysis of Dasein. Jesus is the kerygma and the unveiling of the kerygma is an eschatalogical event realized in the present. But Bultmann is vague on the nature of this kerygma and its appearance because he fails to analyse the problem of theological language in any depth.[10] Paul Ricoeur has pointed out in his 'Preface to Bultmann', 'A complete meditation on the word, on the claim of the word by being, and hence a complete ontology of language is essential here if the expression "word of God" is to be meaningful, or, in Bultmann's term, if this statement is to have nonmythological signification. But, in Bultmann's work, this remains to be thought'.[11] What he looked for from Heidegger, Ricoeur claims, is 'essentially a philosophical anthropology' rather than a model for an ontology of language, so that 'In order to avail himself of Heidegger's "existentials" he has taken a short cut.'[12] Ricoeur states, in the same essay, that 'The claim (*Anspruch*) which God's word addresses to our existence, if it is to

[10] See Robert Funk's *Language, Hermeneutic and the Word of God* (New York: Harper & Row, 1966), p. 35.
[11] *Essays in Biblical Interpretation*, ed. Lewis Mudge (London: SPCK, 1981), p. 70.
[12] Ibid.

be thought, presupposes not only that the meaning of the text is constituted as an ideal correlate of my existence. It presupposes also that the word itself belongs to the being who addresses himself to my existence.'[13] If there is to be knowledge of God, if there is to be theological realism, then a relation must be found between the human word and the word of God. That is not the intention of Heidegger's analysis. Nevertheless, as we shall see in chapter 5, Heidegger's analysis of Dasein's experience of alterity, Heidegger's ontology of language (particularly as it develops in his later work), does suggest a *model* for the relationship between words and the Word for theological thinking which refuses to take Bultmann's short-cut.

In brief, for Cassirer the logos is a common language, a collective structure of consciousness; for Heidegger it is an event, an authentic experience of the human condition. The first is the form of knowledge and the second is the primordial existential state. Between the two – its initial platform in Cassirer's neo-Kantianism and its subsequent development in Heidegger's authenticating discourse (*Rede*) – we discover a third form of logocentric thinking: dialogicalism.

REDEPHILOSOPHIE

The Hebrew form of Logos, *Dabar Elohim* (which relates Logos to a phrase more frequently found in Barth, the Word of God) was being rethought just before, during and after the First World War by several young Jewish and Jewish–Christian theologians and philosophers who constituted an association known as the 'Patmos Group'. Barth met some members of this group in 1919 – the Ehrenberg brothers, and Rosenstock-Huessy,[14] and along with Buber and Rosenzweig he contributed to the journal they edited, *Die Kreature*. Barth left the group three years later because 'they wanted to overwhelm me and choke me with [their] gnosticism',[15] but Rosenstock-Huessy and, subsequently,

---

[13] Ibid.
[14] All three were Jewish converts to Christianity. Rosenzweig also came very close to following their lead but in fact had a reconversion experience to Judaism.
[15] See Busch, *Karl Barth: His Life*, p. 141.

Rosenzweig were developing their ideas on the sacramental value of language years before Barth, Heidegger, and Bultmann.[16] We must assess the model and theology of language developed by these philosophers of dialogue and map out the alternative form logocentrism took as a consequence of their work.

What remains common between these thinkers and the *Sprachphilosophie* of Cassirer and Heidegger is their dependence upon Hamann, Humboldt and later the Marburg School (in particular Hermann Cohen). What essentially makes the group distinctive is their Jewish reinterpretation of Logos. As one scholar has summed this up: 'In contrast to the logos philosophy that has the nature of monologue, Rosenstock reinterpreted the biblical "word" as part of a dialogue.'[17] Theirs is a methodological change which involved not simply a move from neo-Kantianism to phenomenology, but a shift from transcendental subjectivity to dialogicalism. In idealism's exalted subject Rosenzweig saw only an 'eloquent silence' (*SR*, p. 80). In contrast, the dialogical philosophy of language developed a form of social ontology not founded upon the intentionality of the subject (what Rosenzweig termed the 'worldly logos'), but grounded in the communication between the I and the Thou. The in-between was the reality, objective and concrete, and this reality was identified with language as address, discourse or *Rede*. '[T]he I and Thou of human discourse is without more ado the I and Thou between God and man ... the distinction between immanence and transcendence disappears in language' (*SR*, p. 199). On the basis of this analogy between human dialogue and human–divine dialogue, language becomes the organon for revelation, the analogue or *via media* between the language of revelation which speaks and the language of creation which de-lineates, re-counts, de-termines (*SR*, p. 185). Two forms of Logos encounter each other – God's and creation's.

Dabar is both 'word' and 'deed'. It is 'annunciation'. It is

[16] See Harold Stahmer's 'Introduction' to *Judaism Despite Christianity* (Alabama: University of Alabama Press, 1969), p. 14.
[17] Nahum Glatzer, *Rosenzweig: His Life and Thought* (New York: Schocken Books, 1976), p. xiv.

Dabar which brings together the Lutheran emphases of Hamann's philosophy of language and the revelation-as-spoken word theme developed in the Jewish and Judaeo-Christian 'New thinking'(Rosenzweig's term from his essay with that title). An Athens–Jerusalem split was not intended, and that is why I have continued using the word Logos and will continue to use the term logocentrism.[18] But the intention of this group was to focus upon and describe the operation of a Logos beyond the logocentrism of subjective idealism. A philological search for an alternative understanding of Logos was in evidence before their work. This can be seen from the number of academic studies on Logos–philosophy published in Germany at the time. The classical scholarship of Heinze's *Die Lehre vom Logos in der griech Philosophie* (1872), Reinhardt's *Parmenides und die Geschichte der griechischen Philosophie* (1916) and Hoffmann's essay '*Die Sprache und die archaische Logik*' (1925) is summed up in forty double-columned pages for the entry on Logos in Pauly-Wissowa's *Real Encyclopaedie der Classischen Alterums-Wissenschaft* (1929 edition). Here we find: 'But the origin and sense of the Logos doctrine can first be discovered by returning to the original meaning of Logos as "discourse" (*Rede*).'[19] The Logos as speech was seen as distinctly related to an understanding of Logos pre-Parmenides, in the philosophy of Heraclitus. It is thus not insignificant for theologies of the Word that under the heading '*Christliche Theologie*' in the same encyclopedia we read: 'Even Christianity's oldest documents, the letters of the apostle Paul, bear a close relationship to Greek Logos teaching. Paul has the same way of thinking (*Denktechnik*) – the logic of antithesis and the circular form of the evolving process – as Heraclitus.'[20] This account interestingly identifies Paul as a proto-Hegelian.

---

[18] There is something of an Athens–Jerusalem split in Rosenzweig's work. In a manner which is not unlike that of Levinas and Derrida, he will speak of 'philosophy – that is Hellenism' (letter to Rosenstock–Huessy, undated, in *Judaism despite Christianity*, p. 157) Rosenstock-Huessy, as we will see, wished to retain something of the Greek Logos in relation to his understanding of the significance of the Johannine Christ. But Rosenzweig, in his Introduction to Hermann Cohen's *Judische Schriffen*, wrote, pointedly, that 'Had Philo not invented the Logos, no Jew would ever have fallen away from God.'   [19] Vol. 13. p. 1036.   [20] Ibid. p. 1078.

The later work of Buber and Rosenstock drew upon the distinction between Heraclitian and Parmenidian logocentrism. Ernst Hoffmann fleshes out the differences. For Heraclitus, 'Discourse as Logos is a complete Whole.'[21] 'Speaking is also for Heraclitus the essential function of the soul. The ordered world (*Weltgesetze*) shares in speech and participates in God.'[22] He concludes: 'There are hardly two thinkers like Heraclitus and Parmenides who in their significance for metaphysics establish such a sharp and pronounced contrast ... The Heraclitan Logos is life, the word (*die Vokabel*) of the multitude is lifeless and only through the Logos can it become animated; the Parmenidian Logos *is*, words do not have true Being, only relative existence [to it].'[23] His conclusion, with its distinction between the liveliness of the spoken word and words which only have meaning in relation to Logos as Being, between the spoken and the symbolic, encapsulates the difference between the *Redephilosophie* of Rosenzweig and Rosenstock and the *Sprachphilosophie* of Cassirer and Saussure. It is the difference between the word as sacrament and the word as symbol. And Hoffmann's sympathies are with the latter. In terms of dialogicalism, *Sprachphilosophie* is based on an I–It epistemological model which develops an abstract and static picture of language. *Redephilosophie*, in identifying language with discourse, meaning with use, is based on an I–Thou ontological model. It develops a phenomenology of language, an account of the experience of the heard and the spoken. Language is viewed as functioning less as part of a semiotic system, and more as a relational matrix inseparable from our experience of life. Rosenstock called this the 'grammar of being'. In foregoing any analysis of the signification process, it often foregoes any deep appreciation of hermeneutics, of interpretation as being part, if not the heart, of the encounter. We will look more closely at this elision of time between the moment of discourse and the moment of understanding, later, and also the role of the representational in creating that temporal lacuna. For now, it is enough to suggest the latent iconoclasm in *Redephilosophie*.

---

[21] '*Die Sprache und die archaische Logik*' (Tübingen: Heidelberger Abhandl., 1925), p. 5.
[22] Ibid. p. 7.   [23] Ibid. p. 25.

What this return to speech gave rise to, as it had done earlier with Hamann and the *Sturm and Drang* movement, was a critique of Enlightenment reasoning and dialectical methodology. Rosenstock-Huessy: 'my thoughts are haunted by the struggle against dialectic and tabulating conclusions' (in a letter to Rosenzweig dated 29 May 1916). Rosenzweig: 'The Greek spirit, that is the type of the scientific mind looks for mediation ... between man and God. To this Greek charm, the Jew Philo and his Logos fell victim' (*KS*, p. 337). But with the New thinking the '*anthropos theoretikos*, that greatest and most enduring achievement of the Greeks ... has now at last *cessé de regner*' (letter to Rosenstock-Huessy dated 5 September 1916). So, likewise, had monologue ceased to govern the models and methods of thinking and the transcendental 'I' was seen as 'a later discovery' which 'the ancient philosophers did not know as yet'.[24] The I is seen as incomplete. It receives its soul, its authenticity, only in conversation with another and the recognition of a Thou external to itself. Language becomes a vehicle for self-transcendence (and salvation). Taking up a line of thought developed in Humboldtian linguistics, the authentic I is viewed as *within* language, caught in its syntax and grammar, an accusative or 'nominative of passive construction' (*SR*, p. 152).[25] It is embraced in an ongoing dialogue that is historically and culturally contextualized. Rosenstock–Huessy: 'the living language of people always overpowers the individual man who assumes that he could master it ... it guides his concepts unconsciously, towards an unknown future' (*SR*, p. 144).

The historicism of these philosophers of dialogue cannot be underestimated. It marks one of their major differences from Barth's thinking and also their inability fully to outwit Hegelian metaphysics. Rosenzweig writes that 'language is the carrier and messenger of time-bound, flowing, changing, and, therefore, transitory life' (*SR*, p. 302). History and time are reflections of

---

[24] Ebner, *Gesammelte Werke* (Wien: Thomas Morus-Presse, 1952), p. 25.
[25] We will meet this and many other lines of Rosenzweig's thinking later in our analysis of the work of Levinas. See *Correlations in Rosenzweig and Levinas*, Robert Gibbs (Princeton: Princeton University Press, 1992) for an excellent analysis of the parallels in their thinking. See also Nahum Glatzer's essay 'The Concept of Language in the Thought of Franz Rosenzweig' in *The Philosophy of Franz Rosenzweig*.

language; discourse is the inner dynamic constituting time. But it is time always moving towards timelessness, '[f]or the state is the ever changing guise under which time moves step by step toward eternity' (*SR*, p. 332). In revelation the moment is made eternal. There is an experience of immediacy, of the present. 'Eternity is a future which, without ceasing to be future, is nonetheless present' (*SR*, p. 224). In authentic speech, the I–Thou encounter, each moment is new and issues 'into a *nunc stans*, into eternity' (*SR*, p. 29). The I–It constitutes the past tense; it can therefore only represent. A realized eschatology prevails within the horizons of a future *eschaton*. What Buber termed 'the moment of surprise' (in which concrete otherness is encountered) emerges from the tension between the spoken now and an always impending, immanent future in which the Other's response is anticipated as a taste of the eternal.

The logocentrism of the *Redephilosophie* presupposes therefore a doctrine of Providence and establishes language as a *tertium quid*: 'The ways of God are different from the ways of man, but the word of God and the word of man are the same. What man hears in his heart as his own human speech is the very word which comes out of the mouth of God' (*SR*, p. 151). We will return to this statement later, for even 'analogy' seems to dissolve here into 'identity'. Dialogue here is conceived as a sacramental act. In the interweaving of speech, the Jewish notion of the Breath of God and German romantic *Lebensphilosophie*, language as spirit (and the anthropological/theological ambivalence of the German '*Geist*' cannot be undervalued) comes to be seen as the dynamic for historical change, for universal and personal salvation. Rosenzweig: '[W]e disavow a God in history in order to restore Him in the Process by which [history] becomes' (*B*, p. 53).

Rosenzweig's statement introduces the model of revelation as it is conceived by dialogicalism, the model within which Christ has to be placed in the *Redephilosophie* of Christian thinkers like Rosenstock–Huessy and Ebner. This is Hegelianism transformed – by faith – and Christology provides a cutting edge for analysing the differences between Jewish and Christian dialogicalism. Revelation and Christology are the two major concerns in the correspondence between Rosenzweig and Rosenstock conducted throughout 1916, a correspondence which was viewed as a paradigm for dialogical method. Rosenzweig requests, with disarming simplicity: 'please explain to me your present idea of the relation between Nature and Revelation' (*JC*, p. 117). Rosenstock's reply indicates how uncomfortable he finds being put on the spot:

Nature and Revelation: the same material, but opposite ways of being exposed to this light . . . Christ has mediated to us the breaking through into the universe in a heavenward direction of this force, which was latent and imprisoned in the earth. Where hitherto was only Abraham's bosom, there is now a living eternity and an ascent of spirit from star to star. Revelation means the linking of our consciousness also with the union between heaven and earth that transcends the world. The question you put, 'Nature and Revelation', I can only understand as 'natural understanding' and revelation. Nature and Revelation are not comparable. Natural understanding, then . . . helps itself in this enclosure with a net of analogies. (*JC*, p. 119)

The ambivalences are those of a writer thinking on his feet. What is 'this light'? The 'ascent of the spirit from star to star' reminds us that Barth left the Patmos group because of its gnostic tendencies.[26] How far is the figurative language to be understood as prescriptive? How does the idea of nature and revelation as 'the same material, but opposite' relate to nature and revelation as 'not comparable'? But despite the ambivalences a picture emerges of both Rosenstock's Christology and theology of language. 'Natural understanding' with its 'net of analogies' mediates between Nature, on the one hand, and Revelation on the other. Christ incarnates Logos, the perfection of that 'natural understanding' (there are shades of Schleiermacher here), His ascension has broken through the barrier between heaven and earth (the early gnostic images in John's Gospel and

---

[26] In a collection of essays, *Das Geheimnis der Universität* (Stuttgart: Kohlhammer, 1958), Rosenstock-Huessy is still fighting the spectre of gnosticism. This is especially so in the essay '*Dich und Mich*' in which he sets out '*gegen das Unkraut der Gnosis verteidigen*' (p. 149). He distinguishes his form of dialogism from Buber's where '*Ich-Du durchschlingen sich zwei Wesen*' (p. 150). However, with Rosenstock's insistence that the Thou is above the world and the *Dich* and the *Mich* are accusatives of this Thou, we seem far closer to the gnostic barriers than with Buber's insistence that 'the pure relation' is 'not to renounce the world but to establish it on its true basis' (*IT*, p. 79).

the Letter to the Ephesians are not far away) and so we have access to that 'consciousness' which recognizes 'the union' that 'transcends the world'. The sacramental character of the 'analogies' is emphasized in a later letter, where, in discussing religious language and the use of the term 'worm', he writes: 'Don't imagine that by "worm" and suchlike I am spinning allegories; these things have come into existence in the external world, so that we can now possess and use them as symbols for our innerworld, as *significatio* and *explicatio*' (*JC*, p. 123). The tension here seems to be one between existentialism and Platonism – the desire to awaken to the eschatological significance of the present and to embrace the particularity of the world, on the one hand, and the desire to transcend the world completely, on the other. It is a tension evident in the Incarnation, and it led to a Christology which emphasized a theology of history and understanding of the working of the Spirit in the contingency of the world and time, only to effect a salvation which is a transcendence of history, the world and time. This same crux appears in another guise, i.e.: why Jesus of Nazareth? Could it have been anyone? For a doctrine of providence provides criteria for understanding the unique appearance of Christ, while a transcendence of history implies that the contingency of Christ, the story of Jesus of Nazareth, is merely propaedeutic, that the history was not intrinsically necessary at all. Analogical thinking steers the way through troubled waters here. As Rosenstock expresses it later, 'Jesus became the centre of history by being the human soul made visible' (*CF*, pp. 189–90). The Christology here has its counterpart in Rosenstock's presentation of language as a medium whereby Nature and Revelation mirror each other. Language, like Christ, is fundamentally analogical in that it establishes the correspondences between the terrestial and the Divine, so that, for us, now one person has done it, we all have the opportunity to develop the logos potential within us.

The gnostic echoes may arise from the figurative nature of Rosenstock's language, although we find similar accounts of the *logos spermatikos* in Rosenzweig: 'The new creation of revelation is the soul, which is unearthly in earthly life' (*SR*, p. 326) But in both thinkers the stoicism is endemic – we are perfected within our histories by the empathy between the logos principle within us (within our consciousness) and the divine mind beyond us. All is synecdoche and typology – this will be an axiom of Rosenzweig's Jewish theology. In the stoic elements there is the possibility of a balance between a present and a future eschatology. But, and this is typical of the writings of dialogical philosophers, frequently the historical and material teleology is consumed by a realized eschatology. It is through a present and continuous unveiling that we are made to inhabit a sacramental world where the significance of the concrete lies solely in its constituting an analogy, an entrance to that which is eternal. The thinking in this letter wanders between pantheism, panentheism and the need to find some specific function in history for the Incarnation. And the function Rosenstock gives Christ, as revealing the way of ascent 'from star to star', coupled with the idea of Jesus as our analogy, can only lead to gnosticism.

I have drawn this out because it is precisely the ambivalent position of Christ in this picture that enables Rosenzweig to see that the only people who need Christ are the pagans, not the Jews. To the Jews the particular revelation in Christ is not necessary; they need no such propaedeutic in order to enter the universe's dialogue with the divine. The anthropology informing Rosenstock's Christology has always been known to the Jews. 'Man is a natural being (part of creation); the receiver of Revelation (Priest and Prophet); the agent of Redemption ... Why just Jesus and not (or at least, not also) Goethe?' (*JC*, p. 74). The Jews have always lived with their eyes towards an Eternal horizon. Creation has always been the place of revelation; there has always been that speech, that Word made flesh. Buber would agree: 'Israel taught and showed: the real God who can be spoken to, because He is the one who speaks to Men.'[27] Rosenstock considers that the dialogue began with the Incarnation. Rosenzweig and Buber see the dialogue as having begun with creation and with God's call to the Jews to be witnesses. For all three of them, this is the point of their departure from neo-

---

[27] Quoted by H. Stahmer, *'Speak that I may see thee!' The Religious Significance of Language*, p. 198.

Kantian linguistic relativism – the relativism which eventually
Saussure develops into the idea that there is no reality to which
words refer, that in fact words create an infinite number of
realities. The absolutizing of speech, the *a priori* revelation-as-
speech, entails that all our words are God's words and in their
reference to God's Word they redeem themselves and creation.
It entails also that all languages are one (which provides a
theological guarantee for the possibility of translating the Scriptures). 'The ways of God are different from the ways of man, but
the word of God and the word of man are the same. What man
hears in his heart as his own human speech is the very word
which comes out of God's mouth . . . that word of creation which
reverberates within us and speaks within us' (*SR*, p. 151). In the
I–Thou dialogue the It of creation is redeemed and history
moves towards silence.[28] This is the point at which dialogical
sacramentalism moves into iconoclasm, and its commitment to
the contingent and material dissolves into 'the silence of consum-
mate understanding' (*SR*, p. 295). Language is intimately
involved in the process of becoming, Rosenzweig's 'Becoming-
unity', until All is 'coalesced in the One' (*SR*, p. 238), but
language must eventually usher in its own destruction. For '[i]n
eternity the spoken word fades away into the silence of perfect
togetherness ... the word unites, but those who are united
fall silent' (*SR*, p. 308). All the pronouns – I–Thou–It – act
inter-dependently to bring about this final, eschatological
consummation.

At this point perhaps a warning is needed: there is no

[28] The motif of silence is fundamental to Rosenzweig's and Buber's work, as it is also to
the philosophies of language conceived by Cassirer and Walter Benjamin. For all four,
silence indicates a Messianic triumph over representation, the apotheosis of an
iconoclasm we noted earlier. Representational language locks communion into the
sphere of intentionality which for Buber is defined as an I–It universe. Cassirer, as we
have seen, conceives an evolving purification of language in a movement towards a
silent future. Language, in Cassirer's strict Kantian framework, is representational,
but not re-presentational. Walter Benjamin, in his 1916 essay 'On Language as Such
and on the Language of Man', conceives language as 'imbued with ... the residue of
the creative word of God' (*One Way Street and Other Essays*, London: Verso, 1985, p.
123) which will be apocalyptically clarified in the Messianic dawn. Language here is
re-presentational. Only Buber sees the operation of that silence in the present, in the
I–It discourse. For Buber language is both re-presentational and representational.
See chapter 6.

uncomplicated homogenizing of the *Rede* philosophers' project. We will examine more closely in chapter 5 the distinctiveness of Martin Buber's work and its influence upon contemporary Jewish models of the Word in human words. Furthermore, both the work of Ferdinand Ebner and Gabriel Marcel was executed in ignorance of German dialogicalism. For Ebner speech is not *ipso facto* sacred; it becomes a vehicle for the Logos on the basis of our being created *imago dei*. Therefore only 'man, not the animal, has the Word – because God is the object of man and only man ... But God is man's object because man has the word – not as his own invention, but from God' (*S*, p. 681). Logos 'means discourse, Word, but also reason. Reason is the inward sense of man for the Word, it is that in him which advances toward the Word and its meaning' (*S*, p. 417). With Ebner, therefore, the dialogical method is integrated into the dialectical method: man has broken free of his subjectivity through speech but moves towards the transcendental Christ, the Thou, the spiritual being of man. An individualism remains central as one internalizes the Scriptures as a form of personal address: 'one places the word of Christ back into the personal actuality of its being spoken (by making oneself the person to whom it speaks immediately, whom it concerns personally ...) ... then the human–spiritual reality of Christ becomes visible' (*S*, 1, p. 460). Creation and community do not become sacramental; in fact, a much more vivid gnosticism looms here because all social and historical contingency is swept up into a transcendental focus. The Incarnation is 'now', the word is consumed in the Word, the Word has no historical or social context – Christ is a universal referent, not in any sense an historically contingent one. Ebner here is in line with the hermeneutical task of Rosenzweig and Buber as they approached translating the Bible, the 'task of recapturing the original, audible, dialogical quality'. Where the former talks of the voice of Christ, the hearing of the Word, the latter are talking of the voice of God, which is also a hearing of the Word. Furthermore, Ebner's Christology returns us to the core problem tackled in Rosenstock–Rosenzweig letters. Is the historical appearance of the Christ really necessary? Or may there not be several appearances of Christlikeness? Either way, no grounds are provided for the uniqueness of Jesus Christ.

By way of summary, let us then proceed to clarify the character and some of the consequences of dialogical logocentrism. First of all, despite Rosenzweig's attempts to examine the Nay and the Nought, in the earlier part of *The Star of Redemption* (an attempt to become more negatively dialectical); despite also moments when he recognizes the 'Perhaps, perhaps . . . We have ended in a maelstrom of contradiction' (*SR*, p. 85) – the book ends at the gate of heaven. The movement of dialogical thought is towards synthesis, a synthesis immanent throughout. Nevertheless, Rosenzweig wishes to distinguish this synthesis from the 'synthesis' of Idealism in which the 'antithesis is reduced to merely mediating between the construction and the reconstruction of the thesis' (*SR*, p. 229). He wishes to maintain the dialectic in which the Nay and the Yea are equivalent (*SR*, p. 230). But the 'and' which synthizes the Nay and the Yea lies in the root word of creation, 'Good'.[29] In other words, the Nay is never seriously considered as outside the goodness of creation as God first envisioned it. All differences are finally to be embraced by the one, 'all these [independent] melodies adapt themselves to the same rhythm and unite in the single harmony' (*SR*, p. 237). The world indwells a soteriological process that will lead to its redemption – where the gate of heaven is also the gate of Eden.

Secondly, the relating of these independences is performed through language as it establishes a web of analogies. The authentic *Rede* is synecdoche and typology, for it clarifies and promotes human eternity in the very soil of creation (*SR*, p. 259). At times analogy dissolves into identity, differences collapse into sameness: 'The love of the human, the earthly lover – that was a counterpart, nay more than a counterpart, it was a direct likeness of divine love' (*SR*, p. 212).

Thirdly, in a way which relates back to both Rosenzweig's affirmation of ultimate synthesis and *analogia entis*, the emphasis upon immediacy and directness skips over the thorny paths of self-reflection and hermeneutics in its beautification of present

---

[29] Compare Barth's 'antithesis between equals', *GD*, p. 210.

experience. The rhetoric of representation is consumed in epiphany. 'God ... can make himself known without danger to the immediacy and pure presentness of experience' (*SR*, p. 182). The instant, the moment, the Now of revelation bears all time and circumstance towards the eternal 'light of the divine sanctuary' (*SR*, p. 424). *Redephilosophie* diminishes the problem of time.[30] This immediacy is a facet of the reception and response in dialogue.

The centrality of dialogue, of the spoken word, even when referring to the textual, is closely related to hearing as receiving immediately and knowing as instant recognition of the other's intention.[31] Speech appears to require no interpretation; its event, rather than its content, is the focus for dialogical attention, and it is this which allows speech to become a pre-hermeneutic experience. It is not the phonetic sign that signifies but the exchange. The material phonetic sign vanishes into its own presence, a presence that is a moment of living, a moment of creation in its redemption. In fact, the signifier–signified model of language belongs to the I–It relationship. The I–It implies a mastery of the world by the ego. The I–It is a neo-Kantian world. We will examine Buber's understanding of this in more detail in chapter 5, for to some extent Buber departs from dialogicalism. He recognizes that 'we are continually making the eternal Thou into an It' (*IT*, p. 143). Reification is unavoidable. The signifier–signified model of language presupposes that significance lies in exchange. There could be no exchange unless there were an understanding of how to read the signs in the exchange, even if by those signs we understand gestures and inflexions of voice. That the signs are part of a language game rather than fixed in meaning can be accepted. Meaning is not necessarily prior to use and each exchange must involve a modification of what was pre-understood. There is a learning of the game whilst being involved in the game. But we could not join the game without being able to make the signs ourselves,

---

[30] See Karl Löwith's essay 'M. Heidegger and F. Rosenzweig or Temporality and Eternity', *Philosophy and Phenomenological Research*, vol. 3, 1942–3, pp. 53–77.

[31] See Derrida's essay 'Tympan' (*MP*) for a critique of the metaphysics of the ear and eye.

without some knowledge that signs 'refer', without some knowledge that what is, is in fact an address that involves us in making a response which we are capable of making. The significance of the exchange cannot be separated from the referential content of the exchange. And yet one finds in these phenomenological accounts of speech that this tends to be forgotten. In the emphasis upon I and Thou, the ontology of the interhuman, the immediacy of the encounter is all-important. One can see why. There is an unbridgeable difference between the I–It and the I–Thou. Immediacy cannot logically be immediate and yet to admit mediacy is to admit defeat, because it admits a subject–object split.[32]

It seems, then, that there is a problem in analysing the experience–thought–word–object matrix in dialogicalism. These philosophers wish to see experience–thought–word as simultaneous (which they have to be if the communication is immediate) – one hears, one understands, one speaks even when one is heard, one is understood and one is spoken to. There is a distinction between thought and speech, but it is only the distinction between inner and external speech: 'even in the original state of the act of thought the inner action might take place in relation to a genuine and not merely an "inward" *Thou*' (D, p. 27). It is significant that Buber says 'might' here, for what is threatened by dialogicalism's too brief analysis of the experience–thought–word–object matrix is exactly the genuine otherness of the Thou. Otherness can only be constituted as an object other than the I. The otherness of the Thou requires some I–It relationship to validate itself. Even when the Other is taking the initiative, in a pure act of addressing the I, the I can only respond insofar as the Other is now the object of the I's knowledge, the object to be answered. Where the It disappears into the Thou, the Other can never be a genuine Other, can never be the 'thou in opposition'. Heidegger realized this – he often noted the association between '*ein*' *Gesprach* and *das Selbe*, dialogue and sameness. Such dialogue is really still only monological, '*ein*'.[33]

---

[32] See M. Theunissen, *The Other: Social Ontology in Heidegger, Sartre and Buber* (Cambridge, Mass.: MIT Press, 1986) chapter 8, sections 2 and 3.
[33] See Vattimo, *The End of Modernity*, pp. 155–6.

The immediacy of the dialogue can only be achieved by: (a) collapsing the time between being spoken to and speaking; and (b) dissolving that which constitutes time, i.e. the representational nature (phonemes, reference and grammar) of discourse itself. Hence the priority of silence in dialogical thought – a silence which brings the dialogicalism of Rosenzweig and Rosenstock back into the orbit of neo-Kantian thinking, and particularly the teleology of symbolism as Cassirer conceives it.

If the Thou is not allowed to also be an It, an Other over against the I, then, as with idealism, there are no independent objects. And if there are no objects then there are no grounds for validating what is heard or understood. There is no Other whose existence is not already determined by the presupposition of the I. We are caught within a network of continuous dialogues, part of an individual, historical and universal process – hence a social ontology – but as with idealism, ultimately, there are no guarantees we are not simply constructing the reality of the Thou-as-God or the Thou-as-neighbour. Later Levinas, developing the thought of Rosenzweig and Buber, will take up this question and write about 'dia-logue', emphasizing a need to define the rupturing of monologue. Without the freedom of being a reader, an interpreter of the dialogue and therefore both a participant and an observer, there is no guarantee that this encounter does not return to subjective idealism. It is at this point that Barth and Buber with their alternative understandings of 'dialectic' and their emphases upon the negativity of the encounter – the fact the Other does not confirm but annihilates what was presupposed – make their distinctive contributions. The negativity of the encounter is the guarantee that this Other is Other.

Of the three logocentric models outlined in this chapter, it is the dialogical model and Heidegger's (whose later work owes something to the dialogical model) which are struggling to locate a transcendental Logos, a Word beyond and yet discerned within words. Dialogicalism treats the same problematic that lies at the centre of Barth's theology of the Word, a problematic with which Levinas and Derrida will struggle in their own analyses of representation and presence. Significantly, the analysis of the problematic seems inevitably theological. *Redephilosophie* returns us to an explicitly theological account of language and an emphasis – which Heidegger considerably develops (and criticizes) – upon the relationship between language and ontology. For the moment we need to assess Barth's position as it developed in the context of these contemporary logocentric models in order to get a clearer picture of what is happening in chapter 5 of the *Church Dogmatics*.

CHAPTER 4

Barth between Sprache *and* Rede *philosophy*

In trying to cover the immense fields of German philology and philosophy of language between 1760 and 1925 an oversimplification and a radical reduction are certain. Just as certain is an homogenizing of projects in a way that cannot do justice to the rich variety of individual differences. What is being attempted is to define a core problem being treated from various angles by various representative figures or groups, a problem Barth shared, a problem that remains relevant for any theology of the Word being contemplated today. Three forms of logocentric thinking have emerged – Cassirer's 'monadological' account, Heidegger's 'hermeneutical' account and the 'dialogical' account. Deeper in the past, and to some extent influential upon all three, is Hamann's account, which tried to hold together and coherently describe a Christological paradox: Christ as the Logos vertically cutting through the logocentric totality of all human words and thoughts. Hamann's comments concerning entrance into the revealed Logos by faith in Christ (comments arising directly from his Lutheranism) constitute a fourth form of logocentric thinking which had itself been insufficiently developed. What Hamann, Heidegger and the dialogical thinkers share is a common problematic: an attempt to render a coherent account of the transcendental condition that would guarantee the meaningfulness of what can be known and interpreted only immanently. That is, their concern was with the relation between language and metalanguage. And Barth too is examining this problematic.

Philosophically educated in neo-Kantianism, theologically nurtured on the works of Luther, erstwhile member of the dialogical Patmos group, Barth stood at the confluence of at least three of the forms of logocentric thinking outlined in chapters 2 and 3. If the connection between his work and Heidegger's thinking is tenuous from Barth's side, Heidegger, through Bultmann, continued to be influenced by Barth's thinking.[1] In this chapter I set out to assess Barth's association with these different forms of logocentric thinking and trace the extent to which they lie behind his own account of discourse in chapter 5 of *Church Dogmatics*.

BARTH AND *SPRACHPHILOSOPHIE*

It was recognized quite early that Barth 'continuously mixes his philosophical presuppositions, taken from the Marburg school, with the contents of Scripture'.[2] The extent to which Barth was familiar with the work of Cohen and Natorp has been examined more recently.[3] Heinrich Barth was a pupil of Natorp's and Barth certainly owned a copy of Cohen's 1915 work *Der Begriff der Religion im System der Philosophie*. Contrary to the emphasis upon pure thought generating its own objects with no reference to anything external to itself, Wilhelm Herrmann (Barth's teacher at Marburg) wished to place parameters around the realm of thinking. Herrmann was attempting to provide what the philosophies of Natorp and Cohen could not account for, that is, an assessment of religious experience. In particular, revelation for Natorp and Cohen could only be understood in terms of the continuity of creation whereby the ability to reason constituted a correlation between God and human beings as creators. Rosenzweig takes up and develops this position. But for Barth this move issues in a natural theology

---

[1] 'Karl Barth's commentary on *The Epistle to the Romans* appears in 1918. It influences Heidegger's whole style of textual exposition, of word-by-word interpretation, and directs his attention to the radical, psychologizing theology of Kierkegaard. This theological interest, from 1923 on, brings Heidegger into close exchange with Bultmann, and forms the basis for a persistent mutual awareness between Heideggerian ontology and the modern "theology of crisis"', George Steiner, *Heidegger* (London: Fontana, 1978), p. 73.

[2] Paul Schempp, 'Marginal Glosses on Barthianism', first published in *Zwischen den Zeiten* VI (1928), issue 4. Translated for *The Beginnings of Dialectical Theology*, p. 195.

[3] Simon Fischer, *Revelatory Positivism* (Oxford: Oxford University Press, 1988).

already evident in the liberal Protestant tradition which emerged on the rhetorical strength of Schleiermacher's work. It was Herrmann who argued for a distinction between the orders of theology and philosophy. Herrmann re-emphasized Luther's justification by faith (important, as we saw in chapter 2, for Hamann) in order to argue the case for the existence of self-authenticating religious experiences. Thus his work described both an epistemological and an ontological dualism. Revelation here becomes a punctuating experience of God, an event the validity of which Marburg philosophy was unable to assess.[4] Nevertheless, there was still within this dualism a meditation on faith that bore traces of a natural theology given in experience, for there was in the depths of human experience an awareness that the content of certain experiences was divine. In Herrmann's major work, *The Communion of the Christian with God*, he emphasizes the importance of revelation through Jesus Christ for Christians, but is still forced to admit 'that we by no means wish to assert, even for a moment, that the savages of New Holland have no knowledge of God, no pulsation of true religion, and therefore no communion with God'.[5] Such 'pulsations' may not be intelligible to those living within the cultural conditions of Christianity, but they cannot be denied or refuted either.

Barth's understanding of the nature of language is deeply influenced by this neo-Kantian background. It was a background, as we have seen, that led increasingly towards the development of semiotics. Meaning becomes a relation between cognition and culture; it can be neither fixed nor stabilized. But, like Herrmann, Barth also wished to render an account of revelation as a punctuating experience, a means of objective knowledge. He struggled to describe the operation of the Word beyond and other than the immanence of meaning depicted in neo-Kantian logocentrism – an other remaining Wholly Other. In his early work (his 1919 essay '*Moderne Theologie und Reichsgottesarbeit*', for example), faith is understood as an inner exper-

---

[4] Fischer, p. 143.
[5] *The Communion of the Christian with God* (London: SCM, 1972), p. 62.

ience, in a manner close to Schleiermacher and Herrmann.[6] But by 1911, in his essay, '*La Réapparition de la metaphysique dans la théologie*', he was emphasizing the autopistia of revelation which is given expression in symbols having no intrinsic relation to knowledge of God.[7] The naked experience of revelation assumed greater significance in Barth's thinking, while he continued to maintain a commitment to the epistemological idealism of Marburg anthropology. His acceptance of Marburg epistemology remained, but it was juxtaposed to a new appeal to the ontological. The tensions here led to 'dialectical' or 'crisis' theology and Barth's subsequent preoccupation with the connection between revelation and conceptualization, the Word and words.

Already in the first edition of *Romans* (1919) Barth describes 'our position as corresponding to one who waits in the objective space between God and the world' (*1R*, p. 389). He even employs the word *Krisis* in a way that foreshadows his later understanding of the term: 'the identical [*Gleichartigkeit*] crisis in which all human beings of whatsoever rank always stand in opposition to God' (*1R*, p. 441). But we can see why he later felt it necessary to allow the first edition to 'disappear from the scene' (*2R*, p. 2/vi), by comparing his earlier with his later conception of dialectic. In the first edition, the word is consciously employed with Socratic connotations. For example, commenting upon Romans 8.23 and the space [*Lage*] between God and human beings, Barth writes that there is not here 'a deserted, motionless, fixed and complete division of affairs, through the will of God, but in fact a frozen [*augenblickliche*] expression of a movement, like a bird in flight. We need to position ourselves in this movement with the intention of allowing it to move us. The question and answer, through which the will of God is manifested and in which human beings and their kind become what they are, is a Socratic, pedagogical question and answer' (*1R*, p. 384). It is this process of question and answer, in which the questions serve in a negative manner 'to illuminate and open the way forward', that characterizes the movement between these

---

[6] Fischer, pp. 180–1.   [7] Ibid., p. 202.

two poles, God and human beings. The questions 'and their rebuttal demonstrate the sheer difficulty and struggle of those who search for truth ... But ... the dialectical method well maintains the steady progress of knowledge' (*1R*, p. 384). It is by maintaining such an understanding of dialectic that Barth can write in his first Preface that 'historical understanding is a continual, ever candid and penetrating conversation'.

When he comes to rethink and rewrite his commentary on Romans 8.23 for his second edition, nothing of this remains. Or rather, Barth still holds to the dialectical process of thinking and searching, but now as '[c]rossing and dissolving the continuous process of history is the terrible and incomprehensible process of revelation' (*2R*, pp. 359/344). A second 'process' radically disrupts the first, the immanent dialectic ('we are unable to comprehend otherwise than by means of a dialectical dualism' – *2R*, pp. 358/342) is struck through by what Kierkegaard called, and Barth quotes, 'the "infinite qualitative distinction" between time and eternity' (*2R*, p. 10/xiii). The belief in 'the steady progress of knowledge' becomes an acceptance of the inerasable paradox of the human condition: 'the meeting-place of God and man is not an arena ... but a point where God and man meet in order to separate and separate in order to meet' (*2R*, pp. 372/356).

What occurs between the completion of the first edition of *Romans* and the totally rewritten second edition is Barth's direct encounter with *Redephilosophie*.

BARTH AND *REDEPHILOSOPHIE*

In his article on the founding of the journal *Die Kreature* – '*Rückblick auf Die Kreature*' – Rosenstock recalls that Barth was one of its main supporters. Between 1919 and 1920 the Patmos-verlag published *Die Bücher vom Kreuzweg*, to which Barth contributed the long article 'The Christian in Society' (trans-lated in a collection of Barth's early essays *The Word of God and the Word of Man*). Rosenstock characterizes Barth as 'intransigently Confessional', which is not consistently the position evident in his article, as we shall see. The point of the adjective is ideological – the intransigency of Barth's position is expressed in a context where Buber is characterized as 'a Jewish Zionist' and Joseph Wittig as 'a Catholic priest'.[8] Extremes meet. Rosenstock foregrounds the confrontational character of their meetings; their differences substantiated the otherness which gave rise to the need for dialogue. The presupposition of their meetings is the availability of an *Ursprache* that grounds all positions. *Gemein-sprache*, as we have seen, is the term Rosenstock employed. 'They [the editors] were aware that Martin Heidegger's "thrown man" certainly exists, but it is dumb. They were aware that we only speak if others are there; that others speak because we are there.'[9] What was being sought after the First World War by the Patmos group was a new understanding of *Gemeinsprache* and *Gemeinschaft*. The group embraced an ecumenism not founded upon compromise or tolerance, but 'the goal of the struggle' was to become 'the starting point for living thought'.[10] Why did Barth involve himself with such a struggle? Why did Hans Ehrenberg seek out Barth and get him to join the dialogue? The answers to these questions have much to do with a shared understanding of Logos as the transcendental Other.

'The Christian in Society' had been delivered at Tambach in 1919, at the Conference for Religious Socialism, and it was as a consequence of this lecture that Barth became acquainted with members of the Patmos Group. There are elements in the lecture obviously attuned to their own emerging philosophy. The 'meaning of so-called religion is found in its relation to actual life' (*WW*, p. 276). Christianity does not evade the world, it enables a long, hard stare at it. It is in this life that a movement from God to man is evident, a call of the Other to the I, but the immediate and Original 'is never experienced as Form. "Experience" is only a reference to the Original, to God' (*WW*, p. 285). The 'experience', then, is not of any direct object; it is not an It but a relation. The event of the experience has a logic which differs from that of the knowledge of an object in the neo-Kantian economy of knowledge. As such, it is not an experience different from others but 'the world of God ... appearing in

---

[8] *Das Geheimnis der Universität*, p. 208. [9] Ibid., p. 209. [10] Ibid., p. 211.

secular life' (*WW*, p. 268). The experience is characterized negatively. In fact, the lecture foreshadows to some extent Barth's new understanding of 'dialectic' that will emerge more substantially in his revised edition of *Romans*. Where it differs from Barth's later dialectical theology, and looks back to Barth's earlier Christian socialism, is in its emphasis upon 'the miracle of the revelation of God' (*WW*, p. 281) as standing in relation to and inseparable from other I–It relations in the secular world. The revelation of God is made concrete in the community – and this, as we have seen, is a fundamental tenet of dialogicalism.

Another dialogical echo is evident in the essay's antipathy to idealism and espousal of realism. 'True perception of life is hostile to all abstractions' (*WW*, p. 313). Dead is the inner and outer dichotomy as the transcendental ego is ruptured by the Wholly Other whose presence is located in the ordinary and the everyday. There emerges what Barth had already conceived in the first edition of *Romans*, an 'unbroken movement' (*WW*, p. 293) between man and God within which true understanding lies. '[W]e *do* share in the resurrection movement, with or without the accompaniment of religious feeling we *are* activated by it' (*WW*, p. 293). Because of the dynamism of this movement, and because there is no access to some Archimedian point outside this movement, all our knowledge and understanding is incomplete. Final answers are falsehoods.[11] We live amidst transition, but 'in all the social relations in which we may find ourselves, we must perceive something ultimate' (*WW*, p. 300). The present world is 'only a parable' (*WW*, p. 306) penetrated 'by its heavenly archetype' (*WW*, p. 307) and so 'the simple *objectivity* of our thought, speech and action ... contains a promise' (*WW*, p. 308). The logocentrism we have seen as central to dialogical thought becomes more explicit: 'To all our thought, speech and action, there is an inner meaning [*immer nur gemeint ist* – an ever-present suggestion] that presses for expression' (*WW*, p. 317). There is 'the other, for whose actual

---

[11] We can note here how close this thinking lies to that of Gogarten in the important essay 'Between the Times', published in *Die Christliche Welt* in 1920, and one of the early keystones of dialectical theology. See James M. Robinson, *The Beginnings of Dialectical Theology*.

appearing we yearn' (*WW*, p. 320). Therefore, God's 'immanence means at the same time his transcendence'. Christologically, the 'resurrection of Jesus Christ from the dead is the power
which moves both the world and us, because it is the appearance
in our corporeality of a *totaliter aliter* constituted corporeality'
(*WW*, p. 323).

Correspondences with dialogicalism are certainly available,
most particularly in the way Barth distinguishes between two
forms of logos, an immanent and a transcendent one. First the
Word of God, 'the *dunamis*, the meaning and might of the living
God who is building a new world', and society which is 'now
really ruled by its own logos, say rather a pantheon of its own
hypostases and powers' (*WW*, p. 280). Society's logos is the
Parmedian, self-contained reason. God's Logos is described
more in terms of the Heraclitan model, a creative force that
embraces the individual and throws him into a flux. But here the
Heraclitan Logos is not identified with *Rede* so much as *Wort*, a
word with distinct Protestant connotations. In his first edition of
Romans Barth does employ the neuter form *das Reden* to describe
the communication from God, but by employing *Wort* he is still
describing a creative event which vitalizes existence and renders
it meaningful, just like *Rede*. Like the *dabar elohim* of Genesis, it is
pictured in terms of a voice directing its address to the individual. We find this picture recurring throughout Barth's early
work. In 'The Righteousness of God' (1916) it is 'the voice of our
conscience, telling us of the righteousness of God' (*WW*, p. 9); it
is 'God speak[ing] within us' (*WW*, p. 25). In 'The Strange New
World in the Bible' (1916) it is the voice of God coming to
expression in the Bible and projecting a new world into our old,
ordinary world (*WW*, p. 37).

Although there are echoes of dialogicalism in Barth's Tambach
lecture, the theological basis for *Gemeinschaft* between Barth and
these philosophers of dialogue lies in what remains vague in
Barth. In particular, the central axes of both his Christology and
anthropology stand in need of clarification. Barth's presentation
of Jesus Christ as the incarnation of the *totaliter aliter* is, for
example, inconsistent (*WW*, p. 323). At one point Christ is

compared to Socrates, who 'found a direct indication of a general original knowledge of the meaning and aim of life. His findings astonished him. And his astonishment was genuine worship of God the Creator' (*WW*, p. 302). Even so, 'more clearly brought out in Jesus than Socrates is that farseeing happy patience in which all things transitory . . . are seen in the light of the eternal' (*WW*, p. 305). What is significant here is that there is any basis at all for a comparison between Socrates and Christ, that there is an 'even more clearly'. This betrays Schleiermacher's lingering influence.[12] But the comparison stands at odds with an insistence that Jesus Christ is *totaliter aliter*; it is closer to the liberal Barth of 1910 who wrote '*Der christliche Glaube und die Geschichte*'. This is a Christology that Rosenstock could endorse and the Jewish associates of the Patmos Group could entertain. Christ is the perfect expression of an eternity 'man can find . . . in his heart' (*WW*, p. 326). 'We affirm', Barth writes, 'that thesis of humanism that even fallen man is the bearer of the divine spark' (*WW*, p. 310). And so a positive picture of the *imago dei* as the basis for the hearing of divine address by the I, the presence of the Word of God in the words of human beings, is maintained unequivocally. *Gemeinsprache* and *Gemeinschaft*, the Rosenstock–Rosenzweig–Buber ideals, have Barth's support as well. But it is precisely this pietistic, even gnostic anthropology (the divine spark in the human breast) which wrestles in Barth's thinking with a neo-Kantian anthropology that denies its possibility.

It is this neo-Kantian side of Barth that increasingly wishes to place quotation marks around the so-called immediacy and directness of revelation so treasured by the philosophers of dialogue. We recall that it is such an emphasis upon immediacy and directness of revelation that totally compromises any understanding of God as Wholly Other, for the Other is collapsed into the same. Even in his earlier essay 'The Strange New World in the Bible', Barth recognizes that the voice heard within the Scriptures is a product of interpretation. Unlike the

---

[12] See Jeffrey C. Pugh's, *The Anselm Shift: Christology and Method in Barth's Theology* (New York: Peter Lang, 1990), p. 45.

philosophers of dialogue, he emphasizes the need to pass through a hermeneutical stage. There is no immediate access to the voice of God: we have to read the Bible *as* history, or *as* ethics, or *as* ecclesiology before arriving at the place where hermeneutics dissolve into the experience of direct encounter, or hearing. Certainly, when the revelation comes, there 'on the threshold of the kingdom of God! There no one asks. There one sees. There one hears. There one has. There one knows' (*WW*, p. 47). When the eschatological event comes, then, Barth's model for its operation is very close to Rosenzweig's, the revelation that dissolves even analogy into the perfection of what is immediately known. But Barth will increasingly read the character of this revelation dialectically, toning down its positive, mystical quality, as he moves towards the completion of his second edition of *Romans*. And with this move into dialectical theology, his awareness of mediacy, of interpretation, of access only via exegesis deepens considerably. The immediacy and directness of revelation have to be counterpoised by the constitutive consciousness of its human reception. The site which it becomes important to examine now is the realm of the in-between.

Barth, then, never repudiates his neo-Kantian anthropology in the way Rosenzweig and Rosenstock do. Hearing the Word of God, discovering the voice of the author, does not come in moments of pure intuition; hearing and discovering are both interpretations. When Barth comes to write the Preface to his second edition, he makes plain that the speaking of God Himself is not simply available. As he succinctly puts it, 'the question of the true nature of interpretation is the supreme question' (*2R*, p. 9/xii). In other words, as believers we hold that what God addresses to us is true, but the interpretation of that truth always remains questionable. It is the questioning which mediation arouses and which interpretation responds to that is the core of Barth's appreciation of 'the "inner dialectic of the matter" in the actual words of the text' (*2R*, p. 10/xiii). The question of interpretation and mediation pushes Barth towards an awareness of a constant dialectic within theological language. It pushes him too in an opposite direction from the model for the operation of discourse in *Redephilosophie*, for the inner dialectic of discourse implies that the nature of discourse is agonistic, not analogous.

When we ask what is the nature of this 'inner dialectic', then we are asking about the character of both Paul's writing and Barth's theology. The dialectic is not simply the God–human divide, but more the way that divide manifests itself within discourses discoursing about that divide. That, in its turn, is not simply a matter of style – the use of paradox and oxymorons. It is also, and mainly, a matter of a constant and reiterated reflection upon 'the inadequacy of human language' (*2R*, p. 224/206) and the relationship between knowledge of this inadequacy and the divine imperative to speak initiated by the fact that *Deus dixit*. This dialectic, then, manifests itself in the movement within theological discourse between the immediacy of revelation and the mediation of language. Barth reflects upon this mediated immediacy in an attempt to trace the passing of the Word, the testimony to the event of that Word, in human words. '[W]e boldly employ this language, the language of romanticism, because it is impossible to describe the immediacy of the divine forgiveness except by parables drawn from human immediacy' (*2R*, p. 220/202). The 'perception breaks upon us' and as '[b]roken men, we dare to use unbroken language. [But] we must not forget that we are speaking in parables and after the manner of men' (*2R*, p. 221/202). The dialectical movement of theological discourse manifests itself as *both* assertive claims to the immediate *and* a recognition of its own rhetorical mediation.

That injunction not to forget has important consequences throughout the second edition of *Romans*, which Barth completed in September 1921, on the eve of leaving the Patmos Group. It is that injunction which separates him from dialogical philosophy (and also other dialectical theologians like Gogarten and Bultmann[13]). As the second edition unfolds, tracing the dialectic of the human and the Wholly Other, a separation is being announced. As it unfolds so Barth interprets the two pillars of dialogical thought – the nature of the *imago dei* and revelation – in a radically different manner.

[13] See my article 'Theology and the Crisis of Representation' in *Literature and Theology Towards 2000*, ed. R. Detweiler (Atlanta: Scholar's Press, 1994).

In 'The Christian in Society', as we saw, Barth is still working with a pietistic, Romantic notion of the *imago dei*. While Christ is Wholly Other he is also the divine spark within us all. In the second edition of *Romans* Barth considerably reworks his understanding of the *imago dei* as the subjective possibility for the reception of revelation. The impression of a general revelation, in accordance with the Pauline teaching in Romans 1.19–20, is retained, but the contents of this general revelation are interpreted negatively. What we know is that 'we are not'. What we know is the 'recognition [*die Einsicht*] of the absolute heteronomy under which we stand' (*2R*, p. 46/21). Our 'memory of God' is one of absence, not ontological participation. Our memory, which is that which enables the subject to receive the revelation, is the 'memory of that lost relationship with God' (*2R*, p. 230/212). It is a memory that invokes a desire, 'the longing for the recovery of the lost immediacy of my life in God' (*2R*, p. 256/238).[14] The *imago dei* is the negative side of immediacy, the recognition of always and only having mediation. The consciousness of mediation is the recognition of the 'lost immediacy'. What innate knowledge of God there is in human beings, then, is the knowledge of our own inner dialectic, our own proximity to and yet alienation from God – the contradiction and questionableness of selfhood which is a dominant theme of the book. Unlike Platonic recollection and Augustinian memory, Barth's *imago dei* is more akin to Kierkegaard's dread or Heidegger's care (which, of course, it pre-dates). It possesses none of the liberal optimism still fervent in Rosenstock and Rosenzweig. There is no ontology of the in-between for human dialogue is not an analogy for God's relationship with creation. Rather, God challenges the possibility of any dialogue at all: 'our ignorance is precisely the problem and the source of our knowledge' (*2R*, p. 45/21). The revelation of God, of which we only have a memory, a mediation, is the Archimedian point which both confirms and in its confirmation dislodges the Kantian transcendental ego. It

---

[14] Barth's notion of 'memory' (*Erinnerung* rather than *Gedächtnis*) owes much to Hegel's distinction (as does Heidegger's notion later). In his *Encyclopaedia*, Hegel defines *Erinnerung* as interiorizing memory 'recollection as the inner gathering and preserving of experience' (p. 771). Walter Benjamin called this 're-membering'. *Gedachtnis* is the mechanic faculty of memorization. The two operate dialectically.

confirms it by revealing how we can only 'make of the eternal and ultimate presupposition of the Creator, a "thing in itself" above and in the midst of other things' (*2R*, p. 47/23). Even 'mankind becomes a thing in itself' (*2R*, p. 48/23), isolated, their thinking is 'merely empty, formal, critical and unproductive' (*2R*, p. 48/23). It dislodges it by showing us 'the incomprehensibility, the imperfection, the triviality of human life' (*2R*, p. 47/23) which is the 'memory of eternity breaking in upon our minds and hearts' (*2R*, p. 48/23). There is no immediate or natural dialogue in such a *Weltanschauung*, either between human beings and God or among human beings themselves. Chaos and meaninglessness are simply held at bay by the transcendental operation of consciousness. This is what revelation reveals and this is what human beings have an innate memory of. In the *imago dei* there is a recognition of the problem of time, of time divorced from eternity. There is only a 'memory of God' that revelation awakes, which is a memory of separation from what is immediate. Later, in *Anselm: Fides Quaerens Intellectum*, Barth will considerably develop this notion of 'awakening' in terms of a potential in human beings that revelation actualizes.

As we saw, for *Redephilosophie*, there is a triumphant evasion of the problem of time in a simple appropriation of the present, the eschatological *nunc*. Barth's appreciation of the problem is a consequence of a second major difference between his theological thinking and that of dialogical philosophy: the character of revelation. For Rosenzweig, the temporal becomes an analogue for the eternal and therefore revelation is continuous: there is always the present and access to the present. But for Barth, the advent of the eternal within the temporal is described as punctiliar, cutting vertically through a horizontal plane. These two forms of time are heteronomous. The 'knowledge of God is eternal and unobservable: it occurs altogether beyond time. It must therefore be distinguished absolutely from the temporal human knowledge, of which it is the KRISIS, the presupposition, and the dissolution' (*2R*, p. 325/309). The point of crossing between these two forms of time occurs in that word 'presupposition' – the temporal presupposes the eternal and hence can be dissolved into (that is, cannot remain indifferent to) the eternal.

But revelation 'can never be extended on the plane of time, so as to be thought of as a concrete possession' (*2R*, p. 322/306). It can only be the event of a question that by faith is received as God's address. Later, in his first attempt at dogmatics, the lectures given at Göttingen entitled *Instruction in the Christian Religion* or *The Göttingen Dogmatics*,[15] Barth clarifies his understanding of this. Too often the KRISIS has been interpreted as immediate and interventionist. 'There is no question of direct communication in revelation, of an end of concealment ... Fundamentally, we can construct only *a posteriori*. All reflection upon how God *can* reveal himself is in truth only a "thinking after"' (*GD*, pp. 148–50). The 'indirect relation may not be changed into a direct relation' (*GD*, p. 178). To make that change is to fall on to the rhetorical cushions of Romanticism, while to refuse to make it is to accept the paradox, 'the antithesis, the tension, or friction between the divine moment and the human moment from which the presence of revelation springs' (*GD*, p. 210). Because of this repeated reminder of mediation and memory, there is no movement towards the transhistorical, no movement from Rosenstock's 'star to star'. The eternal is always in critical conjunction with the contingent; revelation always takes place in an historically conditioned moment (*GD*, p. 210). For Barth, then, revelation is not continuous but, because of its human mediation and recollection, broken. It has to be returned to and recalled again and again within what is representational and human.

Ultimately, it is the sheer agnosticism of Barth's position as it developed in the writing of the second edition of *Romans* and its exposition in dialectical theology, which distinguishes Barth from the philosophers of dialogue. The phenomenology of dialogue, nevertheless, lies behind Barth's analysis of God's address to human beings. In his second attempt at dogmatics, *Die christliche Dogmatik im Entwurf*, he explicitly states: 'Dogmatic thinking is, in view of its object, part of a continuous conversation, not monological, but dialogical, dialectical thinking' (*CDE*, p. 579). Direct verbal encounter remained Barth's model

[15] Trans. Geoffrey W. Bromiley, William Eerdmans, Michigan, 1991. Volume 1 contains chapters 1 to 6 of the three-volume German edition, two of which are available at the moment published by Theologischer Verlag, Zurich.

of revelation.[16] He was in fact aware, through his reading of Feuerbach, of the I–Thou relation as early as 1914,[17] but it only develops into a major idea in the second edition of *Romans*, in *The Göttingen Dogmatics*, in *Die christliche Dogmatik im Entwurf* and on into the *Church Dogmatics*, where Barth's distinctive interpretation of that relation is found in III.2. The priority of the speech act as event, of revelation as personal encounter (rather than Schleiermacher's impersonal and absolute dependence), of the relation as 'a conversation ... [in which] our other partner is God' (*GD*, p. 180) – these characteristics of Barth's analysis of the Word are shared with *Redephilosophie*. But his is a dialogicalism struck through by a dialectic which insists that faith is the condition for reception, 'faith and faith alone is our true and direct relation to [revelation]' (*GD*, ibid. p. 171).

It is the necessity of coming to some assessment of the Word in human words, an assessment of the 'inner dialectic of the matter', that pushes Barth into dogmatics, for as he writes in *The Göttingen Dogmatics*, 'God's own speaking [is] the problem of dogmatics' (*GD*, p. 11). It is a problem because 'the audible and visible word are still a human word, with the implied concealment of the divinely posited reality' (*GD*, p. 24). There are, then, two addresses, the specific one and 'the original kerygma', and appropriating the latter is not simply a case of copying or recitation. Barth's appreciation of the mediation of revelation (which is the main theme of his *Göttingen Dogmatics*) leads to the value he places on the dialectical in-between which makes Christian speech a 'very ambiguous phenomenon' (*GD*, p. 24). Theological language is both Word and rhetoric, and so the 'Christian rhetorician might also be a Gorgias' (*GD*, p. 25). It is to prevent the church being seduced by mere rhetorical enthusiasm that there is dogmatics: the examination of this dialectic within Christian speaking in order to assess 'how far the Word of God is, or is meant to be, identical with it' (*GD*, p. 25). If, in the *Göttingen Dogmatics*,[18] Barth has not yet arrived at his distinctive understanding of analogy, much of the spadework has been

---

[16] See David Ford's, *Barth and God's Story* (Frankfurt: Peter Lang, 1981), p. 24.
[17] '*Der Glaube an dem personlichen Gott*', *Zeitschrift für Theologie und Kirche*, 1914, p. 67.
[18] In so far as we have a complete text yet. See note 15.

done. Certainly, his book on Anselm, *Fides Quaerens Intellectum*, cannot be seen as the critical turning point in his theology.[19] Despite Barth's own convictions, the Anselmic shift was not nearly so dramatic.

The Anselmic shift is allegedly responsible for five new theological positions.[20] First, it is viewed as responsible for a new found theological realism that enables Barth to replace dialectical negativity with a positive knowledge of God. Secondly, and consequentially, there is a new confidence in theological reasoning; for faith is understood to have a rational basis. Thirdly, there is a new emphasis upon the presupposition of faith. This is grounded in, fourthly, an insistence upon the particularity of Jesus Christ; what will later be termed the *analogia Christi*. Each of these new positions implies, fifthly, the rejection of dialectical method.

The *Göttingen Dogmatics*, however, reveals Barth already reflecting upon faith in the divine Word as the transcendental condition for human words and thinking about God (*GD*, p. 237). There is clearly a recognition here that dogmatic thinking can only be 'the thinking of faith' (*GD*, p. 308), a theological reasoning. There is likewise an emphasis upon the uniqueness of Jesus Christ (*GD*, pp. 110–30) and the centrality of the historical incarnation (section 6). Furthermore, dialectical thinking is never superseded in Barth. In chapter 1 I have already drawn attention to the dialectical structure of chapter 5 of the *Church Dogmatics*. Too many scholars bracket dialectical thinking with existentialism and conclude that Barth's rejection of the latter as a mode of theological analysis entails the rejection of the former. But Barth's dialectical theology always insisted that the existential analysis and the dogmatic or objective analysis must be kept in balance. Account must be taken of the human perspective, but only once one had already taken account of the divine perspective – the one cannot be had without the other. God is both the subject and the object in dialectical theology.

In Barth's later theology there is a shift away from existential language, and he acknowledges as much in his famous Preface to

---

[19] Cf. Daniel L. Migliore's Introduction to *Göttingen Dogmatics*, p. lxi.
[20] Cf. Pugh, pp. 94, 108, 109, 111, 125, 138.

Church Dogmatics. But two points need to be made concerning this Preface. First, he described the difference between his dogmatic work in 1927 and his dogmatic work in 1932 as 'saying the same thing, but in a different way' (I, I, p. xi). It is the vocabulary which changes rather than the theology. And the reason for disassociating himself from such existential vocabulary is to distinguish his work from 'those who are commonly associated with me as leaders or adherents of the so-called "dialectical theology"' (I, I, p. xv). He wishes, then, to draw a firm line between what he is doing and the dialectical theology of Gogarten and Bultmann. Secondly, he rejects the vocabulary of existential vocabulary because he does not wish to be misunderstood as providing theology with 'a foundation, a support, or justification in philosophical existentialism' (I, I, p. xiii). Such a provision was exactly what Bultmann was engaged upon. In his 1928 essay, 'The Significance of "Dialectical Theology" for the Scientific Study of the New Testament', he states unequivocally the centrality of 'the insight into the dialectic of existence, into the *historical nature of man's existence*'.[21] In his 1931 essay, 'The Crisis of Faith' , the *Krisis* is read fundamentally in terms of an insecurity that breaks into the human situation as the consciousness of finitude and the 'constant struggle of self-will'.[22] This is the kind of thinking Barth wishes to disassociate himself from – the kind of thinking currently understood as 'dialectical theology'. Barth is not rejecting an analysis of the human situation *vis-à-vis* revelation – the concern with being insecure, of being constantly questioned, and the repeated use of *Dasein* in the closing pages of chapter 5 are sufficient evidence of this. He is only too aware that revelation can only be made comprehensible and makes itself comprehensible within the metaphysical structures of human thinking. What the dialectical theology of Gogarten and Bultmann shows him, between 1922 and 1932, is that his earlier existentialist vocabulary had been read as providing a philosophical foundation for 'a negative natural theology'.[23]

[21] *Faith and Understanding* (New York: Harper Row, 1969), pp. 163–4.
[22] *Essays Philosophical and Theological* (London: SCM, 1955), p. 15.
[23] The phrase belongs to William Nicholls, in his admirable *Systematic and Philosophical Theology* (London: Penguin, 1969), p. 102.

I would argue that Barth's existentialism, and likewise his understanding of dialectic, remain fundamental for his dogmatics. They provide the reason for dogmatic thinking itself.[24] Too many critics have drawn a sharp distinction between Barth's dialectical and dogmatic thinking, emphasizing the negativity of dialectics and the positive theology that issues from the *analogia fidei*. But in *The Göttingen Dogmatics* Barth draws together and demonstrates the complicity of dialogical, dialectical and dogmatic thinking. '[D]ialektein means to converse with others ... thinking in such a way that there is dialogue ... True dialectical thinking ... means that dialogue is carried on in my own thinking. But I have to let this other, who is not myself, really speak, with all that that distinction implies' (*GD*, p. 309). The dialectic is, then, the relation of self or same with other. It is not simply a style of writing (though this relationship will manifest itself in a style that installs its own self-questioning by paradox and oxymoron). It is not simply a theological method (though the dialectical relationship must be examined in a dialectical manner and this *manner* must be a way of investigation, a *methodos* for treating the subject). The dialectic is a condition of Christian existence, a condition of distance-in-relationship to God. Dialogue takes place within this condition or relation, and dogmatic thinking is the critical exegesis of this 'dialectical dialogue' (*GD*, p. 311). In terms of Barth's relationship to *Redephilosophie*, dialogue was Barth's exit from nineteenth-century liberal theologies of consciousness (which were monological). Dialectic was a consequence for Barth of a theological reasoning in which the other of dialogue remained other, and the transcendent address of this other became the condition for thinking and speaking from the human and subjective side. Dialectical theology was Barth's way of avoiding the immediacy and directness of dialogicalism. Dogmatics became the exegesis of the dialectical relation, the dialogue between the transcendent other and the immanent self.

---

[24] Pugh admits, 'One dialectic that Barth never abandoned was the distance between God and humanity seen from our side' (p. 162), but he fails to realize that *this* dialectic is the founding one.

DIALECTICS AND THE *ANALOGIA FIDEI*

It is, in fact, in the existential and dialectical dogmatics of 1927, *Die christliche Dogmatik im Entwurf* (published more than three years before his book on Anselm) that Barth introduces the notion of *analogia fidei*. His use reflects his preoccupation throughout the 1920s with Reformation theology. But the term *analogia* (in its Latin rather than its Greek form) came to mean something quite different in the sixteenth and seventeenth centuries than the term *analogia* in Aristotle's *Metaphysics*. In its Greek, philosophical sense it was understood as 'proportion' or 'ratio'. It implied ranking within a hierarchy, and to the Hellenistic mind that hierarchy was a cosmic one. Analogy became part of a whole (and Aristotle employs it in *Poetics* as a master-concept in his analysis of poetic diction, where analogy is associated with metaphor through synedoche and metonymy). Analogy was not merely a figure of speech, or an illustration, it was a form of arguing for the nature of what is (as is evident in Plato's sun analogy in *The Republic*). But there appears to be a semantic shift when we compare the phrase found in Paul's Letter to the Romans, 'analogy of faith', in its koine Greek with its Vulgate translation. In 12.6 we have the injunction by Paul *'eite prophetian kata ten analogian tes pisteos'* which the Vulgate translates as *'sive prophetiam secundum rationem fidei'*. But *'ratio'* here, as a translation for *'analogia'*, presents us with a different set of connotations: it speaks of rational statements in contrast to ecstatic and prophetic utterance. Furthermore, *'ratio'* is a technical, business term with the sense of 'account' or 'computation'. The phrase at the end of verse 6 now, in the Vulgate, comes to parallel a phrase at the end of verse 3, where the Greek *'metron pisteos'* is translated *'regula fidei'*. In fact, it is as 'measure of faith' that Barth comments upon verse 6 in his second edition of *Romans*. By the time of the Vulgate, then, *'analogian tes pisteos'* is moving towards meaning *'regula fidei'*, a theological norm (*quae creditur*) in the form of a proposition. It still maintains the sense of a 'proportional resemblance', but this is losing much of its ontological impact. Lisa Jardine, in an illuminating account of humanism and logic in the sixteenth century, points out that logic gives way to rhetoric and that the point of argumentation was no longer to ascertain the truth, to prove it, but to persuade, to render probable.[25] It is no longer, as it was for the Greeks, a way of discovering and expressing the nature of what is, the correlation of the All; 'analogy' is a rhetorical technique for the presentation of an argument, synonymous with 'simile'. And it is this conception of the word that lies behind the Reformer's use of the term '*analogia fidei*'.

One of the most influential books on Barth's understanding of Reformation Protestantism was Heinrich Heppe's *Reformed Dogmatics*,[26] for which Barth wrote a Forward when the book was reissued in 1935. Heppe outlines in his book the move away from Calvin's position on the inspiration of Scripture, in the seventeenth century, towards a more mechanistic conception of verbal revelation. It is verbal revelation that Barth lampoons throughout his *Göttingen Dogmatics* – which by its German title announced a return to Calvin's position.[27] But it is in the context of the verbal inspiration of Scripture that Heppe defined the hermeneutic of '*analogia fidei*', which is rooted in the presupposed unity of the biblical revelation. The contents of Scripture must form a perfect and harmonious presentation of doctrine, and so faith harmonized any apparent contradictions. Hence, like the Catholic *regula fidei*, *analogia fidei* named a form of exegesis by cross-reference and contextualizing. Thus we find Wilhelm Bucanus understanding *analogia fidei* as 'namely, the constant and unchanging sense of Scripture expounded in the opening passages of Scripture and agreeing with the Apostles' Creed, the Decalogue and the Lord's Prayer'.[28] Charmier writes that 'The analogy of faith is the argument from general dogmas which contain the norm of all that is to be taught in the Church.'[29] And the Second Helvetian Confession explains it as 'the comparison

---

[25] *The Cambridge History of Late Mediaeval Philosophy*, ed. N. Kretzman, A. Kenny and J. Pinborg (Cambridge: Cambridge University Press, 1982).

[26] Trans. G. T. Thompson (London, 1950).

[27] Barth's appointment was to a chair of Reformed theology and Calvin's classic statement of such a theology is his *Institutes of the Christian Religion*. The *Göttingen Dogmatics* were entitled *Instruction in the Christian Religion*.

[28] Heppe, *Reformed Dogmatics*, p. 35.   [29] Ibid., p. 36.

of the more obscure with the more manifest'.[30] In all three definitions 'faith' is understood as the rational, *a priori* acceptance of a set of theological norms or propositions and 'analogy' is a method of comparing them. '*Analogia fidei*' is an exegetical technique, similar to the employment of analogies in an act persuasion. It does not, therefore, have anything to do with ontology, but describes a formal comparison whereby certain biblical ambiguities are resolved through placing them in terms of the whole intention of the Scriptures, a holistic intention that is presupposed.

When we meet *analogia fidei* in *Die christliche Dogmatic im Entwurf*, it is employed in a similar sense – as a means of regulating and deciding upon a biblical crux. But Barth extends the notion considerably and one has the first intimation that a more complex and nuanced understanding of the term is being developed. It is mentioned in the context of a discussion on the concrete authority of God's Word in the Scriptures. Barth states that it is the Church who dictates 'to what extent, and in what form the Scriptures are known as the Word of God' (*CDE*, p. 481); the Church then must make decisions on the Canon and on the authoritative text of the Scriptures. He then provides an illustration of the means whereby a decision is taken. The text of Romans 5.1 is unclear and raises a question of 'whether we read *exōmen* or *exomen*' (*CDE*, p. 483). Does the authoritative text understand the verse as 'we have (peace with God)' or 'may we have (peace with God)'? Is the verb indicative or subjunctive? Barth declares that 'what is correct, that is the form of the testimony to revelation . . . must be the object [*Sache*] of an act of faith by the Church' (*CDE*, p. 483). The '*analogia fidei*' accepts that 'this text is a testimony to what has been revealed [*dass dieser Text Offenbarungszeugnis*]' (*CDE*, p. 483). Accordingly, the case for the subjunctive, in the context of the Scriptures-as-testimony, is deemed foolish. For the authority of revelation means that the peace between human beings and God is not a subjunctive possibility, but a concrete fact, although even then, because of the fallibility of such argumentation and persuasion, what can

---

[30] Ibid., p. 39.

be decided is only 'the form of testimony to revelation most likely [*wahrscheinlichsten*] in the text' (*CDE*, p. 483).

The *analogia fidei* thus involves a comparison whereby a textual crux can be resolved, along lines similar to the technique practised by the Reformers. But there is also an extension evident in Barth's handling of the notion, which appears at the point where he emphasizes the Church's act of faith. Only upon the basis of this act of faith by the Church (not on the basis of 'the faith of the private individual') is the establishment 'of a "received text" and a normative translation' (*CDE*, p. 484) possible. The *analogia fidei* is not simply a technique for clarifying the meaning of obscure texts by comparing them with clear prescriptive statements of the faith. Faith is not a set of such prescribed statements to which the Church adheres (or not simply that); it is also a relation that enables there to be a right analogy, enables there to be a normative translation (and translation is concerned with locating in the receiver language analogues for what is communicated in the original language). Thus a 'received' and definitive text is established. Faith bears upon a relationship with God that does have both noetic and ontological implications, for the comparisons which issue from such an act of faith are not merely formal (as they were for the Reformers); they are in fact substantial. As Barth came to understand this, having developed his understanding of it while meditating upon Anselm's work, these analogies create a 'fully efficacious ... substitute for the missing (and necessarily missing) experiential knowledge of Him' (*A*, p. 167).

When Barth embarks upon his commentary upon Anselm's *Proslogion* it is the noetic and ontological implications of that act of faith which preoccupy him. It is in this book, *Anselm: Fides Quarens Intellectum*, that he works out the distinction between *analogia entis* and *analogia fidei* – although neïther of the terms appear. On the debate between the notions of *analogia entis* and *analogia fidei* in Barth, the most renouned critics (Balthasar, Bouillard, Gottlieb Sotingen and Walter Kreck) all concur with Sotingen's conclusion that 'Without the *analogia entis* there is no *analogia fidei*.'[31] What I believe they fail to appreciate is the dialectic of being, or in Heideggerian terms, the ontological

---

[31] *Antwort: Karl Barth*, p. 217.

difference, which is Barth's main argument throughout his book on Anselm. Anselm did not teach Barth anything about theological method, the *a priori* of faith for knowledge of God or the provisional nature of all theological statements, but he did strengthen and confirm what Barth had already understood about reasoning on the basis of faith, reasoning as the intrinsic desire of faith, and he did this by teaching Barth about the ontological difference and how this was associated with two antithetical modes of thinking. He supplemented Barth's epistemological dialectic (worked out thoroughly in the second edition of *Romans*) with an ontological dialectic. In brief, for Anselm, as Barth read him, the being of objects in the world and the existence of God are not the same. One is not quantitatively different from the other – they are dipolar. 'God does not exist as other things exist . . . But God exists – and He alone – in such a way that it is impossible to conceive the possibility of His non-existence' (*A*, pp. 134–5). God's existence 'is therefore independent of the antithesis between knowledge and object' (*A*, p. 141). It is this form of existence, which is caught up in the processes of verification and adequation between the intramental and the extramental, between what is known and the independent reality of the object 'in itself', which constitutes existence as we know it and reasoning as we practise it. 'If God were to exist merely generally, in the manner of all other beings, then not only would he not exist as God, but according to Anselm . . . he would not exist at all' (*A*, p. 154). It is on the basis of this ontological distinction – a God who is totally other than beings as we conceive them, a God beyond or otherwise than Being – that Barth restates his epistemological distinction: '[t]he identification of two possible *modi* of thinking (of existence) of an object' (*A.*, p. 163). For the fool 'thinks on a level where one can only think falsely – though without violating the inner consistency of that level' (*A*, p. 165). For theologians, for Anselm (for Barth), these two *modi* cannot be separated *de facto*, only *de jure*. The dialectic between the man of faith and the fool, Anselm and Gaunilo, is an 'inner dialectic', for the theologian is also always the fool, the *insipiens*. Hence 'there are no theological problems that are finally settled' (*A*, p. 159).

The dialectic of being, the ontological difference, reinforces the dialectic of knowing, the epistemological difference. There is no ontological participation or correspondence which is other than by faith. As such the *analogia fidei* operates within both this ontological and epistemological difference, and therefore has nothing to do with *analogia entis* or the possibility of knowledge of God via the representations of the human mind. The concept of the *analogia entis* has no purchase within the ontological difference, as Heidegger understood.[32] *Analogia entis* can only function in an onto-theology and it is onto-theology which the ontological difference radically questions. The *imago dei* too participates in the economy of these radical differences – only faith awakens its potential to *be* an *imago dei*. Outside faith it cannot be what it is because it is caught up in existence as we know it and not God's existence. The *analogia fidei*, then, is both the product and the promoter of a dialectical theology and a dogmatic theology which examines Christian talk about God in the light of the ontological and the epsitemological differences. *Analogia fidei* is that which constitutes the realm of the in-between, comprehends that there is an in-between, negotiates 'the way from Word to counterword' (*CDE*, p. 582). The *analogia fidei* announces, contrary to *analogia entis*, that '[t]here is not then *one Word*' (*CDE*, p. 582) – there is always, this side of the Parousia, heteronomy. There are always, to return us to where we began in chapter 1 of this book, two antithetical languages.

When we place Barth in the context of German philosophy of language (and discourse), then, we see that his problematic remains the same as that of both the philosophers of dialogue and Heidegger. They are each examining and attempting to clarify the transcendental condition for language. Barth's is a very specific use of language – Christian speaking about God – but insofar as in chapter 5 of the *Church Dogmatics* he is making a statement about language *tout court*, and insofar as Christian speaking about God can only be understood within a more

---

[32] See Heidegger's essay 'The Onto-Theological Constitution of Metaphysics' in *Identity and Difference*, trans. Joan Stanbaugh (New York: Harper and Row, 1969). The difference is prior to onto-theology and metaphysics and yet at the same time it creates and confirms the onto-theological constitution of metaphysics. In terms of Barth's theology of language, *analogia fidei* too precedes *analogia entis*, precedes onto-theology, and yet simultaneously constitutes it. *Analogia fidei* is the condition for *analogia entis*.

general economy of representation, then his problematic is identical to that analysed in *Redephilosophie* and Heidegger's ontology of Logos. Unlike *Redephilosophie*, he wishes to emphasize the mediation of all revelation, the need to take account of the *homo hermeneuma* of neo-Kantianism. His grasp of the 'inner dialectic of the matter' is a grasp of the operation of two antithetical forms of logocentric thinking – one summed up by Cassirer's 'monadology' and the other best expressed by *Redephilosophie*. Here, with these two models for the operation of discourse, each arising from different philosophical approaches (idealism on the one hand, phenomenology on the other), each moving in contrary directions (one towards pure semiotics, the other towards pure semantics), the axiom of endless mediation crosses (crucifies) the axiom of immediacy and presence. The examination of *christliche Rede* and *Rede von Gott* (the task of dogmatics) is the examination of the agonistics within discourse itself, the crossing through and the resurrection of discourse itself. It is this grasp of the agonistic nature of discourse that draws Barth into the orbit of postmodern thinkers such as Emmanuel Levinas and Jacques Derrida, for they too share his problematic. It is the reoccurrence of the same problematic, read theologically by Barth, that concerns the rest of this book. For with Barth we may be able to glimpse a postmodern theology of the Word.

The Jewish philosopher, Emmanuel Levinas, sums up what we have learnt from Barth and what we have yet to learn about postmodern models for the operation of language. He describes the operation of '*le logos de l'infini*' which 'will differ from theoretical intentionality and . . . the unity of the transcendental apperception of a sovereign I in the exclusive isolation of its cogito and its collective [*assemblant*], synthetic kingdom' (*TI*, p. 25). This is a transcendence that 'will be no longer an immanence *manquée*', but a '*relation to the other as such* and not with the other as simply part of the world' (*TI*, p. 27). This is an alterity which is 'prior to the interpersonal order of the otherness of the other man'. This logos shatters the transcendental ego as it proceeds 'from the idea of the infinite, from theological attachment, beyond the *Jameinigkeit* [literally, mineness] of the Cogito and its immanence ... towards a thought which thinks more than it thinks – or which does better than thinking' (*TI*, pp. 26–7). Here is a Word operating in but also beyond words; a description of a relationship between the '*logos de l'infini*' and the finite. Levinas terms this relationship the 'attachment [*affection*] of the finite by infinite' (*TI*, p. 26). But the story of that relationship is another chapter.

Part II
Dialogues with difference

An examination of Levinas's dialectic between the *logos de l'infini* and the *logos du fini* is the central concern of the following three chapters. His work issues from sustained meditations, first on the writings of Heidegger and subsequently on Buber, and in this second stage in the examination of the transcendental otherness of discourse, the Word in words, the distinctiveness of his position will emerge by comparing his thought with that of both these philosophers in turn. In chapter 7, I will return to Barth, and the parallels between his theology of the Word and Levinas's philosophy of Saying [*le Dire*] will be systematically drawn and examined. The reason for the similarities in the structures of their thinking lies in the fact they are each tackling the same set of problems, a set of problems rooted in a shared historical context. That context, the crisis of enlightened liberalism, was the one within which Barth framed his own understanding of language and its relation-in-difference to the Word and also the one out of which Levinas (and later Derrida) is working. Adorno and Horkheimer summed up the historical situation in 1944: 'There is no longer any available form of linguistic expression which has not tended toward accommodation to dominant currents of thought.'[1] There was no longer any Other. Their own response was the development of what Adorno later called 'Negative Dialectics'. The examination of Levinas's work in the context of Heidegger's, Buber's and, finally, Barth's, serves to emphasize the continuous obsession with alterity that we find emerging in post-Great War Germany and issuing into today's postmodernism. The parallels and contrasts between Barth's thinking and Levinas's point the way toward a postmodern theology of the Word.

[1] Introduction to *Dialectic of Enlightenment*, tr. John Cumming (London: Verso, 1979), p. xii.

CHAPTER 5

Heidegger's dialogue with difference

Levinas's *logos de l'infini* has emerged only recently, in 1984, but it issues from an interest in the nature of signification and language that began in *Totality and Infinity*[1] and becomes the dominant theme of *Otherwise than Being*. It issues also from a sparring with Heidegger that began in his post-War books *Existence and Existents*, *Time and the Other* and *En Découvrant l'existence avec Husserl et Heidegger*. In so far as the *logos de l'infini* is a manifestation of what is wholly other, Levinas continues that line of thought discernible in Rosenzweig, Buber and Barth which wanted to champion a dialogical or a dialectical relation with otherness yielding to no synthesis. But Levinas, unlike Rosenzweig and Buber, levels his attack at the problem of ontology, at the *analogia entis* which has underpinned so much of Western metaphysical thinking. He wishes to assert a transcendence that cuts diachronically through 'the unity of being and the univocity of *esse*' (*OB*, p. 94/p. 151).

The 'otherwise' (*autrement*) than being is fundamental. What Levinas is not positing is some Nonbeing, or a negative ontology as that which is prior to Being – as absence rather than a presence. He is attempting to describe a site outside ontology, anarchic to the totalizing of ontological categories, but a site which nevertheless is the condition for Being. What he is positing – and here he takes his cue from Plato's *Republic* and *Parmenides*, Plotinus' distinction between the One and the Nous and Kant's separation of the ethical from the ontological – is a Good beyond Being. Ethics, not ontology, has priority: 'Proximity is ...

---

[1] In particular, see Levinas's Preface and the sections 'Discourse Founds Signification' and 'Language and Objectivity' (pp. 204–12/179–87).

anarchically a relationship with a singularity without the mediation of any principle, any ideality. What concretely corresponds
to this description is my relationship with my neighbour' (*OB*, p.
100/p. 159). This anarchy of proximity 'brings to a halt the
ontological play which, precisely *qua* play, is consciousness,
where being is lost and found again, and is thus illuminated'
(*OB*, p. 101/p. 160). The circle where being is lost and found
again (Heidegger's hermeneutical circle and Hegel's circle of
consciousness where the thesis meets its antithesis in order to
emerge into a new synthesis), remains, is even necessary. But
Levinas locates the condition for its appearance in the rupture of
proximity where 'the neighbour strikes me before striking me, as
though I had heard before I spoke' (*OB*, p. 88/p. 141). This is a
relation of one-for-the-other which is prior to time, representation and phenomenality. 'It is the very transcending characteristic of this beyond that is signification ... My responsibility
for the other is the *for* of the relationship, the very signifyingness
of signification, which signifies in saying before showing itself in
the said. The one-for-the-other is the very signifyingness of
signification!' (*OB*, p. 100/p. 158).

There is then, according to Levinas, a Saying [*le Dire*] prior to
any said [*le dit*]; a signification in the responsibility one-for-
another that is prior to the signifier/signified schema of discourse; a Saying prior to transcendental subjectivity and therefore outside representation and ontology. Levinas describes it as
a 'voice coming from horizons at least as vast as those in which
ontology is situated ... that orders me to the other [and] does not
show itself to me, save through the trace of its reclusion, as a face
of a neighbour' (*OB*, p. 140/p. 220). In a remarkable passage
that assembles many of the themes of Levinas's work – the
philosophies of personhood, ethics and signification – Levinas
writes:

Saying is this passivity and this dedication to the other, this sincerity.
Not the communication of the said, which would immediately cover
over and extinguish or absorb the said, but saying holding open its
openness, without excuses, evasions or alibis, delivering itself without
saying anything said. Saying saying itself, without thematizing it, but
exposing it again. Saying is thus to make signs of this very signifyingness of the exposure; it is to expose the exposure instead of remaining in
it as an act of exposing. It is to exhaust oneself, to make signs by making

oneself a sign, without resting in one's every figure as a sign. (*OB*, p. 143/p. 223)

There are messianic echoes here which Derrida will comment upon. But for the moment, it is sufficient to bring out how this Saying emerges from the command of the Infinite Thou to the accusative 'me'. The encounter with the neighbour as Other [*Autrui*], a neighbour who has priority over me (and thus grammatically places me in the accusative), speaks to me of the wholly other [*autre*]. The I remains forever open to the impress of this Other/other, because it is never fully in command of its own situation while it remains in the accusative. It is only a subject as *sub-jectum*, as passive and dedicated, to alterity. This openness or exposure witnesses to the passing of the Infinite which finds expression in the said, in communication, in a linguistic system. The said is inevitable because signifyingness provokes significa-tion; it provokes it by provoking the responsibility of the-one-for-the-other which is the structure of both ethics and (Saussur-ian) linguistics. The diachrony of personhood repeated itself in the diachrony of language. The Saying is not the Infinite but it bears witness to the Infinite: 'It is by the voice of the witness that the glory of the Infinite is glorified' (*OB*, p. 146/p. 229). But like the Infinite it is outside representation. Its presence, then, in the said is termed a 'trace' of the Infinite. The 'trace' is identified in the ambiguities, the insurmountable equivocation and excess of signification in every said, and it is particularly present in the poetic said where interpretation is called for *ad infinitum* (*OB*, p. 170/p. 263). The Saying 'is the meaning of language, before language scatters into words . . . But the trace of the witness given . . . is not effaced even in its said' (*OB*, p. 151/p. 236). The Saying is not effaced in the said – it is thematized and in so far as it is thematized its infinity is betrayed. There is a sacrifice, an inevitable kenosis, because the system of language means that discourse forever domesticates the rupture that has given rise to it – the rupture which breaks with 'the immanence of represen-tation' (*TO*, pp. 102–3). The said 'retains in its statement the trace of the excession of transcendence' for 'signification has let itself be betrayed in the logos only to convey itself before us' but this '[t]hematization is then inevitable, so that signification can show itself' (*OB*, p. 151/p. 236).

When, in *Transcendance et intelligibilité*, Levinas adopts the expression *logos de l'infini* he is announcing a logos which is other than the logocentrism of the said. Elsewhere this logos of the said is characterized as 'the kerygmatic logos', the 'ideality of logos', the 'logos of response' and the 'narrative to which the logos belongs'. The Saying and the said distinguish then between a *logos de l'infini* and a *logos du fini*. With Levinas's Saying we are on the very threshold of a theology of language. We return to the older traditions of the divine origins of signification. Saying is 'an extraordinary word, the only one that does not extinguish or absorb its saying, but it cannot remain a simple word. The word of God is an overwhelming semantic event' (*OB*, p. 151/ p. 236).

The relation of this distinction between the Saying and the Said and Barth's distinction between the Word and words, I will draw out in chapter 7. For the moment I wish to examine more concisely how this project differs from Heidegger's, for the distinction between the Saying and the Said is Heidegger's before being Levinas's.

The distinction between the Saying and the Said seems to have emerged for Heidegger from his reading of the poet Stefan George. 'Saying' occurs as a concept in *Being and Time* when Heidegger writes that '[i]n clarifying the third signification of assertion as communication (as speaking forth), we were led to the concepts of "saying" and "speaking" [*des Sagens und Sprechens*]' (*BT*, p. 203). But other than developing the idea that 'The existential-ontological foundation of language is discourse [*Rede*]', there is little beyond the relation between logos, saying and apophansis, which develops the concept of saying as aboriginal utterance. Even the German is different. In *Being and Time*, Heidegger uses the German infinitive as the noun form. Later he develops the use of a separate noun (*die Sage*). The difference between the two in Heidegger's mind is nowhere made clearer than in 'A Dialogue on Language', where the untouchable is described as 'veiled from us by the mystery of Saying. A mere clarification of the difference between saying [*Sagen*] and speaking (*Sprechen*) would gain us little' (*OWL*, p. 50/148). The act of saying and the mystery of Saying are related, but not the same.

Both in his 1957 essay 'The Essence of Language' and his 1958 essay, 'The Word', Heidegger quotes Stefan George and draws attention to the capitalization of *Saga*. Normally, George places all words in the lower case, but *Saga* is capitalized because in a poem concerning the stirring of language into an awakening 'Saying ... tells of the origin of the word' (*OWL*, p. 153). The poem comes from Stefan George's last book of poems *Das Neue Reich*, published in 1928, a year after the publication of *Being and Time*.

The first developed look at *die Sage* as 'Saying' arises in Heidegger's 1944 essay 'Logos' where it is associated with logos as the aboriginal Utterance. Before it arrives in his 'A Dialogue on Language' (1953/4), then, it forms part of Heidegger's sustained meditation on Logos which we outlined in chapter 3. 'A Dialogue on Language' itself makes this plain in its explicit references to Heidegger's work on the concept of Logos in *Being and Time*. But what has changed since 1927?

Quite evidently, the form of the discussion – in fact, the nature of 'discussion' itself. '*Die Erörterung*' in Heidegger's 1937–8 lectures '*Aus einer Erörterung der Wahrheitsfrage*' has not the same meaning (and therefore the lectures take quite a different form) as '*die Erörterung*' in Heidegger's 1953 analysis of Georg Trakl's poetry, '*Eine Erörterung seines Gedichtes*' (translated as 'Language in the Poem'). There is, in his essay on Georg Trakl, little sense of discussion, or debate, or argument. There is little in the way of analysis or exposition in the traditional understanding of such terms. In this later work there emerges a more evocative connative reading of '*die Erörterung*'. The prefix expresses a certain inchoate nature in perceiving the object and a move-ment towards a siting (*der Ört* – the site or locus; *örten* – to navigate or orientate), a definition. There is even the echo of *hören* (to hear or listen to) and *das Öhr* (the ear) in this later use of the word. Heidegger listens to 'the ambiguous saying character-istic of Trakl's poems' (*OWL*, p. 192). In fact, his whole essay on Trakl is an attempt to locate 'the site of his poetic work' (*OWL*, p. 159), concluding that such a location is unsayable, for 'the poetic work speaks out of an ambiguous ambiguousness' (*OWL*, p. 192). Like Barth listening for the Word in Paul's words to the

Roman Christians, Heidegger listens in the poetry to what is unsayable. And a literary exegesis that could be expressed discursively in the 1930s is no longer an appropriate method for handling texts in the 1950s.[2] What has changed is signalled to us in Heidegger's observation about his own work in 'A Dialogue on Language'. The recognition of the deeper implications of the hermeneutic circle in the statement 'the language of our dialogue might constantly destroy the possibility of saying that of which we are speaking' (*OWL*, p. 15), has led to the decision that 'in my later writings I no longer employ the term "hermeneutics"' (*OWL*, p. 12). Heidegger is moving beyond hermeneutics, towards that which is the condition for hermeneutics.

Heidegger's statement is significant for our analysis of his later position *vis-à-vis* Barth. We saw in chapter 4 that Barth criticized the neo-Kantian emphasis upon the *homo hermeneuma* as inadequate, and Heidegger's earlier logocentrism was a variant of the neo-Kantian *homo hermeneuma*. In rejecting the employment of 'hermeneutics', in attempting to locate a place prior to hermeneutics, Heidegger must subsequently modify his logocentrism, and it is this modification that interests us.

It was William J. Richardson who distinguished Heidegger I from Heidegger II on the basis 'that the method characteristic of Heidegger II is the process of thought, of Heidegger I the process of phenomenology'.[3] Heidegger in his Preface to the book observes, significantly: 'The distinction you make between Heidegger I and Heidegger II is justified only on the condition that this is kept constantly in mind: only by way of what Heidegger I has thought [*Gedachten*] does one gain access to what is to-be-thought [*Denkende*] by Heidegger II.'[4] We move from

[2] There are already indications in *Being and Time* that in pursuing the question of Being this would become inevitable. In the section 'Assertion as a Derivative Mode of Interpretation' and in the 'Introduction' we read: 'Whenever a phenomenological concept is drawn from primordial sources, there is a possibility that it may degenerate if communicated in the form of an assertion ... And the difficulty with this kind of research lies in making it self-critical in a positive sense' (p. 61). Heidegger, then, already saw the process of *Destruktion* his own writing and method would have to undergo. There are similarities between Heidegger's positive understanding of *Destruktion* and Derrida's *déconstruction*. See R. Gasché, *The Tain on the Mirror*, (Cambridge, Mass: Harvard University Press, 1986), pp. 109–20.

[3] William J. Richardson SJ, *Heidegger: From Phenomenology to Thought* (Le Hague: Martinus Nijhoff, 1963), p. 623.   [4] Ibid., p. xxii.

'thought' (past participle) to 'thinking' (present participle), from observation and representation to experience and presentation, from speaking about language to speaking from language. We move from what Heidegger in 'A Dialogue on Language' describes as 'the attempt first of all to define the nature of interpretation on hermeneutic grounds' (*OWL*, p. 11) to a clearer recognition 'that hermeneutics means not just the interpretation but, even before it, the bearing of a message or tidings' (*OWL*, p. 29). We move beyond the *homo hermeneuma* where the phenomenology of Dasein 'is a hermeneutic in the primordial signification of this word' (*BT*, p. 62) towards a recognition that the primordial signification of this word is man as a messenger appropriating the 'message of unconcealment' (*OWL*, p. 53), listening to the Saying which calls out to him.

Heidegger moves towards the condition for hermeneutics. He recognizes that in order to manifest 'the presence of present beings, the two-fold', the relating of the ontological to and in the ontic, 'what prevails in and bears up the relation of human nature to the two-fold is language. Language defines the hermeneutic relation' (*OWL*, p. 30). Hence Heidegger explores language in order to locate the transcendental condition for language. He enters into the very nature of the hermeneutic circle and discovers that 'the word is a hint, and not a sign in the sense of mere signification' (*OWL*, p. 27). He discovers what Saussure himself had suggested, that the signifier is more significant than what it signifies; that there is always surplus. Talk of hints, trails and traces betrays a growing agnosticism, or rather, a 'growing insight into the untouchable which is veiled from us by the mystery of Saying' (*OWL*, p. 50) And therefore Heidegger's earlier 'necessary acceptance of the hermeneutic circle' as giving 'us an originary experience of the hermeneutic relation' (*OWL*, p. 51) is radically qualified. When his Japanese partner in the dialogue asks, 'How would you present the hermeneutic circle today?' (ibid.), Heidegger can only answer 'I would avoid a presentation as resolutely as I would avoid speaking *about* language' (ibid.). The Japanese friend is quick to respond:

J   Then everything would hinge on reaching a corresponding saying of language.

I   Only dialogue could be such a saying correspondence.
J   But, patently, a dialogue altogether *sui generis*.
I   A dialogue that would remain originarily appropriated to Saying.
     (*OWL*, p. 52)[5]

And a dialogue is what we read, a dialogue whose structure charts an exploration towards an understanding of, even an annunciation of, the Japanese word 'that says the essential being of language, rather than being of use as a name for speaking and for language' (*OWL*, p. 23), *Koto ba*. The essay is a meditation, then, on 'translation' in two related forms. The first is the translation from the original language into the receptor language; the second is the translation of Saying into the said. The latter provides the possibility for the former, presents the possibility of an *Ursprache*.

The ability to translate and to say are associated. But we do not arrive at a definition of *Koto ba* (or the other Japanese word *Iki*) without clearing the ground. This 'clearing of the ground' fundamentally defines the essay's structure. Part of that clearing is removing misconceptions – about aesthetics, hermeneutics, the nature of language and modern understandings of words like 'grace'. But the clearing is executed by the dialogue itself – where the partners 'confidently entrust [them]selves to the hidden drift' (*OWL*, p. 30). Since the nature of language is Saying and

---

5   It is far too easy to quote this text without examining its complex nuances. The complexity is far more evident in German. First, there is the linguistic play through the essay between *sprechen* (to speak or talk), *entsprechen* (to correspond), *die Sprache* (language), *Gespräch* (dialogue) and *Sage* (Saying). Each word relates to the others not merely phonally but ontologically. In *What is Philosophy?* (1955), Heidegger, concerned with *philein* in the word 'philosophy', wrote that 'it signifies here ... *omologein*, to speak [*sprechen*] in a way in which the Logos speaks, in correspondence [*entsprechen*] with the Logos' (p. 47/46). Saying in 'Dialogue' and Logos in *What is Philosophy?* are the same, then. Both institute a correspondence [*Entsprechen*] that constitutes the path of the dialogue [*Gespräch*] in which two people talk [*sprechen*]. Logos *qua* Saying institutes analogies [*Entsprechung*]. Secondly, there is the German verb 'to appropriate' [*vereignen*], which becomes *Ereignis* as a noun (an appropriating event or the event of appropriation). In his lecture 'On Time and Being', Heidegger attempts to clarify his thinking on 'Appropriation' in a way that pushes beyond presence in a Levinasian manner. He discusses 'Being itself as the event of Appropriation' (p. 21), for 'Being belongs to Appropriating. Giving and its gift receive their determination from Appropriating ... Being would be a species of Appropriating.' Being is a gift of a prior relevatory event [*Ereignis*] or Appropriation. This event 'withdraws what it most fully its own from boundless unconcealment' (p. 22). This passage from 'Dialogue', then, is a very condensed piece of writing, which sums up many of the late Heidegger themes.

this Saying beckons in and through language, then there is always a movement towards, as a response to, this Saying. The dialogue is not a 'pumping each other', but a 'releasing into the open whatever might be said' (ibid.). The hidden drift is the passage of Saying. The arrival at the Japanese word and its translation, through the dialogue, becomes an exercise in attempting to let Saying say. Each of the partners participates in that manifestation. Thus, increasingly towards the end of the test, the Japanese professor and the Inquirer finish each other's statements and attain a mutuality of understanding, a pure translation of thought. Being *qua* Logos constitutes the human nature: 'Man, to the extent that he is man, listens to this message' (*OWL*, p. 40). Saying is the 'voice that determines and tunes his nature' (*OWL*, p. 41). In the manifestation of Saying through dialogue the partners come to realize their universal fellowship; that which is beyond and grounds the subjective ego.

We have returned to the *homo hermeneuma*, but this is not the same *homo* as the subject of transcendental phenomenology. Human beings are located within language, and language betrays the 'hint' that points beyond the phenomenological. Human beings remain creatures who necessarily interpret, but hermeneutics is now seen as message-bearing and human beings as essentially messengers. We communicate as well as, and in the very act of, projecting. There is a signification beyond us – a Saying. The *homo hermeneuma* remains, but there has been an anthropological shift towards viewing human beings as open, to some extent, to apprehensions of Being. The intentionality that directs the movement of the hermeneutic circle is no longer simply Dasein's, for 'that-which-regions turn[s] towards our representing' (*DT*, p. 72). So the method has changed becoming more indirect in line with perceiving language as 'hint'. And Heidegger's logocentrism has changed also. The fulcrum for that change is a deeper appreciation of dialogicalism.

Dialogicalism is embryonic in *Being and Time*. The 'existential–ontological foundation of language is discourse [*Rede*]' (*BT*, p. 203). Discourse articulates Being-in-the-world, Being-with-one-another belongs to Being-in-the-world and 'Such Being-with-one-another is discursive' (*BT*, p. 204). But it remained the complaint of first Buber and then Levinas that Heidegger's emphasis even with *Miteinandersein* is upon the subject alone: 'it is in terms of solitude that the analysis of Dasein in its authentic form is pursued' (*TO*, p. 93).[6] Discourse only becomes discourse when there are partners, when there is an Other to which the subject either relates (as in Buber) or to whom the subject is related (as in Levinas). Dialogue only emerges as a methodological principle in Heidegger when we move beyond the phenomenology of Dasein to Dasein as the addressed one and the recognition that 'one's own efforts alone are never adequate' (*OWL*, p. 48).

Dialogue *is* now the vehicle for the 'event of Appropriation' [*Ereignis*], and 'A Dialogue on Language' is the narrative of such an 'Appropriation'. The Saying is not isolatable from the said; in fact, it only takes place in the said. The 'dialogue *of* language' takes place in the dialogue *about* language, and therefore there is no 'pure gift of the messenger's course that the message needs' (*OWL*, p. 53). The Saying is given in the process of the dialogical event, but its presence is always an appearance: 'this clearing itself, as occurrence, remains unthought in every respect' (*OWL*, p. 39). It is not the ego working in isolation which interprets the said as the Saying. No method of interpretation employed by the subject can identify and domesticate the object. The Saying of Appropriation remains other;[7] it remains concealed, even in its appearance. It appears in authentic dialogue as a given, not as a definition worked at by the dialoguing partners. The nature of Saying in itself is unknown and unrepresentable, for the authentic saying is 'silence about silence' (*OWL*, p. 52). Elsewhere, in 'Language', discussing Georg Trakl, whose poetry forms another of Heidegger's dialogue partners, he speaks of language 'as the peal of stillness' (*PLT*, p. 207). 'Speaking occurs in what is spoken in the poem. It is the speaking of language. Language speaks. It speaks by bidding the bidden, thing–world and world–thing, to come to the between of the dif-ference [*der Unter-*

---

6 This is also Karl Löwith's conclusion in his article 'M. Heidegger and F. Rosenzweig'. See pp. 51 and 63. But significantly Löwith is only analysing *Being and Time*.

7 For a more thorough account of Appropriation, its Otherness and its event see 'On Time and Being' and the summary of the seminar which took place following the lecture. See also Heidegger's *Beiträge Zur Philosophie: Vom Ereignis*.

Schied]. What is so bidden is commanded to arrive from out of the dif-ference into the dif-ference' (*PLT*, p. 206). The appearance of Saying is, therefore, the appearance of dif-ference, the appearance of a fissure between ontic and ontological, beings and Being, world and thing, totality and infinity. Man is 'he who walks the boundary of the boundless' (*OWL*, p. 41). Dialogue becomes the first step beyond subjectivism, the constructed worlds of transcendental phenomenology. The possibility for translation is constituted by the space, the site, the between, in which dialogue manifests the dif-ference. With the manifestation of dif-ference the otherness of Saying announces itself. The dialogue presents a paradigm of the rift itself. In 'The Origin of the Work of Art', the rift [*Riss*] is between the world and the earth and it constitutes 'the intimacy with which combatants belong together. This tear pulls opponents together in the origin [*Herkunft*] of their unity' (*PLT*, p. 63). Dialogue now is both method and expression – *it is* the hermeneutic now, not Dasein.

Logos *qua* Saying, then, is not quite the same as in section 34 of *Being and Time*, where '*logos qua logomenon* means the ground, the *ratio*' (*BT*, p. 58). Heidegger's understanding of Logos has deepened. It has become one of a list of 'words of Being as answers to a claim which speaks in the sending concealing itself' (*TB*, p. 9), a list which would also include Plato's 'idea', Aristotle's '*energeia*', Hegel's 'absolute concept' and Nietzsche's 'will to power'. Logos issues from a profound and unrepresentable concealment.[8] This is not the logos Levinas portrays in phrases like 'the kerygmatic logos', 'the ideality of logos', 'the logos of response' or the 'narrative to which the logos belongs'. A greater degree of agnosticism marks the presence-in-its-absence of this logos; the logos is a 'trace' of transcendence in immanence which dialogue (whether between the world and the earth which is the origin of art and poetry or between the Japanese and the inquirer) presences. Put another way, the ontological fissure issues in 'a dialogue altogether *sui generis*' (*OWL*, p. 52), it is 'the

---

[8] Compare this with Levinas's Saying as it issues from *illeity* (discussed in chapter 6). The economies are very close.

authentic dialogue *of* language' (*OWL*, p. 53): the Logos is dia-logical, is two-fold.

In Heidegger's earlier social ontology, the other is always a modification of Dasein and Dasein is never modified by it. The other is never entirely other while the Husserlian ego lives in a transcendental community of monads. But now the perspective has changed and with it there emerges a new understanding of dialogue. The other (which is always hidden and never appears as other) substantiates the self, substantiates man 'in the region-ing of releasement by that-which regions' (*DT*, p. 74). What '"determines" him from beyond the phenomenological horizon is "other-than-itself"' (ibid.). The other is beyond represen-tation and 'neither an ontic nor an ontological relation' (*DT*, p. 77).

The importance of those last words cannot be minimized, for Heidegger is expressing here a movement towards an exteriority that is beyond ontology. The ontological difference between Being ('"Being" remains only a provisional word', *EGT*, p. 78) and beings, the ontological relation ('if it can still be considered a relation', *DT*, p. 76) presents an 'other-than-itself'. The Saying is not appropriated to the said, language is not a *tertium quid* between Being and beings, and the ontological relation itself 'is not a causal relation' (*TB*, p. 52). The ontological difference that comes to expression in language only provides a hint, a hint of absence, of *Nichtigkeit*, of a Saying beyond the ontological relation. In his later writings Heidegger associates this unrepre-sentable Saying with the event of Appropriation (*Ereignis*). It is *Ereignis* – which in chapter 7 we will relate to Barth's *Krisis* (which becomes *Ereignis* in *Church Dogmatics*) – that names the experience not of Being but 'the difference other than [*als*] difference' (*ID*, p. 117).

Heidegger's logocentrism profoundly changes through his exploration of Saying and, later, *Ereignis*. Now he announces a dialogue in and from and with difference. A 'dia-logue', in which there is a 'hint' [*die Spur*] of an other beyond the difference between presence and absence. But the question is how does this Saying differ from Levinas's? More than one commentator has said that there is no difference.[9] It has even been suggested that Levinas is deliberately misreading Heidegger in order to provide his own work with a foil.[10] But the misreading is not deliberate. Levinas has consistently coupled the Heideggerian project with Husserl's. His criticism of Husserl is that 'nothing can ever be known in its totality for an essential character of our perception is its inadequacy' (*LR*, p. 15). For Levinas, a certain agnosticism is not only evident – it is constitutive (of ourselves and our relations with the world and our neighbours). In attempting to investigate a fundamental ontology, Heidegger, according to Levinas, is attempting to know things in their ontological totality, and Levinas radically questions the nature of this totality. The crux of his criticism is summed up in *Otherwise than Being*: 'Heideggerian ontology subordinates the relation with the other to the relation with the neuter, Being, and it thus continues to exalt the will to power, whose legitimacy the other alone can unsettle' (*OB*, p. 52). Levinas reads Heidegger as the final expression of the ontological tradition from Plato through Hegel to Husserl, on the one hand, and as Nietzschean, on the other. This is how Buber will interpret Heidegger in his 1938 essay 'What is Man?' Against his 'relation with the neuter', Levinas levels his own emphasis upon ethics as prior to ontology.

Levinas's interpretation is based upon Heidegger's early work, but it is also a typical French reading which is the result of two contemporary trends. The first trend was the reading of Heidegger's work as the continuation of the German Romantic tradition. German Romanticism was understood to have prepared the soil for Nazi politics, and at the very least Heidegger was believed to have thrown in his lot with 'the political fiction of the German myth'.[11] This is Heidegger prior to his break with Jünger and the 'political transformation which occurred in Heidegger's "late work".'[12] This is not the place to

---

[9] For example, Derrida and Philip Lacoue-Labarthe. See also D. Boothroyd's article 'Responding to Levinas' in *The Provocation of Levinas: Rethinking the Other*, eds. R. Bernasconi and D. Wood (London: Routledge, 1988), pp. 15–31.

[10] This is the essence of Boothroyd's argument in the article above.

[11] Philip Lacoue-Labarthe, *Heidegger, Art and Politics*, tr. Chris Turner (Oxford: Blackwell, 1990), p. 93.   [12] Ibid.

enter into the researches of those who have seen Nazism and the Jewish question as the apotheosis of modernism; all I wish to illustrate (and I think Philip Lacoue-Labarthe and Derrida would agree) is that Heidegger's career in some way maps out the move from modernism to postmodernism, and Levinas rarely appreciates this.

Paralleling Heidegger's shift, and the second major trend which has affected Levinas's reception of Heidegger, is a shift in the interpretative tradition. Vincent Descombes charts the move from modernism to postmodernism through the 1960s and the reaction against Kojève's Hegelianism: 'The generation after 1960 ... condemned dialectics as an illusion';[13] 'the generation of 1960 renounced the ideals defended by Merleau-Ponty in 1964 of a "new classicism", an "organic civilization"';[14] after 1965 '"Humanist" became a term of ridicule, an abusive epithet.'[15] In this philosophical context, interpretations of Heidegger swung between reading him as an Hegelian and reading him as a champion of difference. Later readings of Heidegger can be summed up in Richard E. Palmer's essay 'The Postmodernity of Heidegger' (1979), where the discussion of *Being and Time* is seen as having 'the appearance of speaking about the subjectivity of the subject, although its actual purpose is the explication of ontological structures',[16] whereas in Heidegger's later work an attempt is made 'to find a standpoint that can think the ontological difference between Being and beings *as* difference'.[17]

Levinas's reading of Heidegger, then, is typical of both the French reaction against Nazism and the growing French reaction against Hegelian metaphysics in which the *'dialectic of identity* ... prides itself on having included everything'.[18]

Despite his criticism of Heidegger there are, surprisingly, moments when Levinas explicitly admits that he is building upon Heidegger's work. In a footnote to the 1967 edition of *En découvrant l'existence avec Husserl et Heidegger*, for example, he calls

[13] *Modern French Philosophy* (Cambridge: Cambridge University Press, 1980), p. 75.
[14] Ibid., p. 109.   [15] Ibid., p. 31.
[16] In *Heidegger and the Question of Literature*, ed. William v. Spanos (Bloomington: Indiana University Press, 1979), pp. 77–8.
[17] Ibid.   [18] Descombes, *Modern French Philosophy*, p. 114.

attention to Heidegger's antipsychologism which questions whether all meaning is a projection of the ego. 'Our own inquiry is situated at this point: is not subjectivity ... before "unveiling being"?' (*EDE*, p. 144) Most of Levinas's key terms can be traced back to Heidegger: Heidegger's receptivity becomes Levinas's passivity, Heidegger's *es gibt* becomes Levinas's *il y a, die Spur* becomes *le trace, die Sage* becomes *le Dire,* Being–being becomes existing–existent, the nearness that preserves distance (*die Nahe*) becomes *la proximité.* What each understands by these terms is slightly different, but, on the whole, Levinas's work can be viewed as a Jewish midrash on Heidegger's.[19] Both philosophers work at the limits of phenomenology (this is where Levinas differs from and has the philosophical advantage over Buber), which they both see as providing access to the limits of metaphysics. Both thinkers, working within phenomenology, are metaphysicians of transcendental desire, concerned with origins and concerned with understanding the location of the flash-point of experience (where the immanent touches the transcendent). Heidegger, as we saw, calls that point *Ereignis* and Levinas, being explicitly theological, speaks of the 'God that reveals himself and puts truths into us' (*EDE*, p. 49). Derrida puts his finger on exactly what draws together Heidegger and Levinas when he speaks of the interminable dialogue of phenomenology and eschatology (*WD*, p. 133/p. 196). Both thinkers treat concealment, view the history of metaphysics as a history of concealing, and wish to find a way beyond Western philosophy in order to locate the place of the unthought, the wholly other. Heidegger's process of thinking deliberately uses the traditional

---

[19] This is particularly evident in his early work *Time and the Other*, where Levinas examines Heidegger's analysis of Dasein and Time. Levinas, unlike Heidegger, explicitly does not define the self in terms of the weight of the past and anxiety for the future (p. 56) or the experience of being-toward-death (p. 58). Levinas defines the self in terms of a 'profound unhappiness' with its materiality and its solitude. This unhappiness in everyday life provokes a preoccupation with salvation (p. 58). The difference between Heidegger and Levinas here lies not in the existential analysis, but what is existentially analysed. Similarly, Levinas defines the world not (like Heidegger) as an assemblage of tools, but 'an assemblage of nourishments' (p. 63). But we are only turning the phrase 'we eat to live' into the phrase 'we live to eat', turning praxis into enjoyment. Levinas is aware of this. The difference lies in the ethical charge which Levinas gives to 'nourishments', the materiality and solitude of the self and its enjoyment [*jouissance*].

vocabulary, deconstructing that vocabulary by showing its ambiguity (what remains concealed in the expression). In this way, he attempts to arrive at a postmodern, postmetaphysical conception of 'Being'. But, as Derrida has said, 'Being is transcategorical, and Heidegger would say of it what Levinas says of the other: it is "refractory to the category"' (*WD*, p. 140/ p. 206). Lacoue–Labarthe makes a similar point, 'I have a lot of trouble not seeing in Heidegger's "Being", if it is still Being and if it is Heidegger's Being, the same thing as (if not the very possibility of) Levinas's "otherwise than Being".'[20]

Where there is a difference is in Heidegger's insistence that the process of thinking is forever governed by its historicity and so the questioning that galvanizes it can never come to an end. There is, for Heidegger, no moving beyond the process of thinking itself. There is no alterity, only the suggestion of alterity which questioning itself installs. Heidegger's attention is fixed upon the immanent process of thinking itself. In wishing to read the otherwise than being as ethical, as a responsibility for the other, commanded by the other prior to time and context, Levinas's attention is fixed upon the transcendent. It is not an impersonal transcendence, but one that determines our concept of selfhood, in fact, our concept of concept. Levinas's thinking is always moving beyond self and its representations, beyond phenomenality.

Heidegger and Levinas share much, then, in the movement of their dialogues between phenomenology and eschatology, but where Levinas differs significantly is in determining the post-metaphysical as an ethical and, ultimately, like Buber, a theological *a priori*. Heidegger stops short of being theological. 'The existential involvement of fundamental ontology brings with it the semblance of an extremely individualistic, radical atheism,' he wrote in 1928.[21] '"Being" is an untheological word. Because revelation itself determines the manner of manifestness and because theology does not have to prove or interpret "Being", theology does not have to defend itself before philosophy', he

[20] *Typology: Mimesis, Philosophy, Politics*, p. 23.
[21] *The Metaphysical Foundations of Logic*, tr. Michael Heim (Bloomington: Indiana University Press, 1984), p. 140.

wrote in 1953.[22] 'Faith does not need the thought of Being' he wrote in 1962.[23] Faith is of a different order from Being, for Heidegger. But with Levinas there is a teleology, a movement through a critique of ontology towards theology. That movement towards radical otherness is evident in *Totality and Infinity* as the thinking progresses from interiority to exteriority, from the face to that beyond the face. It is even more evident in the structure of *Otherwise than Being*, where we move from intentionality to the glory of the infinite and the threshold of the divine. We have met the same movement in Rosenzweig's *Star of Redemption*.

It is at this theological juncture that Levinas's Saying of the other differs from Heidegger's. It is the theological perspective that allows Levinas to describe the Saying in profoundly personalist and ethical language. It is in that commitment to a personalist and ethical vocabulary that Levinas's Saying comes closest to Buber's 'saying Thou'.[24]

---

[22] 'Conversation with Martin Heidegger', tr. James G. Hart and John Maraldo, in *Piety of Thinking* (Bloomington: Indiana University Press, 1976), pp. 64–5.

[23] *Seminaire de Zuriche*, French tr. by D. Saatdjian and F. Fedier in *poEsie* 13 (Paris, 1980), p. 60.

[24] This is Richard Bernasconi's argument in '"The Failure of Communication" as Surplus', *The Provocation of Levinas*, pp. 110–11.

CHAPTER 6

Buber's dialogue with difference

It may seem a retrogressive step to return now to Buber. But
Levinas's work on Buber follows after his work on Heidegger,
and more importantly, Buber continued to develop his dialogicalism throughout the years deemed 'late-Heidegger'. It is
Buber's work of that period which we will be examining and it is
a period in which Buber reflected upon Heidegger's later
writings.

In chapter 3, I suggested that Buber maintains something of a
critical stance towards a dialogicalism which dissolved the It
into the Thou far too quickly. As one Buber scholar has
significantly pointed out, 'The Kantian influence was to remain
to the very end of his [Buber's] life.'[1] The Kantian division
between the realm of the phenomenal and the realm of the
noumenal allows Buber to maintain a certain distance between
the I–It and the I–Thou relationships. Nevertheless, throughout
I and Thou, Buber insists that the I–It and the I–Thou relationships, though antagonistic, are not mutually exclusive. The
latter has unavoidably to adhere to the former. For Buber
language in dialogue, moving between self and other, presents
the other and presents the same, hence the wholly other is also
'the wholly same' (*IT*, p. 79). With regard to apprehending the
other in the same, a choice seems to be necessary. 'If you explore
the life of things and of conditioned being [*Bedingheit* –
"relativity"], you come to the unfathomable [*das Unauflosbare*], if
you deny the life of things and of conditioned being, you stand
before nothingness [*das Nichts*], if you hallow this life you meet

[1] Robert E. Wood, *The Ontology of Martin Buber* (Evanston: Northwestern University
Press, 1969), p. 5.

the living God' (*IT*, p. 104/87). Encountering God, then, depends on what 'you' accept or deny; it depends on a prior decision of faith. The Thou is located, for Buber as for Barth, in the unfathomable, which can be either the sounding of the nihilistic No or the mystery of God's grace, either void or plenitude.

There is, as with Rosenstock and Rosenzweig, a radical disaffirmation of the I–It world in the I–Thou relation. Discourse constitutes an encounter with God as a Yes present in the revelation of a radical No. Buber scholars and critics tend either to stress the positive Thou (Robert E. Woods) or the negative Thou (Michael Theunissen). But the Thou is neither positive nor negative for Buber – it is both – and that is why his understanding of dialogue differs from Rosenstock's and develops more consistently the element of 'perhaps' and 'the Nought of our knowledge' in Rosenzweig's thinking.[2] This negativity in Buber suggests that he, like Barth, was moving towards an understanding of dialogue-with-difference, and this influenced Levinas.

Buber, like Levinas, develops his mature thinking on the implicit theology of language in relation to Heidegger's work. We can, in fact, see both 'The Word that is Spoken' and 'What is Common to All' (the essays composing his book *Logos*) and Buber's 1963 essay 'Man in His Image-Work' as specific responses to Heidegger's readings of Heraclitian fragments in '*Aletheia*', '*Logos*' and 'The Origin of the Work of Art' respectively. Buber's later work, I would suggest, is sharper both philosophically and anthropologically through his often inexplicit dialogue with Heidegger.[3]

Prior to examining the extent to which Levinas's Saying is related to Buber's 'Saying Thou', I wish to look closely at the two areas of common ground between Buber and late-Heidegger.

---

[2] See Norbert Samuelson's 'The Concept of "Nichts" in Rosenzweig's *Star of Redemption*' in *Der Philosoph Franz Rosenzweig*, ed. Wolfdietrich Schmied-Kowarzik (Munich: Verlag Karl Alber, 1988), pp. 643–56.

[3] For his earlier estimation of Heidegger's work see his 1938 treatise 'What is Man?' in *Between Men and Man*, tr. and introduction by Robert Gregor Smith (London: Fontana, 1961). He concentrates here solely upon Heidegger's anthropology in *Being and Time*.

The first is their understanding of dialogue itself and the second is their perspective on the relationship between art, particularly poetry, and Being. By comparing their positions and allowing their differences to become evident, we will be able to clarify what each contributed towards Levinas's intellectual development.

For both of them there is otherness because there is dialogue. In Buber's essay 'Elements of the Interhuman' he makes two points about genuine dialogue which are almost simplified abstractions of Heidegger's thesis: first, that 'genuine dialogue is an ontological sphere which is constituted by the authenticity of being' (*KM*, p. 86), and secondly, that in 'its basic order ... nothing can be determined, the course is of the spirit, and some discover what they have to say only when they catch the call of the spirit' (*KM*, p. 87). Being is understood existentially and anthropologically, by Buber, in terms of establishing a social community. That social community is an analogue for God as the Unity of all unities,[4] the wholeness of Being. Authenticity of being is a person's ability to make present 'the contribution of his spirit without reduction and without shifting his ground' (*KM*, p. 85). Being is realized in the act of authentic socializing.

Being has, then, none of the connotations of necessary absence, of being concealed and always only provisionally named (as it does in late-Heidegger). In fact, the question of 'the relation between that-which-regions and releasement, if it can still be considered a relation, [which] can be thought neither as ontic nor as ontological' (*DT*, p. 76) is not a question Buber is pursuing or a question Buber is aware of. Buber is quite content to remain within a Greek ontology while Heidegger is pushing beyond it. Although both share a common starting point, *Faktizität*, Heidegger's concerns are more with the processes of appropriation and forgetting, the engagement whereby one discovers that 'there is' [*Es gibt*]. Buber's concern is with drawing out the social, anthropological and philosophical implications of the fundamental I–Thou relation. Buber's thinking is not

⁴ See '*Das Judentum und die Menschheit*', in *Der Jude und seine Judentum* (Cologne: Melzer, 1963), pp. 21–2.

exploratory, nor does it have the self-reflexive edge which characterizes the hermeneutic back-tracking of Heidegger's thinking.

For both of them dialogue is the location for the ontological, but what each understands by the nature of the ontological differs radically. Buber does not distinguish a rift between the ontological and the ontic; there is no ontological difference. Being is never *questioned* in the manner of Heidegger's thinking. Ontology is a description of the fundament of human experience, for Buber.[5] We begin to recognize how fundamentally this difference concerning ontology affects their work when we ask what happens to otherness in these two types of dialogue. Buber concludes '*Dem Gemeinschaftlichen folgen*' (the English translation, 'What is Common to All', is a modified text) with the words: '*Wir "sind" ein Gesprach* [we *are* a dialogue]' (*L*, p. 72).[6] And to live within that dialogue is to 'be aware of a thing or a being', that is, 'to experience it as a whole ... in all its concreteness' (*KM*, p. 80). The revelation to the I is of the transcending uniqueness of the other. The manifestation 'cannot really be grasped except on the basis of the gift of the spirit ... the spirit sharing decisively in the personal life of the living man' (ibid.). 'Otherness or more concretely, the moment of surprise' (*KM*, p. 113) is mediated by the spirit.

The spirit mediates between the I and the Thou. It constitutes the between, the ontology of the interhuman.[7] This 'between' is the site of language: 'The Word that is spoken is found rather in the oscillating sphere between the persons, the sphere which I call the "between" and what can never be allowed to be contained without remainder in the two participants' (*KM*, p. 112). The 'between' is the site of the spoken dialogue which the spirit inspires and perpetuates. It is a site which emerges because of the distinction between the I and Thou. The otherness arising

---

[5] Wood, p. 120. See also Nathan Rotenstreich's recent book on Buber's ontology, *Immediacy and its Limits* (Reading: Hardwoord Academic, 1992).

[6] The English text has been considerably modified and expanded in its concluding paragraphs. The German text, the second of two essays in Buber's collection *Logos*, ends quite emphatically on the quotation from Hölderlin in the present tense (the English translation puts it into the past).

[7] See 'Elements of the Interhuman' in *KM*.

from this distinction determines 'the tension between what each understands by the concept' (*KM*, p. 114). The grasping of this otherness in any clarity is impossible, because there is always the 'ambiguity of the word, which we may call its aura' (ibid.). The 'between' issues from the uniqueness and therefore difference of the I and Thou and this difference is expressed in 'the ambiguity of the word'. Words are not in themselves ambivalent. In fact, Buber can speak of 'the window of speech' which becomes 'directly perceptible to the hearer' (*KM*, p. 120). But the difference from our point of view arises when we attempt to name the 'aura'.[8] It is not a difference of kind (as in Heidegger's Being/beings dif-ference), but a difference of quantity. It is the absence of a degree of clarity which Buber calls 'the primal phenomenon of speech' (*KM*, p. 118). He attempts to explicate this 'primal phenomenon' by means of Brahmin legends on the relation of truth and falsehood. Falsehood is so intermixed and necessary to Truth that 'the fate of being is determined through the speaking ... [of the] word' (*KM*, p. 119). Dialogue constitutes the very movement, the destiny of Being through language, which clarifies, which clears up, the ambivalence in the representation of the Thou. In another essay with strong Heideggerian themes, 'Man and his Image-Work', Buber writes: 'as my "Thou" the other can be grasped in his full independence' but only 'by freeing it from the sense world, and from its sensible representation ... It exists but not as imagable' (*KM*, p. 157). Buber therefore designates it 'by a small *x*'. He goes on to characterize this *x* as 'unfathomable darkness [whose] being has intercourse with my being' (ibid.). The 'primal phenomenon of speech', the Logos for Buber, is 'that messagelike saying that descends out of the stillness over a disintegrating human world ... [the] indivisible unity' (*KM*, p. 120).

---

[8] Buber no doubt adopts this word from Walter Benjamin where it refers to the ontological mystery pressing in and through language. Benjamin's understanding of language closely parallels Buber's. He too recognized that he was continuing the work of Hamann, Herder and Humboldt; that there is a 'suprahistorical kinship of language'. See 'The Task of the Translator' in *Illuminations*, ed. Hannah Arendt (New York: Schocken, 1969). Benjamin's (and Buber's) views might well be compared with those of Gershom Scholem in his 'The Name of God and the Linguistic Theory of the Kabbalah', *Diogenes* 79 and 80 (1972), pp. 59–80 and 165–94.

The significant words in Buber's descriptions are 'intercourse' (between being and being) and 'indivisible unity', for despite references to the totally other, the unrepresentable, that about which 'we know nothing' and 'the wordless anticipation [*Vorgestalt*] of saying Thou', Buber's prototype for dialogue is Adam in the garden conversing with God. He argues *for* communication, *for* wholeness and unity, *for* dialogue issuing in a greater understanding between human beings and *for* the ontological unity of the human and the divine Thou. Thus Buber too, like the other dialogical philosophers, finally elides the divine address, the divine Thou, into the human address and the human Thou. And he does this by means of the spirit which presences the Thou.[9] His emphasis is upon 'genuine spoken intercourse with one another hav[ing] a share in the consummation of ... indwelling' (*KM*, p. 90). Both 'intercourse' and 'consummation', like his emphasis elsewhere on partnership and reciprocity, elide the difference and, essentially, the otherness of the other. Words and the Word relate through the same spirit; comparisons between the Creator and the created, between the '*Weltprozess*' and '*Wortwerden*', betray a theological schema behind Buber's thinking. It is the schema of the *analogia entis*, where the beneficence of the creator–God is revealed in the *vestigia* of his creation. But considering the depth of Buber's agnosticism, it is a form of *analogia entis*, perhaps, more recognizable by Aquinas than Suarez. The emphasis, and Buber always insisted upon this, is upon the *relation* between the I and the other. It is not upon the otherness of the other, that in the other

---

9 There are two foci in Buber's work which he struggles to mediate: the 'between' which is where Being is located and develops into a social ontology; and the Thou where the transcendent otherness is located, developing a theology of the *imago dei*. There is almost a trinity here – the unrepresentable face of God as Thou, the spirit which constitutes the 'between' and human being (animals and trees) as the incarnate Thou. Of course, Tillich suggested in 1952 that the God of the Jewish experience was not far from the trinitarian God of Christianity as does Nicholas Lash in *Easter in Ordinary* (London: SCM, 1988). Levinas's economy too is trinodal (see chapter 7). What is distinctive about Levinas's position is his castigation of binary oppositions – Same and Other, presence and absence. He wishes to construct analogies through a presence-by-absence. Lash presents Buber as a Jewish Aquinas, but Levinas is much closer to Maimonides. The trinodality of Levinas's economy develops, then, from a different understanding of analogy.

which transcends all possibility of relation and, in doing so, constitutes caesura or rift.

Having said so much, there are moments in Buber's writing when he seems to be pushing at the very boundaries of the ontological idiom he is employing; pushing, that is, beyond his ontological unity towards ontological difference or an *x* beyond Being. It is significant for Levinas's own development that he did not recognize this element in Buber's work at first. In his 1958 essay, 'Martin Buber and the Theory of Knowledge', he criticizes Buber for 'a theology somewhat too well-informed on the nature of God' (*LR*, p. 71) and concludes that although 'Buber has penetratingly described the Relation and the act of distancing, he has not taken separation seriously enough' (*LR*, p. 74). Levinas's appreciation of the negative ontology of Buber's 'Saying Thou' only emerges in his 1984 essay 'Martin Buber, Gabriel Marcel and Philosophy'.[10] There he comments upon the darker side, the negative side of the Thou which runs as a counter-theme to Buber's primary emphasis. There he perceives a transcendental saying of the Thou which lies beyond 'the power of the logos to grasp the world as a world order without which ordering grasp it is not and cannot be a world' (*KM*, p. 91). Derrida is aware of this when he criticizes Levinas's earlier reading of Buber (*WD*, p. 314/ p. 156). The relation *qua* relation in Buber hovers equivocally between being symmetrical and asymmetrical, a Logos establishing the world order and a saying-Thou which is beyond representation.

Thus, for both Heidegger and Buber, dialogue is a means of moving beyond intentionality, and yet, at the same time, it is 'the condition of all intentional relations' (Levinas discussing Buber in *Noms Propres*, p. 34). Dialogue, for both of them, participates in the unfolding destiny of Being. It is given, not found (although Heidegger de-theologizes Buber's concepts of grace and revelation). For both, the recognition of this given issues in a moment of crisis (Heidegger's *Ereignis* – a later development of his moment of authentic insight, *Augenblick* – and Buber's *Überraschung* or 'moment of surprise'). This is an exper-

---

[10] In *Martin Buber: A Centenary Volume* (Jerusalem, 1984), pp. 305–21. The original French article appears in *Hors Sujet* (Fata Morgana, 1987), pp. 34–59.

ience of the rupturing of the transcendental consciousness proceeding from a 'between' – (Heidegger's *Mitte*, the site of 'the peal of the stillness of dif-ference' and Buber's *Zwischen*). The between is the site of language which both receives and speaks, hears and responds. The between constitutes human beings as human beings and language as language and the immediate experience of the between is one of absolute distance.[11] But what is understood by that 'between' is not the same, and this is where they part company. For Buber the between is constituted by a separation, but what is separated still participates in the more fundamental unity of Being itself. The relation, being *a priori*, cannot be represented unambiguously without destroying 'the affirmation of the primarily deep otherness of the other'(*KM*, p. 96), but the relation between human being and human being nevertheless remains an analogue for 'the true being of a common logos and a common cosmos' (ibid.). The between presences the Being of beings. By contrast, Heidegger's between is a caesura. It is the presencing of beings 'in the "between" of a two-fold absence' (*EGT*, p. 48). It is a presencing which 'in both directions . . . is conjointly disposed towards absence' (*EGT*, p. 41), the absence of Being, its hiddenness and non-appearance. For Buber the between is an image of plenitude, and his theology often draws close to a neo-Platonic understanding of *processio*. For Heidegger, the between is a rift, and he avoids trying to give this rift a value as either plenitude or void. It is both and neither:

SCIENTIST   It seems to me that this unbelievable night entices you both to exult.
TEACHER   So it does, if you mean exulting in waiting, through which we become more waitful and more void.
SCHOLAR   Apparently emptier, but richer in contingencies. (*DT*, p. 82)

Buber and Heidegger differ at the point where Buber places most emphasis upon the *tatsachlich*, the existential, the '*Gemeinschaftlichkeit des Logos*'. His agnosticism only occasionally penetrates the main direction of his argument. The difference of

[11] 'Distance', which begins to be a formal concept for Buber is taken up as an important element in Levinas's work and developed further in the philosophical theology of Jean-Luc Marion (see chapter 7, note 11).

emphasis leads to very different types of discourse. Although Heidegger and Buber both begin with facticity and the historical, Heidegger traces the history of Being in dialogue with other philosophers from Anaximander to Nietzsche, tracing transformation in the words for Being and allowing their etymologies to surface. But Buber develops his argument through retelling myths and descriptions of primitive anthropological conditions or states of mind in infancy. The distinction is between a metaphysician working at the 'end of metaphysics' and a philosophical anthropologist. Buber is still working veins of linguistic philosophy opened by Herder and Humboldt, where language is informed by a transcendental wholeness and remains a social construct. His emphasis is upon language's social development in which its opacity becomes increasingly transparent through dialogue. Heidegger is more aware of the hermeneutic circle, the hermeneutics of the facticity that Buber takes for granted, and he is therefore more sceptical of words ever becoming transparent. In fact, *Being and Time* suggests that assertions, in which the meaning of words are frozen, can be obstacles to true understanding. His later work develops the path of thinking (or as a 1954 essay is entitled '*Aus der Erfahrung des Denkens*') into a method. Assertive statements are abandoned, in so far as they can ever be abandoned, as he increasingly realizes that there is no position outside language from which to begin an objective analysis. There are no grounds for analysis as such, only narrative – the narration of one's hermeneutical journeying.

Buber does not take this step – he is still working within prescriptive discourse. In fact, for all Buber's talk of dialogue it is a monologue we readers are presented with. In reading Heidegger's encounters with Georg, Hölderlin or Trakl, we are part of a discussion [*Erörterung*] which unfolds as we follow in the thinker's path, tracing his trace. In a deeper sense this too is monologue – the path, although Being's, is nevertheless Heidegger's. He is the intentional subject giving form to the dialogue. But this is monologue constituted through dialogue, through listening to the voice beyond and other than his own. It is the discourse of an intentional subject in *sub-jectum*. Buber's discourse begins from a place outside both dialogue and his own subjectivity. It is a meta-discourse that provides no grounds for its own privileged objectivity. Heidegger, recognizes there is no dialogue that is not also a dialectic. The dialectic issues from the presence of the unbridgeable rift; it expresses the alterity within dialogue. Buber's dialectic is more Hegelian: the negative moment is synthesized in a higher unity. Commenting upon Buber's dialogical method, Levinas points out that it is evident there is a blindness to 'the ineluctable character of isolated subjectivity' (*TO*, p. 94). In the end, despite Buber's Kantianism and his desire to overcome the Hegelian hermeneutical consciousness through dialogue, he stumbles into Hegelianism by his very method, and dialogicalism returns to the kind of dialectic it has always spurned.

We can see this quite clearly in a second Heideggerian theme taken up in 'The Word that is Spoken', the relation of poetry (which Buber also privileges above other artistic expressions) to thought. Buber writes: 'the earliest speaking ... sets the word outside itself in being, and the word continues, it has continuance. And this continuance wins its life ever anew in the true relation in the spoken word. Genuine dialogue witnesses to it, and poetry witnesses to it. For the poem is spokenness, spokenness to the Thou, whoever this partner might be' (*KM*, p. 119). This sails close to Heidegger. Furthermore 'the name of truth really belongs [*zukommt*] to both, the conceptual and the poetic' (*KM*, p. 118/*L*, p. 24). But when we analyse how it '*zukommt*', how it 'approaches' or 'comes to', we are told quite definitely (though again without mentioning Heidegger by name) that the 'truth is not the sublime "unconcealment" suitable to Being itself, it is the simple [*schlichte*] conception of truth of the Hebrew Bible, whose *etymon* means "faithfulness", the faithfulness of man or the faithfulness of God' (*KM*, p. 120). Here *in nuce* is the difference between Buber and Heidegger. 'The truth of the word', for Buber, 'in its highest form ... [is] indivisible unity' (ibid.). In other words, though the word is 'outside itself in Being', that Being is not understood in Heideggerian terms as hiddenness out of which the thing as thing emerges into 'unconcealment'. That Being is interpreted by Buber as 'indivisible unity'. It is interpreted in terms of totality. It is understood as a truth that is fundamentally historical, for as 'the word continues, it has continuance'. And that indivisible ground of unity which is present in genuine speaking is 'not there and then . . . but here and now' (ibid.). Being, then, does not constitute a dialogue, but it is an address, a 'now', an immediacy of meaning superior to contexts and mediation which is, ultimately, transhistorical and embraces the otherness of dialogue.

What is evident from this is that Buber, unlike Heidegger, does not take time seriously. Again, this is what we found in chapter 3 with other *Rede* philosophers. It is another aspect of Buber's inability to take the subjective conscious seriously – for time, phenomenologically, is the internal structure of Dasein. Time, in Buber, appears as an external stream of instants, rather than (with Heidegger) the perichoretic tension between three *ek-stases*. Consequently, we are never sure whether the relation to the Thou is reciprocal because symmetrical (as in genuine dialogue) or commanded and therefore asymmetrical. The first is existential and historical, the second biblical and transhistorical. Buber does not clearly map out the grounds upon which the second can enter the first, but there is the familiar ghost of gnosticism (and dialogicalism) in viewing language as a vessel for truth and time as a series of nows.

Poetry and language, then, do not emerge from the *a priori* dialogue of beings and Being, an unending unfolding of unconcealment from the ground of hiddenness (of which the poem itself is an example). Poetry is merely a witness (*'das Gedicht bezeugt es'*), not a manifestation (*bezeigt es*). This is why in 'Man and His Image-Making', Buber can write (again *contra* Heidegger) that 'Thinking and art certainly supplement each other, but not like two connected organs; rather they are like the electric poles between which the spark jumps' (*KM*, p. 152). Thinking and art, like meaning and language, are distinct for Buber. Therefore, there is truth 'in poetry and incomparably still more so in that messagelike [*botschaftsartigen*] saying' (*KM*, p. 120). What is given the priority here is *'Spruch'* (which in the context of a voice from heaven comes close to the verbal dictate of God), a definitized content, not Heidegger's *'die Sage'*, the infinite 'Saying' which Heidegger relates closely to *Zeigen* which is the poet's function. Higher than poetry, for Buber, is what poetry bears witness to: the '*botschaftsartigen*' dictum. The adjective is difficult to translate. It describes the dictum as a courteous message, a gracious address. Here is something more defined than Heidegger's trace of the Saying. Here is the movement towards univocity. Here, again, is not dialogue but an appeal to a distinct monologue proceeding from monotheism (Buber's God opposed to Heidegger's gods) – the Scriptural concept of truth as the faithfulness of God. Dialogue moves within the indivisible unity of such a truth, a truth it is always bearing testimony to. It is this truth and its operation that Buber abstracts in his own writings and prophetically announces.

Buber's method, therefore, is not dialogical. Though he speaks of the centrality of dialogue, 'dialogue' is significant only within the context of his own monologue, a monologue that, as we have seen above, proceeds dialectically, proceeds from a critique of Heidegger's position to an overcoming of that position. Buber is unable to overcome the intentionality of the 'I'. For Heidegger, dialogue appropriates Saying because it is fated to do so by its being appropriated by Saying. There is, then, no Saying (no bringing into unconcealment what is recognized in Heraclitus' fragment or Hölderlin's lines) apart from dialogue. Hence Heidegger's interrogatory method. For Buber, the Saying can be distinguished from, abstracted from, the dialogue and its operation in the dialogue described, because the Saying is that of the monological unity of the Thou. Hence Buber's prescriptive method and hence also his closet Hegelianism.

This conclusion brings us to a fundamental question that runs through this study: the relationship between dialogue, ontological difference and the dialectic of non-synthesis. Buber's 'dialogicalism' accommodates the other to the same, alterity to the intentionality of the 'I', because it advocates a dialogue that evades the problems of human consciousness, of human knowing. These are the problems that concerned Husserl in *Cartesian Meditations*, where he sets out to explain 'the mediate intentionality of experiencing someone else' (*CM*, p. 108). Levinas, who translated *Cartesian Meditations* into French, will learn from Husserl. Buber is blind to there being a philosophical and existential problem at all. He evades facing the problem by emphasizing the immediacy, the wholeness of the process, and the directness of the relation in dialogue. Where he does appear to tackle them, for example in 'What is Common to All', it is in terms of Upanishad and Toaist mythology, where the dreamer, caught up in his own image-making, is released into 'the shapeless abiding in worldless being' (*KM*, p. 94). The Kantian anthropology is overcome, but the narrative form in which the overcoming is described takes the place of philosophical analysis. The possibility of analysis is subsumed beneath the story of the hero's victory, his ascension from one realm into a higher. The dreamer, then, only awakes within another dream.

Heidegger is more aware of mediation, more aware of his own discourse and the need for analysis and self-reflection in order to understand what he calls *Ereignis*. He draws attention to this *re*flection by pointing up the role played by 'memory' (which following Hegel – and Barth – is *Erinnerung*) in analysis. We have no immediate grasp of the moment, we have only the *ek-static* tension of time. It is remembering that what is constituted is only constituted *as* memory, *as* mediation, which leads Heidegger to emphasize the dialectical element in every dialogue and the dialogical element in every dialectic. 'If and when dialogue is necessarily dialectic, we leave open' (*WP*, p. 66). In 'A Dialogue on Language' he writes: 'To experience in this sense always means to refer back – to refer life and lived experience back to the "I" ... The much-discussed I/Thou experience, too, belongs within the metaphysical sphere of subjectivity' (*OWL*, pp. 35–6). Heidegger's dialogue within the nature of language has to take place in a dialectical discussion between two subjectivities *about* language. The 'dialogue ... appropriated to Saying' therefore only has form in the dialectic of the Said. Levinas understood this; Buber did not.

But then Buber, like Levinas, does not understand Heidegger's position at all. Like Levinas, he reads Heidegger as standing firmly in the Hegelian tradition (ironically). Despite his knowledge of Heidegger's later writings he does not read

Heidegger's correlation between *Reissen, Aufriss, Grundriss, Riss*. He does not read Heidegger's agnosticism, his alterity. In fact, other than pointing out differences of emphasis between Heidegger's thinking and his own, Buber's main contention about Heidegger's Hellenistic thought is that it is overcomplicated, while his own Jewish thinking is '*schlichte*'. *Schlichte* is a favourite Buber word when distinguishing his own position from Heidegger's (*KM*, p. 153). For Heidegger such simplicity is unavailable because discourse is part of the very problem being investigated. There is no easy escape from the hermeneutic circle. It is because Heidegger is forced to take language seriously and sees language as involved in the very oblivion of Being that the other can emerge as wholly other only in so far as it emerges as a lack, a default, an experience of rift. For Buber, language essentially remains a window, a tool, and so the other of dialogue is ultimately consumed within the indivisible unity of the same. Buber's ambiguities and contradictions emerge because he is caught between the methodological precedence of his 'I' discourse and the ontological precedence he wishes to accord the Thou. Heidegger avoids such a trap by attempting a new form of discourse, a methodology that deconstructs the I. It deconstructs its own voice – revealing the provisional nature of all vocabulary, discourse and understanding – in favour of the voice of the other as its trace appears in the *Riss* between 'the *logos* of *omologein* and the *legein* of the *logos*' (*EGT*, p. 75). For both Buber and Heidegger art, particularly poetry, 'is the realm of the "in-between" which has become a form' (*KM*, p. 165), but Heidegger takes form *qua* form much more seriously than Buber.

Buber's refusal to engage with phenomenological reduction while emphasizing the importance of the 'pure reckoning of the personal existence' (*KM*, p. 120), his epistemologically ungrounded existentialism, leaves him without an adequate account of either the self or language (or time). Ironically, this renders his account of dialogue an idealist abstraction, and therefore his account of an encounter with the wholly other, the transcendent other, lacks coherence. Heidegger's deeper appreciation of the philosophical problem in overcoming metaphysics metaphysically ensures that his trace of the Saying in the said is far better founded than Buber's Saying of the Thou. If their difference can be seen as that between Heidegger's appeal to Hölderlin's gods and Buber's appeal to monotheism's God, their difference is also between Heidegger's Promethean man, guilty that his existence manifests the robbery of *letheia* (concealment), and Buber's Adamic man addressed by the voice of God and naming creation.

Levinas's project, unlike Buber's, does engage with the phenomenological; but Levinas's project, unlike Heidegger's, appeals to monotheism's God. It is this theological appeal that determines the ethical emphasis in his work upon social responsibility and intersubjectivity. These emphases look back to Buber's thinking.

Levinas's work is an attempt at a phenomenology of sociality, distinctive from Heidegger's phenomenology of Dasein and Buber's existential analysis of *Gemeinschaft*. The very tension in the phrase 'a phenomenology of sociality' conveys the distinctiveness, and perhaps the paradoxicality, of Levinas's project. He writes: 'sociality in Heidegger is found in the subject alone ... Against this collectivity of the side-by-side, I have tried to oppose the "I–you" collectivity, taking this not in Buber's sense, where reciprocity remains the tie between two separated freedoms, and the ineluctable character of isolated subjectivity is underestimated ... This [collectivity] is not a participation in a third term ... It is a collectivity that is not a communion. It is the face-to-face without intermediary' (*TO*, pp. 93–4). Levinas is attempting to map out a middle path between the community of transcendental egos (Heidegger's position in *Being and Time*) and the community of intersubjectivities Buber is outlining. He creates this path through the middle by avoiding an underestimation of 'isolated subjectivity' and therefore viewing sociality phenomenologically. In other words, he proceeds through the consciousness of the subject while not locating sociality 'in the subject alone'. It is not 'in the subject alone', because Levinas outlines a schema whereby the two freedoms are not 'separated'. They are related, though not through a mutuality and not through a participation in a third term, but through an absence:

'The relationship with the Other [*autrui*] is the absence of the other [*autre*]' (*TO*, p. 90). We need to clarify what kind of dialogicalism Levinas is describing here.

It is a dialogue that is profoundly asymmetrical. The possibility for such a dialogue is axiomatic for his thesis and so this requires explication. Levinas objects to Buber's 'symmetrical relation' that creates 'the rarefied ether of a spiritual friendship' (*LR*, p. 73). 'The truth is rather obtainable in a wholly different kind of dialogue which does not manifest its concern for Relation so much as it does a desire to assure to the I its independence, even if this independence is only possible in a union (*verbunden*) [*en liaison*]' (*LR*, p. 74/*NP*, p. 42). This wholly different kind of dialogue concentrates on 'a rupture of the individual and the whole' [*la rupture avec la participation à la totalité*] (ibid./ibid.). Levinas, then, like Heidegger is calling for 'a dialogue altogether *sui generis*'.[12]

This dialogue issues from Levinas's phenomenological analysis of the sociality of the I. The I thematizes the communication of the Saying, the trace of the infinite difference, in the said, while the infinite difference institutes the Saying to which the said responds. This participation-in-difference – later to be linked by Levinas to Husserl's analogy of appresentation – constitutes Levinas's understanding of a dia-logue. Following Derrida we can call this 'the dialogue of the question about itself and with itself' (*WD*, p. 80/p. 119). When Levinas points to the symmetry of the relation in Buber's dialogue, he is pointing, then, to Buber's latent Hegelianism and his own break with Hegelian phenomenology. But the break with it is not an abandonment of it; rather, it is a break beyond what Bataille (and after him Derrida) called the 'restricted economy' of the Hegelian dialectic.[13] Levinas, like Derrida (and late Heidegger), recognizes that there is no exit from Hegelian thinking except through and beyond Hegelian thinking.

From the asymmetry of the I–Thou dialogue, Levinas develops the concept of the ego as the accusative 'me' rather than the

---

[12] See his '*Le dialogue*' in *DVI*. He terms his form of dialogue 'dia-logue', to emphasize the rupture and difference.

[13] See 'From Restricted to General Economy' in *WD*.

nominative 'I'; the ego as *sub-jectum*. For subjectivity is 'not a modality of essence' (*OB*, p. 17/p. 33). 'Hegel and Heidegger . . . starting with the object inseparable from the subject, go on to reduce their correlation . . . to a modality of being.' Levinas, on the other hand, deduces that the 'subject already resists this ontologization' (*OB*, p. 18/p. 35). The subject is constituted by a responsibility for the other and this 'exceptional, extra-ordinary, transcendent character of goodness is due to just this break with being and history' (ibid.).[14] Being and signification both become modalities of this *a priori* responsibility – the Good beyond Being – as we saw in chapter 5. The subject is *sub-jectum* – a state which has affinities with Heidegger's *Geworfenheit*. The self is 'from the first in the accusative form (or under accusation!)' (*OB*, p. 53/p. 91). The phenomenological reduction returns us to this *sub-jectum*. It is in the movement beyond this self, towards the other (that which is singular and unique, which constitutes this self), that Levinas moves beyond phenomenology and beyond knowledge. All knowing becomes idealism, that is, the movement towards an endorsement of universals and abstractions. This is because thematization suppresses the singular; it suppresses the otherness, the difference. But though the other is unknowable, ungraspable, that which is known, that which is graspable is a modification of this antecedent relationship. There is, then, 'subjectivity *qua* consciousness' (*OB*, p. 99/p. 157), the transcendental ego, but Levinas is also attempting to describe 'subjectivity that is irreducible to consciousness and thematization' (*OB*, p. 100/p. 157). This is a subjectivity which is already bound to an inter-relation. But where this subject-in-relation differs from Buber's *Gemeinschaft* is in the way Levinas moves through a phenomenological analysis of subjectivity *qua* consciousness towards the other [*l'autre*] beyond and behind the Other person

---

[14] Once more we note the link between Heidegger and Hegel and the levelling of their ontological projects. This consistent misreading is partly because Levinas considers *Being and Time* 'much more significant and profound than any of Heidegger's later works' (interview with Richard Kearney in *Face to Face with Levinas*, ed. Richard Cohen, Albany: State University of New York Press, 1986, p. 15). Levinas does not appreciate Heidegger's 'step back'. Nor does he appreciate that Heidegger's focus is epistemological – that is, how we arrive at a 'new concept of finitude' (*TB*, p. 54). This epistemological enquiry is inseparable from the ontological examination (the concealing and unconcealing of Being).

[*l'autrui*]. The movement towards the other-in-the-self is a movement towards the collapse of phenomenology. In Buber's work the thou of the other person participates in the divine Thou, but this is stated rather than discovered. Levinas investigates the character of this 'participation' phenomenologically and outlines its economy. Where this subject-in-relation differs from Husserl's 'monadological intersubjectivity' (though not Heidegger's *Mitandersein*, despite Levinas's claims) is in the fact that the ego is not a monad placed in a community of other monads. The ego, for Levinas, is not alongside its neighbours, but is actually formed in a response to the neighbour prior to the advent of the neighbour's presence.[15] The self is always, then, hijacked by the other, accused by the other, so that when the face of the neighbour approaches there is a proximity in which 'is heard a command come as though from an immemorial past, which was never present' (*OB*, p. 88/p. 141). The approach of the face undermines all self-identity and imposes the identity of the self as accusative, the self which is a *sub-jectum*. Buber, at the end of his article 'What is Common to All', announces that true transcendence is only established when we stand before the face of God. But, characteristically, this remains an assertion. In Levinas it is a phenomenological reduction.

Because the self is constituted, primordially, one-for-the-other, its fundamental disposition is to be a substitute. Irredeemably open to the Other, the self experiences a 'susceptibility or exposedness to wounds and outrage [that] characterizes its passivity' (*OB*, p. 108/p. 170). 'In the exposure to wounds and outrages, in the feeling proper to responsibility, the oneself is provoked as irreplaceable, as devoted to the others, without being able to resign, and thus incarnated in order to offer itself, to suffer and to give' (*OB*, p. 105/p. 167). There is, then, anthropologically, a kenotic disposition that is prior to any action undertaken by the self or any experience undergone. In fact, this kenosis is *the condition* for any action undertaken or

[15] Compare this with Buber's statement in '*Dem Gemeinschaftlichen folgen*', '*authentischen Gesprochenheit der Sprache in deren Reiche Antwort gehiest wird, und Antwort ist Verantwortung*' (*L*, p. 69). There are similar elements – dialogue with the neighbour, the command to respond, the responsibility for the other – but it is Levinas's analysis of the *a priori* condition for this existential situation that distinguishes him from Buber.

experience undergone. Selfhood, or what Levinas calls 'ipseity' (because the Latin for 'self' has no nominative form), is 'naked to the other to the point of making the subject expose its very exposedness' (*OB*, p. 109/p. 173). The passivity commands a substituting of the self for the other. '[T]he expulsion of self outside itself is its substitution for the other' and this is 'the ultimate secret of the incarnation of the subject', (*OB*, pp. 110–11/p. 175). We need to take note here that the substitution *is* the expulsion. The substitution is not an act in itself, but the 'hitherside of the act-passivity alternative" which conditions all that follows. Levinas stresses how this description differs from Hegelian subjectivity where 'the ego is an equality with itself, and consequently the return of being to itself is a concrete universality' (*OB*, p. 115/p. 182). The self incarnates an anarchy and an origin, an alterity and an identity, a diachrony and a synchrony. It incarnates a substitution for the other, 'an expiation prior to activity and passivity' (*OB*, p. 116/p. 183), prior, that is, to the will. The 'me' is always a substitute and its nature is substitutional. The prior dialogue which constitutes the self structures, therefore, both a horizontal communication with other people and a vertical communication with that which is wholly other. Language, then, 'express[es] the gratuity of sacrifice' (*OB*, p. 120/p. 191).

We examined the nature of this communication in chapter 5. Here, we need to examine how Levinas's wholly other differs from Buber's (before we go on in chapter 7 to examine how it differs from Barth's), for it is with this concept of the wholly other that Levinas, like Buber (and Barth) moves from an ethical to a frankly theological discourse.

Levinas names his concept of the wholly other 'illeity', by which he means the 'detachment of the Infinite from the thought that seeks to thematize it and the language that tries to hold it in the said' (*OB*, p. 147/p. 230). Language (the said) and Saying (the trace of the infinite) are both conditioned by this illeity, this non-phenomenality. And this is where Levinas moves beyond Buber's 'saying Thou'. This illeity 'escapes the objectification of thematization and dialogue . . . in the third person' (*OB*, p. 150/p. 234). In Levinas the dialogue is not I–thou but thou–me. And the condition for the possibility of this dialogue lies outside dialogue altogether, for outside the said's response to and yet betrayal of the Saying, is the infinite, the transcending otherness, the other (*autre*) which is beyond the Other person (*autrui*). Dialogue is not then trying to locate the common ground, the universal, a participation in a third term; it issues from and nourishes difference, the truth in difference. It fosters an understanding of otherness, particularity and uniqueness.

Dialogue is constituted by the rupture of 'thirdness'. This thirdness is Levinas's step beyond the ontology of Buber's 'We-saying'. With the concept of illeity Buber's vision for *Gemeinschaft* and *Gemeinsprache* is now provided with a transcendental condition which, as we saw, it ultimately lacked. Levinas reformulates Buber's vision by means of a more radical understanding of Buber's Thou as 'wholly other'. The mutuality and reciprocity of Buber's 'We' is struck through by a dissymmetry which radically questions such humanism in the name of a much deeper responsibility for the other.[16] The entrance of this 'thirdness' takes the form of 'a third party that interrupts the face to face of a welcome of the other man, interrupts the proximity or approach of the neighbour' (*OB*, p. 150/p. 234). The approach of the third party constitutes that which breaks open any simple oppositional structure between the 'thou' and the 'me'. It constitutes the otherness in the Other, for it is other than the Other. It is that which cannot be held or represented within a binomial opposition; s/he for whom I too am an Other. Proximity, then, births the Saying, but the communication is born because of the presence of the third party, the community that the face belongs to. 'The apparition of a third party is the very origin of appearing' (*OB*, p. 160/p. 249), because it is the origin of difference *as* difference. Incarnate Saying is, therefore, authentic human-beingness as it proceeds from proximity with the Other which recalls the I to a responsibility for that other which is otherwise than Being. Put in a different way, illeity invokes the Saying, which invokes the said, which bears witness to the diachrony of the Saying, which is a trace of the glory of the infinite (illeity). A perichoresis emerges, a perichoresis working

[16] See Levinas's essay 'Humanism and Anarchy' in *CP*.

at the heart of Levinas's anthropology of difference: 'The enigma of the Infinite, whose saying in me ... becomes the contestation of the Infinite' (*OB*, p. 154/p. 240).

Read theologically, here is a picture of the *imago dei*, the 'common root of humanism and theology' (to quote Derrida). Here is discovered a trinodal structure at the heart of discourse (the said), human experience (ipseity) and divinity. It is a structure that operates not just ontologically, but beyond ontology in the non-representational order of responsibility one-for-another. Levinas names this operation of illeity 'God'. 'Illeity overflows both cognition and the enigma through which the Infinite leaves a trace in cognition. Its distance from a theme, its reclusion, its holiness ... is its glory, quite different from being and knowing. It makes the word God be pronounced, without letting "divinity" be said' (*OB*, p. 162/p. 252). The 'word God' is seen as 'the *apex* of vocabulary' (*OB*, p. 156/p. 244).

In an essay entitled '*Démythisation et idéologie*', Levinas asks two highly significant questions: 'is divinity possible without relation to a human Other? Is such a thing possible in Judaism?' (*DVI*, p. 247). He does not directly answer the questions, but he draws a distinction between Judaism and Christianity (in which 'thirdness' plays such a fundamental role). 'The direct encounter with God, *this* is a Christian concept. As Jews we are always threesome: I and you and the Third who is in our midst. And only as a Third does He reveal Himself.' But cannot that 'you' in Levinas's Jewish triad be read Christologically? As Christians we too are 'always threesome: I and you and the Third who is in our midst'. When read theologically, then, how does Levinas's trinodal economy of the Saying in the said differ from Barth's Word made flesh?

CHAPTER 7

Barth's theology of the Word and Levinas's philosophy of Saying

In his essay 'The Linguistic Circle of Geneva', Derrida, comparing the work of Rousseau and Saussure, writes: 'we are concerned ... with discerning the repetition or permanence, at a profound level of discourse, of certain fundamental schemes and certain directive concepts. And then, on this basis, of formulating questions' (*MP*, p. 153). My concern in this chapter is similar to his. What I wish to draw out are parallels in the structures, though certainly not in the details, of Barth's thinking and Levinas's. Then, on the basis of these parallels (Derrida's 'repetition or permanence ... of certain fundamental schemes'), I will ask the question why the structures of their thinking on the Word/Saying are so similar. What I wish to argue is that each thinker is analysing the character and ethical demand of a phenomenology of signification. For both thinkers, I will suggest, the phenomenology of signification (an account of how something becomes manifest and meaningful *for* the human condition) involves a theological account endorsing the ethics of kenosis and exhibiting a trinodal operation. Signification, for both of them, is unavoidably theological. The problem of otherness, which we have seen recurring through the philosophy of language since Hamann, *is* a theological problem.

In wishing to draw out the parallels between Barth's work and Levinas's, I do not wish to collapse their differences. There are important structural differences and it is these differences which draw Barth closer to Derrida. There are other differences: their religious traditions, their idioms, their historical, geographical and linguistic contexts. But some roots are shared: the rejection of totalizing systems, often associated with Hegelian modes of thinking; the influence on Levinas's work of Barth's German contemporaries – Cohen, Rosenzweig, Husserl and Heidegger; the Scriptures as a sphere of unique revelation or testimony. Their similarity lies in a constellation of ideas which cluster around Barth's *Krisis* (later called *Ereignis*) and Levinas 'rupture' or 'diachrony'.[1] Within this constellation three comparable sets of interrelated themes are evident.

First, there is the concern to situate ethics beyond ontology. As we have seen, for Levinas an encounter with what is wholly other is ethical, for it calls into question or acts as a judgement upon the values and philosophies of the self and its world. The ethical claims of this encounter are prior to ontology or anthropology. Furthermore, it is 'in this ethical perspective that God must be thought'.[2] He distinguishes his own positive reading of the crisis this encounter installs from Derrida's: 'he tends to see the destruction of Western metaphysics of presence as an irredeemable crisis, I see it as a golden opportunity for Western philosophy to open itself to the dimension of otherness and transcendence beyond being'.[3] The crisis is understood as a theological judgement and in it is traced the passing of God. It arises from the dialectical tension between totality and infinity. The tension is produced in human existence, and so '[h]istory is worked over by the ruptures of history, in which judgement is borne upon it' (*To.In.*, p. 52/23).

Barth shares this dialectical tension, as we have seen. The

---

[1] Reference must be made here to Steven G. Smith's highly stimulating book, *The Argument to the Other* (Chico, California: Scholars Press, 1983), which, as its sub-title states concerns 'Reason Beyond Reason in the Theological Thought of Karl Barth and Emmanuel Levinas'. Smith's purpose in the book is twofold. First, to outline the historical development of Barth's and Levinas's thinking about the Wholly Other, and secondly, to draw attention to 'their common gesture of arguing to the Other' (p. 242). Insofar as the book focuses upon the method by which Barth and Levinas construct their argument to the Other – the kind of logic that governs their thinking – it differs from this present study. The book does not compare the structures of Barth's and Levinas's thinking with reference to how each understands representation, analogy and the economy whereby representation and analogy become significant *for* us. While drawing attention to their similar ethical positions, Smith's book does not examine the phenomenology of signification which, I argue, is the fundamental concern of both thinkers and the source of their subsequent similarities.

[2] *Dialogues with Contemporary Thinkers* (Manchester: Manchester University Press, 1984), p. 56.   [3] Ibid., p. 64.

asymmetrical relationship between human beings and God means the denial of any *tertium quid*, any ontological relation. 'God is only known through God . . . [and such knowledge] does not have either its basis or origin in any understanding of the human capacity for knowledge' (ii.1, p. 44/47). The encounter with God is also the putting into question of the 'totality of our human will and intelligence' (*2R*, p. 191/170). Nevertheless, as human beings, in order to grasp the otherness this encounter installs we have to have some conception of it and 'the concept of revelation, too, is obviously a general human concept' (ii.1, p. 245/277). So we are inevitably drawn back into 'the immanent truth of a metaphysico-anthropological relation' (ibid.). The crisis is a judgement continually in operation upon this 'immanent truth'. Ethics ('which I regard as the doctrine of the command of God' [i.1, p. xvi/xii]) issues from this judgement, this encounter with righteousness (Levinas will call it the Good) beyond ontology. The 'Word is the ground of our being beyond being' (i.1, p. 444/467). Or, as Barth wrote in *Die christliche Dogmatik im Entwurf*, 'Human existence is put into question by Him as it hears, really hears, God speak; from God, that is, who is Governor of antitheses' (*CDE*, pp. 96–7). The rupture is known existentially and read theologically as God speaking to us: 'in the creaturely form of a historical occurrence (*Ereignis*) or a succession of such occurrences, we are invited and summoned to know Him as the One who acts and rules in these occurrences and relationships' (i.1, p. 201/225). There lies within such a judgement, such a negative moment, a grace which renders everything meaningful and constitutes the significance of all signification. The value of history 'lies in the Krisis within which all history stands' (*2R*, p. 146/123).

Beneath the differences of idiom, the parallels in the structure of their thinking here is evident. For both, the human–God relation is asymmetrical, and the revelation that institutes otherness-in-the-same reveals an otherness beyond being. For both, the effect of what Levinas calls 'diachrony' and Barth first calls 'diakrisis' and later 'the second plane which falls upon [the first] perpendicularly' (i.1, p. 404/424) is a separation and a judgement which are also a summons to recognize the other as other. The call to obey and respond is prior to a metaphysics of being or an anthropology. Yet both thinkers are required to describe some relationship to a metaphysics of being and an anthropology in order for the call to be heard at all, in order for there to be any knowledge of this other *as* other. For Barth, as we know, the *analogia fidei* articulates that relation of the Word in words. For Levinas, it is the 'analogy of apperception' that articulates the relation between the Saying and the said.

This need to articulate the relationship between Word and words or the Saying in the said, is the second structural theme Barth and Levinas share. Both wish to articulate this relationship in a way which radically reorientates logocentrism or models of analogy founded upon logocentric correspondence. For both, the primordial distance between self and other, with the implication that '[c]orrelation does not suffice as a category for transcendence' (*To.In.*, p. 53/54), radically qualifies the adequacy of language to refer, radically qualifies in particular the employment of analogies. Where totality is fissured and there is no *tertium quid*, then grounds have to be sought upon which a valid representation of what is communicated can be made. For both thinkers this entails a close examination and subsequent redefinition of analogy.

Levinas, while insisting there 'is no natural religion', must also insist that the '*idea* of infinity *is revealed* (*se relevé*), in the strongest sense of the term' (*To.In.*, p. 62/33). The infinite cannot become an object of our knowledge, but, following Descartes, Levinas claims that the *idea* of the infinite, while constituting the separation of significance from signs, also constitutes their more meaningful relation. This, as we saw, Levinas terms the Saying in the said which forms 'a veritable conversation (*discours*)' (*To.In.*, p. 70/42), so that, following in the footsteps of Hamann and the dialogical philosophers, he states that 'revelation is discourse (*discours*)' (*To.In.*, p. 77/50). The revelation is based upon the fact that 'language institutes a relation irreducible to the subject–object relation' (*To.In.*, p. 73/45). There is always an excess of significance because of the distance between the finite and the infinite; language issues from this distance, this absence which manifests itself as excess. For this reason language is unstable because it is caught between always being 'to a certain extent rhetoric and negotiation' (*To.In.*, p. 71/73) and yet always pointing to an absence, to what it is unable to say. Hence the paradox of representation: 'expression ... presents the signifier. The signifier, he who gives the sign, is not signified' (*To.In.*, pp. 181–2/157). Representation, then, is always and necessarily open to the dismantling 'trace' of the other which is its very origin and dynamic.

The analogy that is transcendentally established by the Saying in the said, the divine Word within words ('This first saying is to be sure but a word. But the word is God' [*CP*, p. 126]), is 'the apperceiving in discourse of non-allergic relation with alterity' (*To.In.*, p. 47/18). It is, following Husserl, an analogy of apperception.

The analogy of apperception or appresentation is developed by Husserl in his *Cartesian Meditations* (lectures given at the Sorbonne in 1929, published in Germany in 1933, but translated into French by Levinas and Gabrielle Peiffer in 1931). Husserl develops this form of analogy in an attempt to answer the question of how, given his own commitment to a transcendental subjectivity, there can be an experience of and an acknowledgement of someone else. 'A certain mediacy of intentionality must be present here', Husserl writes, otherwise 'he himself and I myself would be the same' (*CM*, p. 109). The question is the nature and status of this mediacy – for that which cannot attain actual presence needs to be both mediated and yet legitimated as an object exterior to that mediation. Husserl concludes that, aware of 'the difficult problem of making it understandable *that such an apperception is possible*' (*CM*, p. 113), 'the body over there ... must have derived this sense by an apperceptive transfer from my animate organism, and done so in a manner that excludes an actually direct and primordial showing of the predicates belonging to an animate organism specifically, a showing of them as perception proper. It is clear from the very beginning that only a similarity connecting, within my primordial sphere, that body over there with my body can serve as a motivational basis for the 'analogizing' apprehension of that body as another animate organism' (*CM*, pp. 110–11). Husserl is quite plain about the limitations of analogizing, for it 'by no means follows that there would be an inference from analogy (ibid.).' Following Hegel,[4] Husserl claims that analogies do not give access to the universal; they remain arbitrary comparisons drawn in the realm of the contingent. But Husserl develops this much further than Hegel, for analogies are 'conceivable only as the analogue of something included in my peculiar ownness'. They occur 'necessarily as an "*intentional modification*" of that Ego of mine ... or as an intentional modification of my primordial "world": the Other as phenomenologically a "modification of myself"' (*CM*, p. 115).

Levinas agreed with this; his own analogy of appresentation is the understanding of a co-presence. But he disagrees with the way Husserl gives priority to the Ego. For Levinas, priority must be given to the Other (the eternal Ego rather than the existential Ego, as Barth emphasizes throughout the second edition of *Romans*). Levinas reverses Husserl: the Ego is now a modification of the infinitely other. Nevertheless, the concept and method of 'analogy of appresentation' remains the same. The Other is recognized as an analogy of apperception by the Ego. For Levinas, the infinity of this other produces a dissymmetry in the relationship which the self is obliged to recognize. Husserl would wish to know how this relationship is understood as dissymmetrical – how one determines that the Other is not only that other body over there, but is the incarnation of an infinity that is absolutely other. Within Husserl's thinking there is no room for an absolutely other that can be recognized as such.

With this we come to a problem at the heart of Levinas's thinking which Derrida has been wrestling with since his first essay on Levinas's work 'Violence and Metaphysics' in 1964. We will investigate this problem, Derrida's response to it and the means by which Barth avoids a similar problem, in the next chapter. For the moment, what is significant for Levinas is that the apperception of the other only becomes perceptible because

---

[4] In *The Phenomenology of Spirit* (tr. A. V. Miller, Oxford: Blackwell, 1977), Hegel, having also spoken about how, from the evidence of one experiment, 'we can then by *analogy* draw an inference about the rest', goes on to compare 'probability' with 'truth' and concludes: 'analogy ... on account of its nature contradicts itself so often that the inference to be drawn from analogy is rather that analogy does not permit an inference to be made' (p. 152).

it is presenced within representation; discourse provides it with a face 'in which he [God] is disincarnate ... [and] is revealed' (*To.In.*, p. 79/51). Otherness is both re-presented in discourse *and* the absence that provokes discourse. Derrida clarifies Levinas's notion of incarnation-as-disincarnation: 'the wholly other ... negotiates the non-negotiable by means of a context, negotiates its economy as the other' (*P*, p. 160). Representation as the context within which Saying occurs draws attention to itself as context alone; that is, it draws attention to the absence of the text, the other for which it inevitably must substitute. There is an endless contextuality provoked by the other's absence. Thus 'the dialogue of transcendence ... is the "dia" of dialogue' (*DVI*, p. 225) and 'I only ever have access by appresentation' (*DVI*, p. 221).

In *Die christliche Dogmatik im Entwurf* Barth, rather than writing 'dia-logue', writes '*diakrisis*': 'in this diakrisis the Word of God is disclosed' (*CDE*, p. 107). Representation here also is both necessary and performs its own deconstruction (Barth employs the Hegelian verb *aufheben*). It is necessary because, as we have seen, the Word of God is not immediately present to us. What is present to us, through mediation, is the absence of immediacy; and so a linguistic system of 'different from' object signs presents the concealment. As we saw, Barth understands this realm of the said as a form of 'secondary objectivity' and emphasizes that this 'secondary objectivity is fully true, for it has its correspondence and basis in His primary objectivity'. Barth's concept of *analogia fidei* articulates the rationale whereby 'different from' objects reveal; the nature of that 'correspondence' whereby the 'fully true' is available for us.

Although, after *Die christliche Dogmatik im Entwurf*, Barth tones down the language of '*diakrisis*', nevertheless the idea of penetration as the constituting principle (and verification) of revelation remains axiomatic for him.[5] We are told that creaturely reality 'represents (*eintritt*) God in so far as it is determined, made and used by God as his clothing' (II.1, p. 17/17). God is represented here by an 'entrance into' objects, an entrance

[5] George Hunsinger, *How to Read Karl Barth: The Shape of His Theology* (Oxford: OUP, 1991), p. 11.

which makes such objects meaningful. This representation-as-entrance is 'an event (*Ereignis*) outstanding (*hervorgehobenes*) in its relationship to other events (*des sonstigen Geschehens*)' (ii.1, p. 29/31). The 'entrance into' is described as *Ereignis*,[6] a distinct and rupturing event that 'stands outside' other 'happening' (*Geschehen*) within a narrative.

The rupturing of representation by the event of the Word establishes analogies in which signs become signifiers of an appresented signified. The analogies established in and through creaturely reality are analogies of God's total otherness from creaturely reality – analogies only seen and read by faith. But most importantly for Barth, and unlike Levinas, the revelation and the reconciliation are 'enacted in Jesus Christ' (i.1, p. 424/446). He is God's Word and 'God gives Himself to be known in His Word, and therefore to be known mediately' (ii.1, p. 12/11). Only in the scandal of Christ does the 'human worldly and historical and "natural"' become a sign. 'But that it is a sign (*Hinweis*) and a parable is surely in no wise trivial' (*2R*, p. 281/263–4). Barth's *analogia fidei*, then, unlike Levinas's 'analogy of appresentation', must also articulate a Christology. Christ is the condition for language. He and He alone is the incarnation of otherness, which makes *the* difference and constitutes *thereby* the meaningful. His advent 'can find force and expression only in the shipwreck of their [men's] words, conferring suitability upon their words, which are impotent as such' (ii.1, p. 221/249). The miracle of His advent institutes the *analogia fidei*, whereby the Word is communicated to human being in words.

There are parallels between these two forms of analogy, but also differences . Both writers are attempting to describe the

---

[6] Interestingly, this 'entrance into', which Barth earlier terms 'the absolute Moment', is called, in *Church Dogmatics* by the very Heideggerian term '*Ereignis*'. A recent volume of Heidegger's work, *Beiträge zur Philosophie: Vom Ereigins* (Tübingen: Niemeyer, 1989) now charts the development of this concept from the early 1930s to his 1962 lecture 'On Time and Being'. There are many points of similarity between Heidegger's later use of this word and Barth's, but the hidden conversation is not between Heidegger and Barth, it is between Barth and his older brother Heinrich, the Professor of philosophy at Basle. The move from the negativity of *Krisis* and *Diakrisis* in the second edition of *Romans* and *Die christliche Dogmatik in Entwurf* to the more positive *Ereignis*, reflects Barth's development of the doctrine of analogy, which was able to constitute a mediation for the ontological difference between human beings and the Creator.

economy of a communication between what Barth calls the
creaturely reality and a transcending other. For both, the event
of this other constitutes the reality of, while not being domesti-
cated by, the immanent. The transcendent remains other which
means that it remains concealed. For both, it is the espousal of a
form of analogy that provides them with ground for a metaphysical (on Levinas's part) or theological (on Barth's part) realism.
Analogy enables them to articulate the coherence of a possibility
that is impossible, a communication in encounter that cannot be
thematized. In fact, this ground – Levinas's philosophy of
Saying and Barth's theology of the Word – becomes the *Grundriss*
(with all the connotations of that word) upon which the rest of
their work is constructed. Both forms of analogy – the analogy of
appresentation and the *analogia fidei* – describe a rupturing or
wrecking of representation that enables the expression of the
transcendent; the transcendent itself cannot be represented. For
both thinkers, this disruption of the immanent values of what is
'creaturely reality' for Barth and 'totality' for Levinas is read
theologically as a revelation of God. Levinas, in words that
might have come from Barth's second edition of *Romans*, speaks
of the 'eschatological notion of judgement' which 'institutes a
relation with being *beyond the totality* or beyond history' (*To.In.*,
p. 22/xi). The theological expression is not merely a rhetorical
flourish. Levinas regards his analogy of appresentation as theologically significant. It is this move from phenomenology to
theology that Derrida comments upon in his essay 'Violence and
Metaphysics'. Having concluded that Levinas's analysis proceeds 'in the form of a negative theology', Derrida continues, the
'"Other resembles God"' ... Via the passageway of this resemblance, man's speech can be lifted towards God, an almost
unheard of *analogy* which is the very movement of Levinas's
discourse on discourse. Analogy as dialogue with God ...
Discourse with God and not in God as *participation*. Discourse
with God, and not discourse on God and his attributes as
theology ... Presence as separation, presence-absence as resemblance, but a resemblance which is not the "ontological mark" of
the worker imprinted on his product ... a resemblance which
can neither be understood in terms of communion or knowledge,

nor in terms of participation or incarnation. A resemblance which is neither a sign nor an effect of God ... We are "in the Trace of God"' (*WD*, p. 108/160). Levinas moves through phenomenology and towards the metadiscourse of theology. This move, as Derrida suggests, is an act of faith: 'independent of its "theological context" does not this entire discourse collapse?' (*WD*, p. 103/152). The analogy of appresentation as Levinas conceives it, then, is a form of *analogia fidei*.[7]

The structures of their thinking are closely aligned, but the details which give meaning to the structures of their thinking are not. Levinas does not espouse the particularism of Barth's Christology, and we will examine this later. For the moment we need to map out the third of the structural parallels in their work.

For both Barth and Levinas, the rupture of revelation fissures the Kantian unity of apperception. Revelation, for both, questions the meaning of all human acts, perception and discourse. Revelation, for both, requires a new grammar of the subject–object relation, a grammar which necessarily works within while deconstructing the ordinary grammar of human discourse. This new grammar is a theology – for it maps out how the term 'God' is given to us and how, consequently, it is meaningfully employed.

For Barth, the 'Word of God ... is a speaking about God [*Reden Gottes*], an act whose subject is God and God alone' (*CDE*, p. 128). God Himself is 'the Subject who absolutely, originally and finally moves, produces, establishes and realizes' (II.1, p. 3/ 1). Yet, in 'His revelation He is considered and conceived', so that 'He enters into the relationship of object to man the subject' (II.1, p. 9/8). Within Barth's all too human syntax 'God' is both subject and object, twisting between active and passive tenses and nominative, accusative, genitive and dative cases. Human beings are accusative within their own testimony to God, or as Levinas can put it in French, '*Me voici*'. In section 4 of his

[7] The question of whether Levinas would accept that one needs to be already working with theological assumptions in order to grasp the validity of his form of analogy, is a different question altogether. *That* question would have to treat more fully the differences between Levinas's and Derrida's thinking and how each has replied to the other's work and since the early sixties. See chapter 8.

Göttingen Dogmatics, sketching a theological anthropology, Barth writes that the concern of such an anthropology is 'the man who is addressed, and is to be addressed' (*GD*, p. 72). It is this theological determination of a human being that gives rise to the 'dialectic of life', for the ' "himself" must be asserted' (*GD*, p. 77) while in revelation the human being is addressed. As accusative, a human being's identity, or selfhood, is a gift from God (subject to object). Thus the ' "himself" [which] must be asserted' is accused, for it stands under the judgement of God (which also His grace).

As we have seen, this map of God and self is the groundplan of Levinas's own redefinition of subjectivity – the self as *subjectum* to the other. This is Levinas's notion of *ipseity*.

On the basis of revelation, both thinkers share a similar conception of selfhood: a selfhood interpreted ethically in relation to the encounter with otherness, a selfhood which is understood existentially as caught between authenticity and inauthenticity, between two truths – 'creaturely reality' and the wholly other. Where the difference unfolds is in how each thinker is understanding the incarnation of otherness, and this we must examine closely. Put briefly, Levinas conceives otherness in terms of Others, or more accurately the 'face' of an Other person. It is in the light of this alterity, evidenced within *socialité*, that ethics and the identity of self are constituted. Barth, on the other hand, from his earliest work conceived otherness in terms of the uniqueness of Jesus Christ. Both Saying and Word is the voice of the other, but only with Barth is Jesus' 'voice the voice of the other' (*GD*, p. 111). Only in the 'face' of Jesus Christ do 'I recognize myself to be confronted paradoxically by the vast pre-eminence of a wholly different man – which I am not' (*2R*, p. 272/255). As with Levinas, the self is composed of the 'EGO which *practises* what I – the other EGO – contemplate with horror' (*2R*, p. 262/244). But it is Jesus Christ who 'is – what I am not – my existential I – I – the I which God, in the freedom of God – I am' (*2R* p. 269/252). Later, when Barth has expunged much of the existentialist idiom, the same anthropology is evident, for in relation to Christ 'man ... is always, and for the first time properly, the one he is' (1.1, p. 449/471). Despite the Christological difference, both thinkers describe living for the Other (the surrender of the ego I am for the ego of the Other) as a state of being 'inspired', as living in the spirit of God. Levinas writes that 'I exist through the other and for the other, but without this being alienation: I am inspired' (*OB*, p. 114/146); Barth writes that 'God's freedom to be present in this way to man, and therefore to bring about this encounter, is the Spirit of God, the Holy Spirit in God's revelation' (I.1, p. 451/473).

This inspiration, for both thinkers, enables a submission of the I to an overriding Lordship; it calls forth, for both Levinas and Barth, a theology and an ethics of kenosis. In Barth's theological idiom, repentance becomes a testimony to grace. In Levinas's phenomenological idiom, the 'consciousness of obligation is no longer a consciousness, since it tears consciousness up from its centre, submitting it to the Other' (*To.In.*, p. 207/182). The call of transcendence is to an emptying, a giving gratuitously and without worrying about reciprocity, to 'the stranger, the widow, and the orphan, to whom I am obligated' (*To.In.*, p. 215/190). In his later work, Levinas calls this 'the state of being in hostage' (*CP*, p. 124). It is the 'ethical event of "expiation for another",' and 'incessant event of substitution' which constitutes the '"egoness" of the I, its exceptional and strange uniqueness' (ibid.).

For Barth this 'uniqueness' is predicated of Jesus Christ alone. In the event of Jesus Christ there was a 'self-abasement of God in His only Son . . . a self-emptying, in a complete resignation not of the essence but of the form of His Godhead, He took upon Himself our own human form – the form of a servant, in complete likeness to other men' (II.1, p. 397/447). The revelation, then, is a kenotic act on behalf of the Revealer. Adopting the form is both pragmatic – that the Godhead might be recognized – and an expression of God's nature: 'the disposition of God in which He acts towards us as the same triune God that He is in Himself' (II.1, p. 51/55). Kenosis is the fundamental operation of the Trinity, but whilst it institutes the revelation, the giving of God Himself, it is also the content of the revelation – the form of a servant which is the true likeness, the true nature of human beings. Jesus Christ is the revelation of the true human nature. In Jesus Christ God presents 'the original and creative I, from whom the I has received and as it were leases its I-ness' (ii.1, p. 59/63).

Kenosis, for Barth, thus not only institutes the revealing event (*Ereignis*), but is the content of that event and, furthermore, promotes the recognition that that content is the primary ethical and existential disposition of human nature (its very I-ness). The commandment to love my neighbour issues from the revelation of Christ in my neighbour's suffering, and this revelation distinguishes him as my 'neighbour' from my 'fellow-man': 'What Is.53 says of the suffering Servant of God is true at any level of any man so far as it simply speaks of his suffering. In the reflection of the prophecy about Christ there is a reflection of my neighbour, if I have the grace to recognize him in my fellow-man. And in recognizing my neighbour in my fellow-man, I am actually [*faktisch*] placed before Christ' (1.2, p. 429/474).

Jesus, then – the 'otherness of man ... his truth, his unveiled reality: the truth and reality also of his cosmos' (ii.1, p. 110/122) – 'actually encounters us in our neighbour, and ... we decide for or against Him in making this decision in relation to our neighbour' (1.2, p. 429/474). The human being only fully realizes her identity in recognizing Christ in the neighbour and serving Him, by being a hostage (in Levinas's language) to the otherness which constitutes her true self.

Ethically and anthropologically, again, we discover the close parallels between the structure of Barth's thinking and Levinas's. Barth's economy of living on to God is structurally close to Levinas's phenomenological account of substitution, of living-for-the-other. For both, the humanism of egology, of Kantian anthropology, of transcendental reasoning – the humanism which, as we have seen, is closely woven with logocentrism – is ruptured by the new humanity of the Other, so that 'the new invisible title of all humanity is made manifest in the "Now" of revelation [*im 'Jetzt' der Offenbarung unanschaulich anschaulich wird*]' (*2R*, p. 421/407). It is the particularity of Jesus Christ as the revelation of the triune God which distinguishes theologian from philosopher. But we now need to consider carefully, first, this Christological and, as a consequence, secondly this Trinitarian difference – for as we will see, parallels in the structures of their thinking still remain.

THE CHRISTOLOGICAL DIFFERENCE

Levinas often appears to model his description of this primordial disposition towards kenosis, this Saying betrayed in representation, on Isaiah's account of the suffering servant and the gospel acounts of Jesus Christ. He will frequently employ terms like 'incarnation' and 'resurrection'. He will describe ipseity as 'the very fact of finding oneself while losing oneself' (*OB*, p. 11/14). Speaking of persecution, accusation and responsibility for others, he describes the self as 'expelled from his place and has only himself to himself, has nothing in the world on which to rest his head' (*OB*, p. 121/155). This human destiny to suffer and to serve, this phenomenological analysis of *passio*, is viewed in terms of 'the God who suffers both through man's trangression and through the suffering by which this transgression can be expiated' (*LR*, p. 234). Derrida has noted 'the messianic eschatology from which Levinas draws inspiration' (*WD*, p. 83). Levinas is Jewish and profoundly schooled in Talmudic exegesis, the language of expiation and redemption is as traditional for him as for Barth. But for Barth '[i]t is in fact the suffering Servant of the Lord of Isaiah 53 who is rediscovered in Jesus' (1.1, p. 387/407). The Servant becomes an historical event in Jesus Christ.

This is exactly the point where care especially needs to be taken – because, to an extent (and it is the extent that is fundamental), Barth's particularism, the unique revelation in Jesus Christ, is paralleled by a particularism of Levinas's own.

In Levinas, as we saw, Saying is the offspring of *illeity* and *illeity* names God. The *il* is the third party, radically 'breaking up the bi-polar play of immanence and transcendence' (*EDE*, p. 199). It is a 'preoriginary saying' (*OB*, p. 151/153), prior even to Saying. It is the Absolute which 'detaches itself absolutely' (*OB*, p. 147/188) and Saying bears the trace. But a particularism (Levinas often uses the term 'singularity') is inherently characteristic of the transcendence of Saying, for Saying is an event in the face of the other person which 'suggests the eventuality of the

Word of God' (*TO*, p. 114). The pre-existing logos is, then, according to Levinas also an event within our history. It is an event in discourse, but it is one that is provoked by the actuality of the neighbour's proximity. In the diachronic encounter with the neighbour as Other lies the concrete encounter with the scandal of God's Word.

In the period of Barth's engagement with the second edition of *Romans*, the particularity of Jesus Christ closely parallels Levinas's particularity of proximity. Jesus Christ is described as the 'existential I', the not-I which I am. He is encountered in the 'Now', in suffering, deprivation and negation. The '"other" man, the man of the world, the outsider, the Gentile, who, unlike the Churchman ... appears before us in visible poverty, evidently abandoned and without protection ... in him the forensic righteousness of God is revealed in all its glory ... God has determined to reveal His glory and His mercy in this "other" man' (*2R*, p. 418/429). The neighbour's 'otherness' 'reminds us of the WHOLLY OTHER' (*2R*, p. 444/429). In language culled from Barth's early association with Rosenzweig and Buber, this is to 'see in every temporal "thou" the eternal, contrasted "thou" apart from which there is no "I"' (*2R*, p. 495/479). An encounter is evident here paralleling Levinas's own description of the self and the neighbour.

In the development of his theological realism (through the doctrine of the *analogia fidei*), Barth's Christological particularism is considerably sharpened.[8] In *Church Dogmatics* (1.1, p. 458/480–1), though 'the Son of God is the prototype of the sonship of believers', Barth distinguishes between Jesus Christ as *Filius Dei natura* and believers as *filii Dei adoptione* (cf. 1.1, p. 458/480–1). Barth's believers-as-sons stand and remain at some distance from the original and proper sonship (which is distinctively the character of Christ). But significantly, this distinction is the cause of much tension in Barth's Christology, for a causal relation associates God with His Son – 'As the Son of God made

---

[8] Barth's Christological particularism and its relationship to his theological realism has been recently examined in two important books: Bruce Marshall's *Christology in Conflict* (Oxford: Blackwell, 1987) and George Hunsinger's book. The former details the logic of Barth's particularist Christology and the later describes its nature.

his own this one specific [*bestimmte*] possibility of human essence
[*Wesen*] and existence [*Dasein*] and made it a reality, *this* Man
came into being, and He, the Son of God, became *this* Man' (1.1, p.
150/164) – but no such relationship associates the original Son
with adopted sons. There is an ambiguity in this particularism,
then, concerning the economic operation of the Trinity as it
affects the salvation of creaturely reality. In terms of the
grammar of personhood expressed in II.1, p. 59, and quoted
above, how does Jesus as 'the original and creative I' relate to or
correspond with 'the created I [who] has received and as it were
leases its I-ness'? How can the humanity of Jesus Christ be
different from and yet identify with our humanity in order to
effect the redemption and our adoption by the Godhead? The
proposed answers to this question and the details of Barth's
theology of reconciliation we will examine in later chapters and
with reference to Derrida. At this point I merely wish to point
out the ambivalence which emerges from Barth's extreme
particularism.[9] It emerges from the ontological difference
between the 'creative I' and the 'created I' which the repetition
of the pronoun 'I' masks. The two I's are not the same and not
naming the same objects. We recognize once more how Barth's
theology is a theology which takes seriously ontological difference.

The ambiguity is significant because Levinas's particularism
runs into a counter-form of ambivalence. It is an ambivalence
which is the polar opposite of Barth's – as a comparison with
Barth's particularism highlights. In the section on 'The Ego as a
Singularity', in his essay 'The Ego and Totality', Levinas insists:
'The other purely as interlocutor is not a content known and
qualified, apprehendable on the basis of some general idea
which governs it'. The ego is an 'irreplaceable singularity' (*CP*,
p. 36). But Levinas's concept of ipseity-as-sonship effectively
means that each person is the Messiah, each stands in an original
and proper messiahship which demands that one substitute

---

[9] Bruce Marshall, in outlining the consistency of Barth's Christology – Barth's answer
to the question how is Jesus Christ, the particular person, *heilsbedeutsam* – does not
touch upon this. It is outside his very specific task which is to clarify the grounds upon
which Jesus Christ can be consistently named as unique and 'alone the definitive
bearer of that which is ultimately significant' (p. 12).

oneself for the Other. For the other is always an Other person. The other is not, as it is with Barth, always and only Jesus Christ. The neighbour, for Barth, is she or he who, by grace, has put on Christ – the form of which 'will always be the form [*die Gestalt*] of the death of Christ' (1.1, p. 458/481). Levinas's self recognizes in the hungry and the destitute its own sonship, its own ipseity, its own state of being a hostage to God and responsible for Others. And Levinas describes this condition in terms of recognizing the Suffering Servant. Barth describes this condition in terms of recognizing the death of Christ. But whereas for Levinas each is called to be the Suffering Servant pouring out her life for others, for Barth the believer only enters into 'the form of the death of Christ'. No human being approximates to the uniqueness of Christ, they only approximate to the 'form' of such uniqueness. Another way of putting this would be to say that sonship is a mode of being, an existential condition for Levinas. The sonship of believers for Barth still participates in the ontological difference – it is living in the form of a mode of being, living as a figure of a person whose own living is original and proper.[10]

There is, therefore, a secondariness, a level of mediation in Barth that is absent from Levinas. As we have seen, this level of secondariness presents the spectre of a disparity that renders the redemption of creaturely reality problematic. But Levinas's lack of such a secondariness, his notion of the Suffering Servant as the proper mode of one's being, presents the spectre of a parity, as Derrida's major criticism of his work makes clear. For in wishing to insist upon a '[d]iscourse with God in the face to face' (*WD*, p. 116/170), Levinas, as Derrida tells us, 'is resigned to betraying his own intentions in his philosophical discourse' (*WD*, p. 151/225), because he must return to the metaphysics of presence and the *analogia entis*.

The Christological difference, therefore, is a parting of the

---

10 This similarity-in-difference reflects, to some extent, their 'different' starting-points for the analysis or exegesis of revelation. Barth's theological starting-point is the *a priori* of faith in God and Levinas's philosophical starting point is the structure of intentionality. But, again, we cannot make too much of this 'difference' insofar as Barth is aware that the tools he employs are metaphysico-anthropological ones and that outside the *a priori* of faith all his thinking might constitute a lesson in human psychology (cf. II.1, pp. 244–5/276–7).

ways between Barth's thinking and Levinas's. But their common emphasis upon forms of particularity mean that there is a certain symmetry in the parting of those ways. Their parting moves in diametrically opposite directions – towards eqivocation that demands faith on Barth's part, and towards assimilation on Levinas's.[11]

THE TRINITARIAN DIFFERENCE

The particularism of Barth's Christology is inseparable from the economic operation of the Trinity. His theology issues from an interpretation of the concrete 'event of revelation' in Jesus Christ (1.1, p. 299/315). As we have seen, Levinas too emphasizes the particularity of Saying and his philosophy issues from a phenomenological analysis of the revelation of this Saying. For both, their work emerges from a reflection upon the phenomenon of a determining revelation. Though, therefore, Levinas maintains no belief in, nor need for, the Trinity, it is significant that the structure of his analysis is also trinodal and that Levinas is aware of it: 'Desire . . . is a plot with three personages' (*CP*, p. 72). We now need to examine this structure carefully to assess the nature of its similarity to Barth's.[12]

Levinas's work is situated between a 'philosophy of transcendence . . . and a philosophy of immanence' in which is described 'the unfolding of terrestial existence, of economic existence' (*To.In.*, p. 52/53). His work describes an economy of separation, or difference, for 'to be economically' is to 'separate oneself, not to remain bound up with totality' (*To.In.*, p. 175/pp. 149–50). In the separation there is an apperception of exteriority, of

---

[11] The theology of Jean-Luc Marion develops Levinas's thinking in terms of Christianity. Although he too wishes to emphasize a radical difference between God and Being, he develops a theology of transubstantiation and the icon which leads him dangerously close to neo-Platonism and the *analogia entis*. See *L'Idol et la distance* (Paris: Grasset, 1977), *Dieu sans l'être* (Paris: Fayard, 1982; English translation *God Without Being*, Chicago, University Press, 1991) and *La Croisée du visible* (Paris: La Différence, 1991).

[12] Raimundo Pannikar might recognize here 'The Trinity . . . as a junction where the authentic spiritual dimensions of all religions meet', *The Trinity and the Religous Experience of Man* (New York: Orbis, 1973) p. 48. But in this essay I am simply drawing attention to similarities in the structure of Barth's and Levinas's thinking.

finitude located in infinity, and it is in this way that transcendence becomes the condition for immanence.

The dynamic of this economy is Desire: 'to apperceive infinity as the Desire for infinity' (*To.In.*, p. 292/268). The Desire for the other *constitutes* the relationship which proceeds by way of an 'inspiration, beyond the logic of the same and the other'. This inspiring Desire is 'the very pneuma of the psyche' (*OB*, p. 141/p. 221) that gives birth to the recognition of being-for-the-other. We have seen this earlier in Levinas's grammar of the divided self, but in the later parts of *Totality and Infinity* he develops this in terms of the family as 'a metaphysically ineluctable structure' (*To.In.*, p. 306/283) and 'resurrection constitut[ing] the principle event of time' (*To.In.*, p. 284/260) – and here lies the heart of what Levinas understands by 'economic existence'.

The economy of separation, the 'relation of rupture and a recourse', is manifest in the 'converse of paternity' which is 'filitity' (*To.In.*, p. 278/255). The unicity of the I, the son, is owed to the father. This is the paradox of created freedom – the repudiation of the father in order to be the elected son. This is 'the permanent revolution that constitutes ipseity' (ibid.). We are all, then, elected to be sons, predestined to sonship.[13] Ipseity is the nature of our election, our election by that which is wholly other. In theological terms, what Levinas is describing is the nature of the *imago dei*. In paternity, then, the I prolongs itself in the other and enters a time not governed by ageing or fate. Levinas juxtaposes the 'discontinuity of Cartesian time' (*To.In.*, p. 58/29) – time as the struggle of the ego to get beyond itself, to be redeemed from its totalizing by grasping the instant; time, therefore, as the experience of postponement, of the 'not yet' (*To.In.*, p. 247/225). This is 'to go back to paternity', where the I is other while also being itself, where the I recognizes its sonship or ipseity. This is the 'time of fecundity ... an existence as entirely pardoned' (*To.In.*, p. 282/259). Levinas describes this as the resurrection of the instant which had died and the very

---

[13] Because of the ontology of sonship and the paternity of *il*leity, Luce Irigaray has criticized the sexism of Levinas's thinking. Cf. her article 'Questions to Emmanuel Levinas: On the Divinity of Love', *The Irigaray Reader* (Oxford: Blackwell, 1991), pp. 178–89.

process of continuation – 'death and resurrection constitute time' (*To.In.*, p. 284/261). Resurrection is the institution of sonship, while the nature of sonship is to recognize its *sub-jectum*, its incommensurate kenosis. This resurrection is the fulfilment of time 'where the perpetual is converted into the eternal' (*To.In.*, p. 285/261). Levinas is aware that his thinking here is eschatological (see his Preface to *Totality and Infinity*).

In *Otherwise than Being* Levinas develops a notion of the feminine found in *Totality and Infinity* in terms of 'maternity'. Maternity signifies that process of Desire which enables the 'gestation of the other in the same' (*OB*, p. 75/95). Levinas writes, 'Incarnation is not a transcendental operation of a subject that is situated in the midst of the world it represents to itself; the sensible experience of the body is already and from the start incarnate. The sensible – maternity, vulnerability, apprehension – binds the node of incarnation into a plot larger than the apperception of the self' (*OB*, p. 76/96). This maternity completes the metaphysics of the family – it is 'the very signifyingness of signification' (*OB*, p. 108/137).

Levinas's trinodal structure, then, functions as three modes of being in the economy of time and Desire – the paternal, the filial and the maternal which gestates the other in the same in a way that relates whilst separating. These three modes are arrived at through a phenomenological analysis of revelation where the paternal is betrayed in the filial and revelation is primary.

In the first volume of *Church Dogmatics*, Barth tackles the question of *vestigia trinitatis* – threefold patterns in nature which have been read as a revelation of the threefold Godhead. His concern is to dismiss 'an essential trinitarian disposition supposedly immanent in some created realities quite apart from their possible conscription by God's revelation' (1.1, p. 334/353). In Barthian terms, then, Levinas's 'family' is not a *vestigium trinitatis*, but the structure of the hegemonic revelation that only revelation itself reveals. The perichoresis of the three elements – the disclosure of the paternal and unpresentable *illeity* in the *ipseity* of the son through maternal Desire – follows the same logic of revelation as Barth's 'three elements of unveiling, veiling and impartation [*die Mitteilung*]' (1.1, p. 332/350).

For Barth, as chapter 2 of *Church Dogmatics* illustrates, a doctrine of revelation is inseparable from the doctrine of the triune God, God's three modes of existence. His dogmatics issue from an interpretation of this 'event [*Ereignis*] of revelation' (1.1, p. 299/315). The verticality of the soteriological 'event' is related to the 'Now' or the 'Moment' in the second edition of *Romans*. In this earlier work, Barth distinguishes between 'unqualified time' – time spent in ignorance and sin – and qualified time – the eschatological 'Now' in which eternity dissolves all past and future (*2R*, p. 500/484). And though *Krisis*, which is the content of the 'Now', is expunged in *Church Dogmatics* and the 'event' is read more positively, still the 'so-called "inner logic"' of the *Church Dogmatics* is the axis of eternity and time unfolded through the motif of the "analogy of faith".[14] The concern with time in Barth's earlier work, as in his mature dogmatics, is with a distinction between time as a string of successive moments bearing unborn potential and the eternal 'Now' of revelation which can actualize the potential of such moments. Revelation occurs as 'completed event [*das abgeschlossene Geschehen*], fulfilled time, in a sea of the incomplete and changeable and self-changing' (1.1, p. 116/119). This 'Now' is the revelation of the Word, of Jesus Christ, in the world. The dialectic of time and eternity is bridged by the paradox of the incarnation, which is a God-event, and the economy of which is trinodal. The incarnation, then, reveals time as the creation of the triune God. 'God's love requires and possesses eternity both inwards and outwards for the sake of its divinity, its freedom. Correspondingly it requires, creates and therefore possesses in its outward relations what we call time' (II.1, p. 464–5/523). 'Our time' – or 'the time of our sin' – is only understandable on the basis of 'His time for us, revelation time'. Through the 'perpetually fresh giving [*das immer neue Gewähren*] of revelation' [my translation], our time becomes a sacramental reality (II.1, p. 62/67). '[O]ur time is conditioned [*motivieren zu lassen*] by the Spirit' (*2R*, p. 457/441).

The logic of this time and eternity relationship has been seen

---

[14] 'The Doctrine of Time in Karl Barth' by Richard Roberts in *A Theology on the Way: Essays on Karl Barth* (T. & T. Clark: Edinburgh, 1991), p. 1.

to be troubled, and a disparity is evident founded upon the disparity we have already seen concerning Barth's concept of analogy.[15] But the parallels between this mode of thinking and Levinas's remain. For both, there is the establishing of a transcendent, or authentic time within an immanent or inauthentic time. A third form of time emerges which Levinas terms the time of fulfilment or resurrection. Barth too will draw attention to the forty days of Resurrection as a time of 'the concrete demonstration of the gracious God' (III.2, p. 450/540) and speak of 'fulfilled time'. For both, history is a predicate of revelation, time of eternity, so that, outside the operation of God or *illeity* there is no real understanding of time, only the empty appearance of time. Levinas would concur with Barth's statement that the advent of the Word 'does not remain transcendent over time, it does not merely meet it at a point, but it enters time; nay it assumes time; nay, it creates time for itself' (1.2, p. 50/55). For both, revelation is explicable in time only in terms of a trinodal operation.

The dynamic of this operation for Barth is God's love in the work of the 'Spirit [which] guarantees man ... his personal participation in revelation' (1.1, p. 453/475), just as between the Father and the Son it 'is the active mutual orientation and interpenetration of love' (1.1, p. 487/511). In the second edition of *Romans* Barth describes this love in terms of Agape and the ethics of Agape are 'to seek and serve the One in the others ... to be related to the Primal origin ... AGAPE is the KRISIS in which the others stand' (*2R*, p. 454/438). Agape is the dynamic of Trinitarian perichoresis and our inclusion within it. It is also the kenotic spirit of Christ, whose disciples Christians are and whose life Christians imitate. The mutual orientation towards the other is rooted then in the Trinity and revealed in the 'event' of Jesus Christ and the proclamation of His Word in the Church. Furthermore, '[t]he work of the Spirit in revelation is presented as a work of creating and begetting' (1.1, p. 485/509) and so 'begetting is originally and properly a divine not a creaturely mystery' (1.1, p. 432–3/455). For Levinas, as we saw, the dynamic of the trinodal operation is Desire and the family as a

---

[15] This is Richard Robert's argument in the essay above.

'metaphysically ineluctable structure'. For him, '[f]ecundity is to be set up as an ontological category ... The fecundity of the I [its sonship, its ipseity] is its very transcendence' (*To.In.*, p. 277/ 254).

For both Levinas and Barth, then, an analysis (what Barth calls 'exegesis') of the event of revelation leads to similar structures in their thinking of the relationship between time and eternity and the threefold economy which accounts for that relationship. Levinas, I repeat, is not accepting the Christian Trinity, but he is, like Barth, 'read[ing] off from revelation ... statements about the being of God' (1.1, p. 480/503), or what he terms *illeity*. And the structure of those statements possesses a trinodal logic.

As I said at the beginning of this chapter, I do not wish to collapse the differences between Barth's theology of the Word and Levinas's philosophy of Saying. There are differences, as we have seen, and they emerge from the particularism of the content of revelation as each understands it. On the other hand, neither, in the parallels we have been tracing, are we simply observing a translation from one idiom to another (although, 'Goodness' in Levinas closely corresponds to 'righteousness' in Barth, 'apology' in Levinas to 'repentence' in Barth, 'fecundity' in Levinas to 'resurrection life' in Barth). The fact that so many terms remain the same for each – sin as atheism and egology, 'revelation', 'God', 'prophet', 'Messiah', 'eternal', 'creation', 'born again' – testifies to their common idiom: the Scriptures. The similarity in the structures of their thinking returns us to Derrida's search for 'discerning the repetition or permanence, at a profound level of discourse, of certain fundamental schemes and certain directive concepts. And then, on this basis, of formulating questions' (*PM*, p. 153). Both thinkers, starting from an investigation into revelation which is a self-manifestation of the eternal and wholly other apperceived or seen by faith, are led to discuss the same problematics and arrive at similar models of language, self, ethics, time and participation in a triadic economy. It is important for the argument of this book that we ask not only *how* the thinking of Barth and Levinas relates to each other, but *why*. The *why* is the subject of this book.

To answer that question we must return to the point from which they both begin. What is being investigated by each is a phenomenon – not the otherness of God, but a revelation, an unveiling of a Logos which remains veiled and hidden within logocentrism. Both analyse how that revelation can be, already has been, significant for human beings; how human beings have been addressed by it. It becomes significant because as it is revealed it reveals; in its manifestation it becomes significant *for* us. It announces something about our human condition (its sinfulness, its guilt, its inauthenticity). It becomes, then, existentially meaningful in the dia-logue it installs and the dialogue it commands. What we are tracing in both Barth and Levinas, therefore, is the grammar of signification itself – the syntax of revealer, revealed, revelation. Their theology, on the one hand, philosophy on the other, are readings of this syntax. They are readings of how something appears as meaningful given the constraints of a Kantian anthropology where 'transcendence means not appropriation of *what is*, but its respect' (*To.In.*, p. 302/279). They are readings of the consequences of that 'meaningfulness' in terms of the categories that govern Christian theology, on the one hand, and metaphysics on the other (soteriological and ethical categories). The logic of this signification is the logic of the possibility for their own discourses – how their own discourses are meaningful because they represent the passing of the meaningful. Both thinkers establish that discourse is only possible when understood in terms of its difference-in-relation to a metadiscourse. For both, divine *fiat* institutes a signifying phenomenon and the phenomenology of signification that is thereby constituted is excavated in order to give some account of this theological economy. There is in the logic of signification, both suggest, a moment which is ineluctably theological. The parallels between Barth's theology of the Word and Levinas's philosophy of Saying issue from this fundament: both present an an-archeology of logocentrism; both argue for an ethics or righteousness beyond and yet constitutive of meaning.

Part III
Différance

Part III

Differentiation

At the end of part I I drew attention to a link between Barth's Word and Levinas's depiction of '*le logos de l'infini*'. At the end of part II, having traced the historical associations between the context of the philosophy of language within which Barth worked and the work of Levinas, I specifically analysed the relationship between Barth's theology of the Word and Levinas's philosophy of Saying. In drawing out the parallels in their thinking I drew attention to their points of divergence, and it is these divergences which I now wish to explore through Derrida's understanding of 'negotiation'.

The word is taken from Derrida's own 'negotiation' with Levinas's work in his essay 'At this very moment in this work here I am [*me voici*]' (1980). There, commenting on an axiomatic phrase in Levinas's work ('*me voici*'), Derrida writes: 'The phrase describes or says what within the said interrupts it and at a stroke makes it anachronistic with respect to the saying, negotiated between the said and the saying and at the same time interrupting the negotiation while forthwith negotiating the interruption itself. Such interruption deals with a language ... which tend[s] to interdict what here *must be said* [*il faut dire*], namely, the astriction to giving and the extradiction of subjectivity to the other. Negotiation thematizes what forbids thematization, while during the very trajectory of that transaction it forces language into a contract with a stranger, with what it can only incorporate without assimilating' (*DR*, pp. 415–16/ *P*, p. 169).

Derrida here recomposes major themes in Levinas's work in terms of metaphors from trading ('deals', 'extradition', 'transaction' and 'contract'). Levinas's concerns then are not explicated but translated into alternative models for their description. The French '*négocier*' still retains stronger mercantile associations than the English 'to negotiate'. The word for Derrida not only acts as a description of the relation-in-difference between the Saying and the said in Levinasian thinking. It describes also the tactic for handling Levinas that Derrida employs. The word 'negotiation', with the metaphorical constellations which it generates, is integral to the form of the *rapprochement* being established. It is integral too to the form of response that Levinas's work solicits. Derrida is not attempting to describe the operation of the Saying within the said. Rather, he raises to the surface an implication about the dislocation-in-correlation of the Saying within the said, an implication about how Levinas has to be read, about how Levinas's texts actually perform in relation to his readers. Similarly, Derrida's own response – the essay was written as a gift for a collection of essays in honour of Levinas – is also performative. What is being suggested is that all reading is negotiation – reading is a process of negotiating between several textualities, negotiating with an otherness inscribed within the operation of this reading.

Negotiation differs from the idealism of both Rosenzweig's and Buber's dialogue, where meaning is fully present and easily exchanged. It also modifies Levinas's conception of dia-logue by placing the emphasis neither upon the Saying nor the said, but the textual interface. In the interface, Derrida traces the alterity which is always at play. It is an alterity evidenced in the way language exceeds and escapes the reasoned argument. The alterity undermines the reasoning of the argument and, therefore, limits the argument's claim to universal acceptance. The interface begins when one text (Levinas's) is recontextualized by another (Derrida's comments). The process bears some similarities with Heidegger's understanding of discussion [*Erörterung*]. What is an important difference between dia-logue and negotiation is that where the former assumes the hierarchy of Saying above said no hierarchy is assumed in the latter. Negotiation is more pragmatic and does not imply the *telos* of a truth to be understood. Negotiation suggests suspicion of intentionality (one's own and the other's); it suggests that each participant in any encounter comes heavily laden with presuppositions and previous contexts; it suggests that the movement in the transfer being performed is slippery and not necessarily progressive. Negotiation is the economy of textuality itself.

Derrida rehearses his concern with the impossibility of dialogue in his exchanges with John Searle (in *LI*) and Hans-Georg Gadamer (in *Dialogue and Deconstruction*, eds. Diane P. Michelfelder and Richard E. Palmer, Albany: State University of New York, 1989). Negotiation enables us to understand Derrida's own work as a supplement to Levinas's. Barth's divergences from Levinas will then be examined in the light of Derrida's negotiation. I will then be in a position to justify my claim that Derrida's economy of *différance* clarifies what is occurring within Barth's discussion of the Word in words. *Différance* renders coherent and necessary the sliding and evasions, the half-suggestions and contradictions evident in Barth's account of the Word in words, developed in chapter 5 of *Church Dogmatics*.

Furthermore, the recontextualizing of Barth's work within Derrida's also allows us to reframe Derrida's philosophical thinking in terms of Barth's theology. The negotiation is thus two-way. In particular, Barth's theology of the Word is a Christology. In negotiation with Derrida's work this Christology will be re-read, and in this way we move through the tradition, and its recontextualization, towards a postmodern Christology. Only such a movement – negotiating the past, the heritage, in a present appropriation – can be legitimate; for every movement is always and only a movement such as this. This is the economy of *différance*. In outlining this economy in Barth we also move towards a deeper appreciation (for this is the nature of negotiation) of the 'theological' horizons within which Derrida's work is situated; we will recognize the theological face of any radical questioning of metaphysics.

CHAPTER 8

Derrida as Levinas's supplement

To situate Derrida's work in relation to Levinas's is a complex
task. Derrida himself has made that plain. 'Faced with a
thinking like that of Levinas, I never have an objection. I am
ready to subscribe to everything he says. That does not mean
that I think the same thing in the same way, but in this respect
the differences are difficult to determine . . . I have tried to pose a
certain number of questions to Levinas whilst reading him,
where it may have been a question of his relation to the Greek
logos, of his strategy, or of his thinking with respect to femininity
for example, but what happens there is not of the order of
disagreement or distance' (*Alt.* p. 74).[1] Recently, there has been
a flurry of attempts to clarify the relationship.[2] Each of these
attempts examines, in varying degrees of detail, seminal texts for
the *rapprochement*: Derrida's essays 'Violence and Metaphysics'
(1964) and 'At this very moment in this work here I am' (1980);

[1] Where texts by Derrida have yet to be translated, or where the translations are not
widely available, the translations are my own, although I have consulted translations
that have been made. This is particularly so with regard to: '*D'un ton apocalyptique
adopté naguère en philosophie*' (translated by John P. Leavey, Jr for *The Oxford Literary
Review*, vol. 6, no. 2 (1984), pp. 3–37; and '*Comment ne pas parler: Denegations*'
(translated by Ken Frieden in *Languages of the Unsayable: The Play of Negativity in
Literature and Literary Theory*, ed. Sanford Budick and Wolfgang Iser (New York:
Columbia University Press, 1989, pp. 3–70).

[2] For discussions of the exchange between Levinas and Derrida see the following: 'The
Trace of Levinas in Derrida', Robert Bernasconi in *Derrida and Différance*, ed. David
Wood and Robert Bernasconi (Evanston: Northwestern University Press, 1988);
'Levinas, Derrida and others' *vis-à-vis*, John Llewelyn in *The Provocation of Levinas*;
'Derrida, Levinas and Violence', Edith Wyschogrod in *Derrida and Deconstruction*, ed.
Hugh J. Silverman (London: Routledge, 1989); '"Bois" – Derrida's final word on
Levinas', Simon Critchley in *Re-reading Levinas* (London: Athlone, 1991 and appear-
ing in his book *The Ethics of Deconstruction: Derrida and Levinas* (Oxford: Blackwell,
1992).

Levinas's note in *Noms Propres* '*Tout Autrement*' and the espousal of certain Derridean terms in *Otherwise than Being*. They are often attempts to uncover a change in Derrida's treatment of Levinas, a treatment accompanied by Levinas's own response to Derrida's work. This chapter must, in part, draw upon these investigations, but the question that will remain foregrounded is a question these critics and scholars have not asked. It is the question of analogy; the possibility of a coherent account of a discourse con-cerned (con-taminated, as Levinas and Derrida might say) with transcending otherness.

<h3 style="text-align:center">'VIOLENCE AND METAPHYSICS'</h3>

For Derrida, as will become increasingly apparent, there can only be quasi-transcendence because there is never any pure reception. This is the point of his remark in 'Violence and Metaphysics' that Levinas is an empiricist.

At the time Derrida's essay appeared (1964) Levinas published, in the same journal, his essay '*La Signification et le sens*' in which he commented extensively upon empiricism and pure reception. There, while developing the concept of the 'trace', Levinas insists that 'there is no given already possessing identity; no given could enter thought simply through the shock against the wall of receptivity' (*CP*, p. 77). But the fact that Derrida allows his statements about Levinas's empiricism to remain unrevised when the essay was re-written for publication in *L'Écriture et la différence* (1967), perhaps reveals again that Derrida is not arguing in 'Violence and Metaphysics' against Levinas's position but within it. He is reading Levinas's statements about non-appearing and absence through the metaphors of light and sound which weave through Levinas's texts and stand in contradiction to its theme. He is not saying that Levinas is wrong, in other words, but he is deconstructing Levinas by raising this contradiction to the surface and supplementing other metaphors, metaphors of writing, which enable Levinas's thesis to be modified and re-read. In the same essay by Levinas, for example, he can still say, 'Whence came this shock when I passed, indifferent, under another's gaze' (*CP*, p. 94). What Derrida is pointing to is not the contradiction which arises when this statement is placed alongside the earlier one, but that this contradiction is an inevitable consequence of a double movement within Levinas's discourse in which the metaphors *do* privilege sensation.

Levinas, as Derrida reads him, implies that there is in his thinking a necessary moment of pure transfer and pure reception which by-passes intentionality and hermeneutics. He privileges an access to a metalanguage of silence, and Derrida, in that early essay, is concerned with uncovering this hidden metaphysics of presence, this dependency upon a language of immediacy and epiphany. He explores both how Levinas articulates revelation within representation and how Levinas is able to think non-violent mediation. Levinas's realized eschatology takes place in 'a space or hollow within naked experience' (*WD*, p. 83/124) and Derrida asks '[h]ow ... will the metaphysics of the face as the *epiphany* of the other free itself of light?' (*WD*, p. 92/137). That is, how will it free itself from a phenomenology, from appearing?

There are two movements of thought negotiating in this essay and they relate to the two-fold nature of deconstruction as both critique and supplement. First, Derrida is drawing attention to what he interprets as an implicit Platonism in Levinas which he relates to the privileging of the moment and the experience of this moment. This is Levinas's emphasis upon the '*present* at the heart of experience. Present not as a total presence but as a *trace*' (*WD*, p. 95/142). This privileging leads 'Levinas [to] describe *history* as a blinding to the other, and the laborious procession of the same' (*WD*, p. 94/p. 139). The experience of the other becomes, then, an experience of the transhistorical. But Derrida points out that such an experience is only possible because Levinas becomes blind to his own metaphors (particularly those to do with hearing), for the face expresses itself without representation only because 'living speech, in its mastery and magisteriality, is able to assist itself; and only living speech is expression and not servile sign' (*WD*, p. 101/p. 150). We are returned to the dominant theme of *Redephilosophie*, which as we saw has influenced Levinas's thinking. Derrida's critique is a critique of this residual dialogicalism in Levinas. 'The face is presence, *ousia*' (ibid.) for Levinas, even though he does not wish it to be, even though what he is attempting to describe is a non-appearing and a dia-logue.

The point being made here by Derrida, and this is fundamental to the nature of the negotiation, is not that Levinas is wrong, that he is a Platonist without realizing it. It is not that Levinas, like Buber, returns to an Hegelianism without recognizing the fact. Levinas is only too aware of his 'return to Platonism by a new way' (*CP*, p. 101). The point of Derrida's critique is that Levinas falls victim to the metaphoricity of his own discourse. At stake for Derrida is the fact that we can never break out of or be allowed to forget this metaphoricity. But we do, inevitably (and much of the profundity of Derrida's remarks arises from this inevitability) become blind to the metaphors our discourses employ. It is this blindness in Levinas that Derrida is pointing to.

Secondly, and concurrently, as Derrida explores these flaws in Levinas's writing (flaws which contaminate the purity of any logically developed argument), he also explores the possibility of modifying Levinas's project. It is a modification which takes place in and because of his reading of Levinas's work, the interpellation of his (Derrida's) voice within Levinas's own. In this way, the essay is both critique and supplement – the kind of supplement which all readings of readings, all recontextualizing of arguments, necessarily constitutes. And so, if Levinas's intention is to articulate that which is 'neither mediate nor immediate ... the truth to which the traditional logos is forever inhospitable' (*WD*, p. 90/134), then Derrida asks whether the thesis might not be more coherent if writing rather than speech was the metaphor it employed in its exploration.

This move substantially modifies Levinas's project, for 'the writer absents himself better, that is, expresses himself better as the other, addresses himself to the other more effectively than the man of speech' (*WD*, p. 102/15). *Redephilosophie* is supplanted by grammatology. The emphasis upon the immediate exchange of speech (which Derrida terms phonocentrism) is related, as we have seen, to logocentrism and pneumatology, while the emphasis upon the mediation of the sign, or writing, is related to the loss of and nostalgia for presence or 'the originary effacement of the proper name' (*OG*, p. 108). Derrida then posits the play of a primary writing, interposing it into Levinas's emphasis upon the primacy of speech. He traces in Levinas's work the play of these two antithetical origins, speech and writing or *ousia* and *grammē* (*MP*, pp. 29–67 where the same operation is traced in Heidegger).

Once Derrida has clarifed that Levinas's project is the call 'towards this unthinkable–impossible–unutterable beyond (tradition's) Being and Logos' the question *for both of them* is whether it is 'possible either to think or to say' this call (*WD*, p. 114/168). 'Tradition' within parenthesis here is significant. Later in the essay, Derrida will speak of 'the philosophical logos' and, comparing Levinas's work with negative theology, he will state that 'Negative theology was spoken in a speech that knew itself failed and finite, inferior to logos as God's understanding' (*WD*, p. 116/p.170). I am not suggesting here that Derrida accepts the existence of a 'logos as God's understanding'. He is quite clear that 'the "interrogation of God" will never belong to a book' (ibid.) – that, in fact, doing theology is impossible. But he is aware of a distinction between 'the philosophical logos' and the 'logos as God's understanding'. He raises the question – it can only remain a question, for him – of an untraditional logos. In his essay 'Cogito and the History of Madness', for example, Derrida speaks again of 'the tradition of logos' (the genitive is both subjective and objective), which he equates with the Greek logos that 'had no contrary ... The Greeks were in the greatest proximity to the elementary, primordial and undivided Logos' (*WD*, pp. 39–40/p. 63). But he contrasts this to 'a self-dividing action, a cleavage and torment interior to meaning *in general*, interior to logos in general' (*WD*, p. 38/p. 62). Here is the logos *sous rature*, a crucified logos which Derrida claims as the 'ordinary logos', the 'common ground of all dissension', a logos prior to 'the Middle Ages and before the classical age' (*WD*, p. 39/p. 63). I do not wish to read too much into these statements. The material I am analysing here is drawn from Derrida's early essays, when the Heideggerian influence is still strong and the 'concepts' of the 'trace', 'supplement' and 'différance' are only beginning to emerge. Towards the end of *Writing and Difference*, in an essay written three years after 'Cogito and the History of Madness', Derrida equates the search for a conception 'of the common ground' as 'the *différance* of this irreducible difference' (*WD*, p. 293/p. 428) – *différance* replaces talk of 'an ordinary logos'. What is significant is Derrida's awareness of an unavoidable metaphysics; even within his own critique of metaphysics there is a movement towards a non-original origin; or a desire for origins is implicit within language itself. Can *différance* be read as an alternative logos? It if has an economy which we can trace then to what extent is it the logos of the other? These are the central questions of the third part of this book. Derrida is not some maverick conquistador of logocentrism. There is no conquest of logocentrism, only the recognition that it is continually fissured. But in the fissuring of self-presenting representation something alternative issues.

The task for both Levinas and Derrida is how to articulate the means whereby this otherness does not appear. *Comment ne pas parler*, as Derrida entitles one of his most recent essays. Though Levinas and Derrida approach this project from different positions – Levinas traces a metalanguage and defines the possibilities for a transcendental signified, while Derrida draws attention to the infection of any metalanguage by metaphor and signifier – both are obsessed by the existence of signs and an inability to 'give up this metaphysical complicity without also giving up the critique we are directing against this complicity' (*WD*, p. 281/412). It is the acknowledgement of an uneradicable metaphysical complicity, which Derrida is concerned to expose as frankly theological in its presuppositions, that gives rise to theological motifs and explicit theological references within Derrida's work. The horizon of the metaphysical complicity is also then the theological horizon within which Derrida is working. These references have baffled and misled a number of commentators.[3] In order to explore this metaphysical compli-

[3] See Kevin Hart's book *The Trespass of the Sign* (Cambridge: Cambridge University Press, 1989), for a good resumé of those who have read deconstruction as an *odium theologiae* and those who have read Derrida as a *liberator theologiae*. See also Susan Handelman's *The Slayers of Moses: The Emergence of Rabbinic Interpretation in Modern Literary Theory* (Albany: State University of New York Press, 1982) and *Fragments of Redemption* (Bloomington: Indiana University Press, 1991). See also Mark C. Taylor's *Deconstructing Theology* (Chico, CA: Scholars Press, 1982) and *Erring: a postmodern a/ theology* (Chicago: Chicago University Press, 1984).

city, without saying anything about it directly, Derrida deconstructs Levinas's work. He proceeds to unveil the fact that
appeal to God as the author of speech leads Levinas back into a
metaphysics of presence, whereas the only coherent appeal is to
God as the author of writing and a metaphysics of absence.
'[A]bsence is the heart of the question ... separation can only
emerge in the rupture of God – with God – ... the infinite
distance of the Other is *respected* only within the sands of a book in
which wandering and mirages are always possible' (*WD*, p. 69/
104). In writing, in the book, there is the endless play of presence
and absence. 'It [life] does not negate itself any more than it
affirms itself: it differs from itself, defers itself, and writes itself as
différance' (*WD*, p. 78/116).

Derrida's essay on Levinas's work is, then, part of a much
larger project of analysing 'the metaphysical exchange, the
circular complicity of the metaphors of the eye and the ear' (*MP*,
p. xiii). Levinas's writings become one among several forms of
textuality upon the body of which Derrida performs his pathology. It is pathology which dissects the way 'the *written* text of
philosophy [or theology] ... overflows and cracks its meaning'
(ibid.). Both men are 'faced by the as yet unnamable which is
proclaiming itself and which can do so ... only under the species
of the nonspecies' (*WD*, p. 293/428). They trace a non-appearance. For both men what is unnamable is the other, but whereas
for Levinas this other is directly associated with the God beyond
being, for Derrida the unnamable is the Book, the appeal to a
quasi-transcendental text, to an *archi-écriture*. Levinas affirms the
existence of a transcendent subject, Derrida qualifies this affirmation in terms of nothing existing outside textuality, and
therefore 'I say that there is no stability that is absolute, eternal,
intangible, natural' (*LI*, p. 151). There always remains for
Derrida an indecidability, and so what is stable is also provisional and finite.

THEOLOGY AND ANALOGY

The privileging of the unmediated experience of diachrony
above synchrony, of antecedent sense [*sens*] above cultural signs
(*CP*, p. 100), betrays a theological presupposition. For Derrida,

the privileging constitutes the theological, for in hierarchy 'the particular sciences and regional ontologies are subordinated to general ontology, and then to fundamental ontology' (*MP*, p. xix). So Derrida questions whether Levinas's thinking is coherent independent of its theological context (*WD*, p. 103/152). It is this move towards, and this presupposition of, a theological grounding which Derrida (endorsing his principle of undecidability) believes unwarranted.

In Levinas's concept of the 'trace' (a concept Derrida owes much to),[4] 'every sign is a trace ... A sign stands in this trace. This signifyingness lies in, for example, the writing and the style of the latter' (*CP*, p. 105). The trace, then, is always inscribed (as with Derrida), but its meaning is prior to and privileged above inscription (a move Derrida could not make). This leads Levinas to conclude that '[o]nly a *being* that transcends the world, an absolute *being*, can leave a trace' (ibid.). The italics are mine but the language of presence is Levinas's. And the language of this conclusion brings Levinas close to a theological argument for the existence of God. It is this language of presence, this return to the notion of the trace of a supreme being, which leads Derrida to suggest that Levinas's Good beyond Being 'would not lead beyond Being itself, but beyond the totality of the existent ... or beyond ontic history' (*WD*, pp. 141–2/208–9). The privileging and hierarchy of presence imply a certain correlation between being and beyond being. 'Between being and (what is) beyond being, a rapport is maintained which is fairly homogeneous, homologous or analogical' (*P*, p. 564). And so Levinas's thinking is founded upon 'a doctrine of analogy, of "resemblance"' which presupposes 'the determination of existent-man, the existent-God and the analogical relationship between them; the possibility of this relationship can be opened solely by the pre-conceptual and the pre-analogical unity of Being' (*WD*, p. 143/211).

Despite, then, espousing Husserl's analogy of appresentation, Levinas cannot articulate such an appresentation without implicitly espousing the analogy of being, and Derrida locates the reason for this in not only the nature of language itself (where

---

⁴ See Robert Bernasconi's 'The Trace of Levinas in Derrida'.

one can never have pure rupture nor pure presence, one can only have both and the violence implicit in having both), but Levinas's debt to dialogical philosophy, to '[a]nalogy as dialogue with God'.[5] For dialogue implies participation on a third and common ground; it implies able 'to find oneself in his trace', as Levinas writes (*CP*, p. 107). Hence, Derrida avoids entering upon a 'dialogue' with Levinas's work and favours a 'negotiation'.

If, then, Levinas is unable to say that which he alleges he is saying (in terms of the coherence of his own thinking), if he is forced by the power of his own discourse to return to *analogia entis*, what of Levinas's espousal of Husserl's analogy of appresentation? We began our exploration of this question in the last chapter, where I drew attention to the difficulties in the way Levinas wishes to appropriate Husserl's form of analogy. We need now to examine this more extensively in order to see the fracture lines in Levinas's philosophy of the Saying within the said.

For Husserl, the analogy of appresentation is and remains an intentionality, a mediation. The developed notion of monadological intersubjectivity – which, it was hoped, would rescue his phenomenology for solipsism – the recognition of the other, remains 'a correlate of my cogito' (*CM*, p. 91). This recognition is part of a wider problematic for Husserl – a transcendental theory of the objective world. Husserl locates, within 'the ego's sphere of ownness' (*CM*, p. 95), a '*founding* stratum' in actual experience within which 'my *animate organism* [is] *uniquely* singled out' (*CM*, p. 97). A sense of one's own uniqueness is also a sense of one's differentiation from the multiplicity of '"objects outside me"' (*CM*, p. 99). Husserl employs quotation marks to clarify that these objects are not outside him in any naturalistic spatial sense; this 'exteriority' remains constituted by him. That which

---

[5] In his essay '*Le Signification et le sens*', Levinas admits to 'interpreting the exceptional uprightness of the thou-saying as an epiphany of him' (*CP*, p. 106) and describes illeity as the condition for the Thou-structure of human encounter developed by Buber and Marcel. But Levinas, like Barth before him, converts the bipolar I–Thou relationship of dialogical philosophy into the trinodal economy of illeity. In doing so positive theology evaporates and the simple dualism of the presence–absence of negative theology evaporates also. What we have left is the trace or the question, the withdrawal from relation of that which is absolutely other.

constitutes the Ego Here is constituted also by that which is There. This sense of one's uniqueness-in-difference is a self-apperception (for it is not perceived, it is rather a reduction of what is always and only perceived intentionally or apperceived). This self-apperception 'constitutes, at the first level, the other in the mode: alter ego' (*CM*, p. 100). In it the *'founding* substratum' is apperceived as 'the *"primordial"* transcendency (or "world") ... [which] is *still a determining part of my own concrete being*' (*CM*, p. 106). The other is a presupposition of uniqueness; the other in ' "the ego of his ownness" ' (*CM*, p. 101) is an analogue of this apperception, his presence is the condition for his appresentation. 'A non-originary making-present can do it only in combination with an originary presentation' (*CM*, p. 109). An 'immanent transcendency' is established which governs physical as well as psychical objects, and so *'each everyday experience* involves an *analogizing transfer*' (*CM*, p. 111). Consciousness continually analogizes, the other can therefore only be a modification of myself, the recognition of my uniqueness. So *'another monad* becomes constituted appresentatively in mine' (*CM*, p. 115).

The question we face with Levinas's adoption of this model of appresentation is whether the model can still function when Levinas's modifications to its economy are supplemented. Levinas makes two major modifications. First, in the manner reminiscent of Buber commenting upon Heidegger, he wishes to replace the community of monads with his concept of *socialité* or *fraternité* (corresponding to Buber's *Gemeinschaft*). A metaphysical ethics of irreducible responsibility one for another is prior to, and diachronically disrupts, intentionality. Secondly, the Other for Levinas is not simply an appresentation of the Ego, but it, simultaneously, appresents and is appresented by the absolutely other (*autre*). Husserl's logic of the Other as a modification of the Ego is both extended and, in its extention, reversed. Thus for Levinas, the Ego is modified by the Other (and the Other by the Ego) which, simultaneously, is a modification of and is modified by the absolute other. Instead of Husserl's centrifugal dynamic, we have Levinas's centripetal economy disrupting the Ego's centrifugence. Levinas wants the activity of the Ego to be constituted by the passivity of its disposition *for* the Other/other. Hence the Ego is never the transcendental nominative, as in Husserl, it is always accusative.

These modifications can be summed up in 'The neighbour is precisely what has meaning *immediately*, before one ascribes one to him' (*CP*, p. 119). Where Husserl would wish to question Levinas's account is precisely at the point where Levinas uses the words 'meaning' and 'immediately'. In Husserl's model, 'meaning' can only be constituted by the mediation, by the analogizing of the Ego. Levinas disagrees and develops his notion of 'proximity', the *a priori* responsibility. But as Derrida comments, 'At bottom, it is the very notion of a "constitution of an alter ego" to which Levinas refuses any merits' (*WD*, p. 315/181). For Levinas the Ego encounters the Other and, in the face of the Other, it is apperceived that the Ego has always already been encountered by the other, always held as hostage by and for the other. Derrida is sceptical that any knowledge of this pure and prior encounter is available. He is sceptical of Levinas's *a priori* meaning and its immediacy of contact. Constitution is not opposed to encounter 'provided that one distinguishes the moments of passivity and activity with intuition' for both 'encounter' and 'constitution' have 'only a derivative and a dependent meaning' (*WD*, p. 316/181). In reversing Husserl, is not the analogy of appresentation reversed also, leaving Levinas open to the re-entry of a metaphysics of presence and the analogy of being? Is 'not the notion of encounter ... prey to empiricism?' (ibid.), Derrida asks.

Levinas moves beyond the experience of Others, which Husserl insists is irreducibly mediate, towards an immediately but appresented ultimate meaning 'in the form of a negative theology' (*WD*, p. 106/157). But in moving beyond, the character of that 'appresentation' is changed. Appresentation for Husserl *is* mediation; for Levinas, it is a form of immediate encounter with an auto-significance which signifies infinite withdrawal. This immediacy destroys the ineradicable difference which constitutes the analogy of appresentation, a form of analogy which 'respects separation, the unsurpassable necessity of (non-objective) mediation' (*WD*, p. 124/182). Derrida adds,

if 'I did not approach the other by way of analogical appresentation, if I attained to the other immediately and originally . . .
the other would cease to be this other' (ibid.). We are reminded
here of Barth's complaint about the *analogia entis* reducing God
to anthropology. It would cease to be the other since the
immediate, the 'now', as Derrida (taking his cue from Hegel)
saw, is a point 'of absolute indifferentiation' (*MP*, p. 41). Other
is always other *than* – it cannot be absolutely divorced from the
play of the same. 'Infinitely other' and 'absolutely other' are
transgressive concepts – concepts which are logically unstable.
They are theological concepts and theology employs them in a
transgressive discourse. Philosophical discourse, and philosophical coherence, which is Levinas's alleged subject, must not be
transgressive. The act of transgression, of crossing the boundary
and affirming an absolutely other and an infinitely other, is an
act of faith. For philosophical coherence, mediacy has to be
accepted. The other is mediated and therefore not immediate.
One cannot, therefore, affirm, without crossing the bounds of a
strictly philosophical discourse and entering the grounds of a
frankly theological discourse, that this otherness *is* transcendent.
For Derrida, Levinas's return to the metaphysics of presence is a
consequence, again, of privileging, and Husserl's phenomenology is 'profoundly foreign to all hierarchies' (*WD*, p. 121/p.
178). 'Encounter' (its purity, its immediacy and, in Derrida's
terms, its empiricism) is elevated above 'constitution'. In the
name of revelation, theology begins with such a privileging and
such a privileging is an act of faith. For Derrida there are no
philosophical grounds for privileging. There is neither pure
encounter, nor pure constitution, only the world 'in which the
absence–presence of God *plays*' (*WD*, p. 107/158).[6]

The crux of Derrida's remarks about Levinas's theological
subtext is the question 'whether the trace permits us to think
presence in its system, or whether the reverse order is the true
one' (*WD*, p. 108/160). That is, whether the trace of the other is
the condition for presence, like the Good that engenders Being
(as Levinas believes) – and so this is the trace of God; or whether

---

[6] Derrida's 'play' here is probably in italics because it is a word used by Levinas which is
often the antinomy of the 'responsibility' or 'gravity' of being a hostage. See *CP*,
p. 123.

presence, in being unable ever to self-present (Derrida's argument throughout his essay '*Ousia* and *Grammē*'), in always being fissured, is the condition for the trace – and so this is the trace of an absolute instability. Or whether, thirdly (and this is where I will position Derrida in the next chapter), the question is itself unanswerable. But despite its unanswerability the economy of such a trace can be outlined. *Différance*, as we will see, becomes the economy of the question itself. The question is the play between the trace as God and the trace as absolute instability, the play between plenitude and void.

We could re-write the question governing the negotiation between Levinas's work and Derrida's as 'What is the difference between the trace for Levinas and the trace for Derrida?' In Levinas, the trace as Derrida understands it is a 'critical and negative moment, within the hollow space of finitude in which messianic eschatology comes to resonate' (*WD*, p. 103/p. 152). As Levinas himself develops his notion of the trace (in his essay 'Meaning and Sense' [*Le Signification et le sens*], it is the very passing of God described in Exodus 33. 18–23: a passing requested by Moses and in which Moses, hidden in a cleft of rock, witnesses only God's back. For Derrida such an eschatology is only possible by freezing the play of differences and becoming dogmatic. He questions whether God can impose meaning in the way Levinas's concept of Saying suggests, for God 'has *meaning* only for an ego in general. Which means that before all atheism or all faith, before all theology, before all language about God or with God, God's divinity . . . must have a meaning for the ego in general' (*WD*, p. 132/193). There can be no reading of the trace as the passing of God otherwise. The point being made is that there can be no pure violent or non-violent intervention, no freezing of the play between violence and non-violence in the agonistics of discourse. The trace cannot be said to be this or that. 'Peace is made only in a *certain silence*, which is determined and protected by the violence of speech . . . One never escapes the *economy of war*' (*WD*, p. 148/p. 220). This economy of war is the agonistics of discourse itself. Levinas expounds a realized eschatology escaping the agonistics of discourse; Derrida suggests that is impossible.

It is important to realize that Derrida is not simply attempting a philosophical critique. He is drawing attention to the presuppositions of Levinas's writing; drawing attention to the writing itself, where it forgets itself. He provides Levinas with a deconstruction which he, Levinas, requires in order to move towards an account of the Saying which is unsayable. Levinas moves (like Barth) between disparity and parity. On the one hand, 'If one thinks, as Levinas does, that positive infinity tolerates, or even requires, infinite alterity, then one must renounce all language, and first of all the words *infinite* and *other*' (*WD*, p. 114/168). On the other hand, there is the fall into the metaphysics of presence and the *analogia entis*. Levinas does not provide us with a negative theology, because negative theology 'never undertook a Discourse with God in the face to face' (*WD*, p. 116/170). He requires, then, the deconstruction which Derrida's essay provides, and so Derrida becomes Levinas's supplement. The burden of this supplement is that 'equivocality is original and irreducible' (*WD*, p. 113/167), that origins are heterogeneous. Such equivocality is at play in Levinas's work and Levinas recognizes it, but because Levinas wishes to privilege, to theologize, there are moments where his discourse ceases to question itself. Levinas is 'inspired by a truth more profound than the "logic" of philosophical discourse' and by 'making the origin of language, meaning, and difference the relation to the infinitely other, Levinas is resigned to betraying his own intentions in his philosophical discourse. The latter is understood, and instructs, only by first permitting the same and Being to circulate within it' (*WD*, p. 151/224).

Derrida's first essay, then, continues to put Levinas's discourse into question at the point where Levinas stops. It is this continuing to question which is central to the style of the 'negotiation' in Derrida's second major essay on Levinas, 'At this very [*même*] moment in this work here I am'.

'EN CE MOMENT MÊME DANS CET OUVRAGE ME VOICI'

The basis of Derrida's 'negotiation' widens in this text. It is still fundamentally a negotiation between Levinas's work and Derrida's, but there is a greater awareness of the slippery nature of both the proper names and the word 'work'. This essay is more deeply self-reflective than the earlier one, its self-reflectiveness issuing from Derrida's insistence that reading is a negotiated space between a text that is always parasitic and therefore supplements another text. There is a deeper awareness of textuality itself – that texts can never be distinguished from contexts and each reading constructs a new text. The essay is a meditation upon reading as negotiation and textuality. There is no original text, nor any text *qua* text – only textuality. Reading as negotiation is necessarily plurivocal: the meeting of several voices. In his essay, Derrida formalizes this plurivocity in terms of a trinity: the absent, but inscribed, Emmanuel Levinas, a male and a female.[7] The question circulating throughout the essay is precisely 'Whose text is it, anyway?' In a profound sense, Levinas's work provides the pretext for this present performance, but also an archetype for the play in all textuality of reading/commentary/critique.

The trinity of voices formalize the deconstructive operation within textuality, and, as such, each voice is characterized by both what it shares with the others and that by which it is distinctive. It is the absence of Levinas himself (and the theological connotations of the forename 'Emmanuel' are also part of the circulation of Derrida's thinking) which propagates supplementary readings. Differences between the readings are polarized here by the male and the female personae in what is, after all, Derrida's interpretation.

Attention is drawn to this absent author by the future anterior of the opening phrase – '*Il aura obligé*'. The *il* is both future and past, but never present. Furthermore, the *il* is indefinite. Is it 'he', and, if it is 'he' who is the 'he'? Is it Levinas or the wholly other, the *il*leity? Is it EL (for the initials occur frequently). Is it

---

[7] This issue of who authors this text is played out through the guise of 'dictation'. There is an act of dictating at the heart of the text. In fact, 'Now I write at your dictation' (*DR*, p. 420'*P*, p. 186) suggests the male and female share the role of amanuensis. There is no direct speaking to each other, for what each says is transcribed. Any clear delineation between who is dictating and who is receiving the dictation is occluded. The strategy is not new, it parodies Platonic dialogues (TA, p. 38).

therefore not only an *il* but an *elle*?[8] Is it a woman who is the
wholly other of the other? The essay returns us to this question at
the end. For the moment, it is sufficient to appreciate the play of
otherness present through absence and present also in the
relationships between the voices which constitute the discourse.
For Derrida is absent as well. Just as there is within the text a
consciousness of the difficulty of knowing when an I is addressing
a you or a you an I or a we is being addressed by a he – so, as
readers, we are implicated in the movement of the discourse
between monologue, dialogue and written address. Hence the
subtleties of negotiation compared with the I–thou dialogue.
For Derrida there is no pure I and no pure thou either, there is
only negotiation. And it is not, as with dialogue, a negotiation
between independent subjectivities. Taking up a theme in
Levinas which, as we saw, is also an important theme in Barth,
there are no subjectivities which are not also at the same time
objectivities. This creates part of the difficulty of reading the
essay and trying to distinguish rhetorical strategy from 'argument', for we are made unsure whether we, as readers, are
addressees or interlopers, hearers or overhearers. The experience of textuality, the experience of siting oneself in relation to
this text, is paradigmatic for Derrida, on two levels.

First, it is a paradigm of the operation of a critique. The
situation performs the difficulty of presenting or representing
another: 'in the same language, in the language of the same, one
may always ill receive what is thus otherwise said' (*DR*, p. 407/*P*,
p. 161). This is an important point within the context of
Levinas's sharp distinction between the Saying of the other and
the said of the same, important because it opens the possibility
for a critique, not directly, but by repeating and recontextualizing Levinas's axiomatic theme '*cet autrement dit*' in such a way
that it becomes increasingly ironic. It is the irony which betrays
another voice lodged somewhere in the difference between what

---

[8] The play on *elle* and Levinas's initials 'E.L.' is perhaps further complicated by
Derrida's Hebrew name Elijah which, in French, is '*Elie*'. The barely suppressed
schizophrenia of discourse is developed in other plurivocal texts, like *Feu la cendre*
(1987). It is related to Derrida's leaning towards untranslatable titles, like '*Des tours de
Babel*'. The theme of 'a dissonant arrangement [*un desaccordement*] of notes and voices in
the head' as it inheres [*tient*] to all language, is central to 'The Apocalyptic Tone
Recently Adopted in Philosophy' (pp. 34–5).

Derrida is 'saying' and what Levinas is 'saying'. The presence of this other voice illustrates an ongoing inability to understand fully what Levinas is saying, a deferral of meaning. If there is a continuous deferral of meaning then that obscures any precise understanding of the character of Saying. The nature of discourse, of textuality, prevents Levinas from defining this origin of this Saying and naming it God.

The essay is paradigmatic secondly, in so far as it articulates, while performing (deconstruction is only a concept to the extent that it is always already an operation in operation), the economy of *différance*. But now we begin to move towards a Derridean thematic, and we will say more about that in the next chapter. For the moment it is important that negotiation as a strategy implies that there can be no final critique or judgement of Levinas's work, because there is no 'outside' of Levinas when reading Levinas which could facilitate a final decision. Neither is there any critical dialogue with Levinas, where the I receives cleanly the gift of Levinas's work as an object to examine and responds cleanly and simply with a gift of its own.

If, on the first paradigmatic level, Derrida draws attention to the impossibility of describing analytically the movement of the Saying in the said, the other in the same, on the second paradigmatic level he draws attention to the difficulty of receiving the Saying in the said, receiving the gift as a purely given: 'in order to give without restituting, I must still conform to what he says of the Work in his work, and to what he gives there as well as to the re-tracing of the giving' (*DR*, p. 409/*P*, p. 162). Both paradigms reveal an inability to construct a grammar of giving, a grammar of the relationship between self and other: 'I don't know yet how to qualify what is happening here between him, you and me' (*DR*, p. 413/*P*, p. 166). Both paradigms inscribe de-construction.[9]

---

[9] Derrida's deconstruction programme is based upon his insistence that any text is constituted by more than one language or voice: 'If I had to risk a single definition of deconstruction, one as brief, elliptical, and economical as a password, I would say simply and without over-statement: *plus d'une langue* – more than one language, no more of one language' (*'Des Tours de Babel'* in *Difference in Translation*, ed. Joseph F. Graham, Ithaca, N.Y.: Cornell University Press, 1985, p. 206). One voice deconstructs another. But this is a positive *de construction* as much as a negative *déconstruction*. See his *'Lettre a un ami Japonais'* in *P*, translated in *Derrida and Difference*, and his essay 'The Ends of Man' in *MP* (p. 135).

Derrida's work renders explicit the wider significance, hence the paradigmatic nature, of Levinas's thinking. The questions he addresses to Levinas, such as 'How, then, does he write?' are reflected back upon himself.[10] These questions arise from the specific commission to write a tribute to Levinas's work for a volume dedicated to him. But Derrida clearly does not know how to write the essay that has been asked for, how to respond to Levinas's thinking. And in that specific problem of how to write a response he locates a more general problem of the economy of writing itself. The essay is, then, caught up in its own negotiations – it both pays homage to and thereby affirms Levinas's understanding of responsibility ('he will have obligated') while also, ironically, displaying an ingratitude by drawing attention to that which is other than Levinas's thinking. The ingratitude does not arise from an external critique of Levinas but arises from an internal analysis that concludes by questioning the otherness of the other in Levinas's work. Homage and ingratitude, agreement and difference, and the movement between them, the slippage between them, constitute the rhythm and the economy of the essay. In 'the wake of the gift I commit a fault . . . I let it, as they say [another irony], slip by . . . I don't write straight [*droit*]' (*DR*, p. 411/*P*, p. 164). It is the inescapability of that slipping (highlighted in his earlier essay on Levinas's work) which Derrida now recognizes is also an aspect of his own work. There is no right [*droit*] writing, or reading. There is only 'negotiating the non-negotiable with a context' (*DR*, p. 406/*P*, p. 160).

The focus for this negotiation of the non-negotiable (which is, in fact, the problematic we have been tracing throughout this book) is the repetition, with increasing irony, of an insistent phrase in Levinas's work: '*en ce moment même*' – at this very moment, or in this *selfsame* moment. Like the undecidable distinction between the telling and the told in Derrida's analysis of Ponge's 'Fable' (in *Psyche: Inventions of the Other*), that which both correlates and separates the Saying and the said is time – the present and the past. The deferral of this present (the

---

[10] In *Psyche* Derrida explores the 'coimplicity' of a text which is both performing and describing.

inability to make present even in the act of seemingly presenting) infects presenting with an irony, an irony which the essay
'At this very moment' deepens as it repeats it.[11] The additional,
and inevitable, irony is that Derrida himself requires some such
phrase to speak about the simultaneity of differing and deferring
in the economy of *différance*. *Différance* is in operation because of
the simultaneity of both presence and absence in any act of
writing or representing. The one cannot be separated from the
other. Throughout the negotiation, therefore, is a realization
that Derrida's text has no more privileged a grasp of the truth
than Levinas's (an important reminder to those who would see
Derrida's work as a development of, a logical 'progression'
beyond, Levinas's).[12] Derrida draws emphatic attention to a
certain forgetting that occurs in language, the forgetting that
what is presented is in fact re-presented.[13] There is 'the false
appearance of a present' (*DR*, p. 413/*P*, p. 166), an infection of
immediacy by mediation, the absence of direct rupture by its
inscription in language, its repeatability. Tropology ensures
that meaning is never stable, never fully self-presented. It is
always deferred. Writing and reading are both negotiations
between what has already passed and 'the false appearance of a
present'. And so Saying never appears as the original language.
Nevertheless, it haunts the said and its haunting is intrinsic to the
economy of supplementarity.

Derrida's negotiation in this essay on Levinas is, therefore,
paradigmatic of both 'interrupting the negotiation while forthwith negotiating the interruption itself. Such negotiation deals
with language, with the ordering of a grammar and a lexicon . . .
which tend to interdict [*interdire*] what here *must be said* [*il faut*

---

[11] Hence Derrida's insistence on the relation between deconstruction, time/spacing and
historicity (including the historical contingency of his own work).

[12] This is exactly what Marion does in his book *L'idol et la distance*, where Derrida's
différance is seen as going one step further than Levinas's *différance*. See Simon
Critchley's book for a much more insightful commentary on the relationship between
Levinas's work and Derrida's.

[13] One could compare this with Karl Barth's emphasis upon not forgetting the crisis,
which he saw as central to dialectical theology. '[W]e [dialectical theologians] wished
and do wish with this really dialectical "transcendence" nothing else than to warn
against a forgetting of the crisis' (*The Beginnings of Dialectical Theology*, ed. James M.
Robinson, John Knox Press, 1968, pp. 145–6).

dire] . . . The negotiation thematizes what forbids thematization'
(*DR*, p. 415–16/*P*, p. 169). It is Derrida's overriding concern
with thematizing that which forbids thematization which makes
his work relevant for the theologian. Negotiation, as Derrida
portrays and understands it, has the economy of a theological
investigation. Derrida uncovers in writing the inerasable
interdiction (a prohibition which is also an inter-diction and – in
French – a disconcertion, a surprise that stops one speaking).
Writing is always partly a form of dictation.

In this essay the levels of dictation are manifold and Derrida
uses them to display the difficulties of assigning authorship, the
difficulties of being an independent subject, a self. There is,
within Levinas's thinking, a dictation prior to time and being by
the other. There is a dictation from Levinas to Derrida and from
Derrida to us. There is also a dictation performed within the text
between the two voices, male and female. The inability in the
text to define that *il*, which we saw earlier, uncouples and
obfuscates the relation of author to work. The work is Levinas's
but also Derrida's. Levinas's economy of the trace is inter-
woven, inter-spoken, with Derrida's economy of *différance*. What
is common to both economies is that 'to hear the absolute . . . one
must have read the serial work that displaces, replaces and
substitutes this word "absolute" . . . the dislocation is to be found
in the interior without inside of language which is yet opened out
to the outside of the wholly other' (*DR*, pp. 421–2/*P*, pp. 186–7).
The dislocation is literally found in that 'interior without inside
. . . which is yet opened out'. Here the utterance desists from its
saying – it fissures *en abîme* its intention, while ironically (and this
is the inescapable point) saying what is unsayable. The dislocation is performed, presented here in this essay by a textual
strategy which represents the trace and economy of the other.

It is admitted (for who is it who speaks in this text?) that
'What the work of E.L. will therefore have succeeded in doing –
in the unsuccessful act it claims to be, like any work [including
Derrida's and Barth's] – is to have obligated us [*c'est d'avoir
obligé*] . . . to this dissymmetry' (*DR*, p. 428/*P*, p. 192). The
dissymmetry is unavoidable and we must respond to it: 'The
variation is not arbitrary [*libre*], the transformation is regulated

in its irregularity and in its disturbance' (*DR*, p. 429/*P*, p. 193). The questions then multiply: 'But how? By what? By whom?' It is this continual return to questions which distinguishes Derrida's thinking from Levinas's (and perhaps philosophical thinking from theological). The return to the act of questioning, the unfinished and open nature of interpretation, is called for and instanced by the indefinition (and untranslatability) of *il*. For Levinas the *il* is the wholly other, 'he', illeity, God, and therefore, as Derrida points out, if 'he is not the agent or creator of the work . . . it must immediately be specified that this letting is not a simple passivity' (*DR*, p. 424/*P*, p. 189). Within the context of the essay, Levinas's designation of the 'he' as the unnamable God is an illegitimate leap beyond the slipperages of contextuality towards 'an eschatology without philosophical teleology' (*DR*, p. 425/*P*, p. 190).

The illegitimacy of Levinas's move is brought out by Derrida by bringing into the debate that which has been forgotten in the designation of *il* – that is, sexual difference.[14] In the essay one of the voices is an obligated female reader [*lectrice obligée*], who has been dictating the essay to a male addressee. She now raises her suspicions and draws out the implications.

The means of defining otherness (an other beyond the male otherness in Levinas's thinking) is associated with introducing the female voice into the text. The male voice in negotiation with Levinas's work can lose himself because of the sameness, the identity he brings to Levinas's work. It is at the point where Derrida's male voice seems almost to synthesize with Levinas's that the female interlocutor inter-locutes: 'In listening I was nonetheless wondering [*je me demandais*] whether I was comprehending myself [*j'étais comprise, moi* – *comprendre* is also 'to include'], and how to stop' (*DR*, p. 428/*P*, p. 192). The point for the critical incision is to insert the female other into the male dominated discourse. We have seen in the last chapter that the feminine is secondary and derivative, the masculine is master, in

---

[14] Luce Irigaray points to Levinas's lack of awareness of sexual difference in her essay 'Questions to Emmanuel Levinas: On the Divinity of Love', translated by Margaret Whitford in *Re-reading Levinas*, ed. Richard Bernasconi and Simon Critchley (London: Athlone, 1991), pp. 109–18.

Levinas's writing. By this strategy, Derrida once more exposes the implicit hierarchizing and naming of that which cannot be named (certainly not as 'Father'). 'How can one mark as masculine the very thing which is anterior, or even foreign, to sexual difference?' (*DR*, p. 430/*P*, p. 194). 'The very thing that *ought not to have been* mastered and which – therefore – could not avoid being mastered, or at least attempting to be mastered' (*DR*, p. 433/*P*, p. 197 – translation slightly altered). Our attention is drawn, once more, to the theological presuppositions, principally Jewish warnings about idolatry. Nevertheless, Derrida is not altogether countering Levinas's thinking. In some ways (and this is the positive side of de-construction), he is deepening Levinas's thinking by pointing towards a more profound alterity, a 'surfeit [*surcroît*] of un-said alterity ... The other as feminine ... would become the other of the Saying of the wholly other' (*DR*, p. 433/*P*, p. 197).

This essay too, then, is both a critique – of Levinas's theological movement towards a masculine arche – and a supplement. Textuality and its negotiation become interminable. Levinas's desire to overthrow the metaphysics of presence and reveal the otherwise than Being necessitates the interrupting of presence and the disruption of *analogia entis*. 'Yet the analogy once interrupted is again resumed [*on la voit renouée*] as an analogy between absolute heterogeneities by means of [*à travers*] the enigma, the ambiguity of uncertain and precarious epiphany' (*DR*, p. 436/*P*, p. 200). What this means – and we will return to this passage later when discussing Barth's Christology in terms of Derridean *différance* – is that 'the other as other will be kept in guard, wounded, wounding, impossible utterance' (*DR*, p. 435–6/*P*, p. 199).

Derrida's project remains the same in both of his essays on Levinas. He himself defines the project in his 1982 lecture '*D'un ton apocalyptique adopté naguère en philosophie*': 'the tropological transfer, both metaphorical and analogical, is precisely our problem' (TA, p. 43). The site for the critical incision into Levinas's corpus is the metaphorical and analogical which encourages and defines its theological horizons. Derrida consistently points to these very horizons within any writing: 'The mystagogues of modernity ... are the men of the impending [future] and the trace ... [T]hese people delude [*abusent*] with metaphors and figurative expressions ... in order to represent to us this presentiment ... We know this scene only too well today' (TA, pp. 43–5). It is not the theological in itself which Derrida is saying anything about. There is, in fact, nothing theological in and for itself which can be spoken about (that is one of the corollaries of Derrida's thinking). Nevertheless, the impossibility of the theological necessarily infects and colludes with our metaphors and analogies. Theological questions are a necessary effect of writing – something writing must remain continually aware of. There is no room here for either dogmatism or scientific empiricism: 'our mystagogues ... substitute 'analogies' and 'resemblances' for evidence and proofs' (TA, p. 45). We are betrayed by our own metaphors and we forget this. It is a forgotten metaphoricity which leads to dogmatism and empiricism, for it leads to a belief in transparency and an immediacy which fosters the privileging of an arche, the access to an origin. Philosophy which forgets its own rhetoric, its own textual strategying, wanders into the domain of theology; its thinking becomes governed by an implied onto-theology. All texts, Derrida claims, proceed as an analysis of the metaphors which compose them, they investigate their own metaphoricity and 'philosophy is incapable of dominating its general tropology and metaphorics. It could perceive its metaphorics only around a blind spot of central deafness' (*MP*, p. 228).[15]

As we saw in our last chapter, Levinas's philosophy of Saying and Barth's theology of the Word are both descriptions of a metalanguage within the operation of human representations (human thought and words). The question now is whether the deafness Derrida locates in Levinas's work might also be found in Barth's.

[15] Several of Derrida's own essays proceed by stating the guiding metaphor at their inception. 'White Metaphor', for example, is an analysis of 'exergue' (the 'outside the work', an epigraph, and 'the space on a coin or medal reserved for an inscription'. It has the subtitle 'usure' (meaning both 'usury' and 'deterioration through usage'). In fact, the book *Margins of Philosophy* proceeds as an extended analysis of the metaphor 'tympan' which is the title of the opening essay.

CHAPTER 9

Barth and Levinas: their difference as différance

As Barth is reintroduced, there are certain similarities – which become more prominent in the light of Derrida's work on Levinas – between the why and the way Barth is unable to give a fully coherent account of the Word in words and the why and the way Levinas is unable to give a fully coherent account of the Saying in the said. We will develop these similarities in this chapter, opening further the differences between these two thinkers which we began to see at the end of chapter 7.

In his essay 'White Mythology', Derrida examines the temptation *'to take the metaphor for concept'* (*MP*, p. 261). He distinguishes (unfairly in view of theologians, like Barth, who are preoccupied by the problem of language) between Descartes's discourse as a philosopher and 'a theologian's: that is, the discourse of someone who is satisfied with metaphors' (*MP*, p. 267). Equivocality 'is original and irreducible' (*MP*, p. 277) and so the source of language is always heterogeneous. Barth, as we saw in our first chapter, has a double origin for language, and it is this which constitutes his problematic concerning the relationship between the Word and words. Between the interstices of *Sprachphilosophie* and *Redephilosophie*, Barth forges his *analogia fidei*, whereas, as we have seen in the last chapter, Levinas, despite wishing to rupture the omnipresence of *analogia entis* nevertheless is forced to return to it. This is because Levinas develops his understanding of the economy of signification in terms of one particular model. That model was introduced by Saussure, who, as we noted in chapter 3, continued in the traditions of *Sprachphilosophie*. Unlike Derrida, Levinas never questions this model of language.[1]

Saussure examines the economy of signification by means of an oppositional structure between '*la parole*' and '*la langue*'. The former is operative within the latter as a vertical or diachronic axis penetrating a horizontal or synchronic axis. For Saussure this bipartite structure corresponds to 'the individual act of will' (*CGL*, p. 14) in the context of the community. It is a sociological and anthropological structure as well as a linguistic one. Other correlations also emerge: what is 'more or less accidental' (ibid.) in contrast to what is essential; the immediacy of speech (*Rede*) compared with the mediation of a language system made up of representative signs (*Sprache*). Although between the two poles there is an absolute distinction (*CGL*, p. 19), the possibility of the one is the presupposition of the other. The synchronic and the diachronic moments find their focus in the sign itself, which 'associates' a signifier with a signified, a 'sound-pattern' (or the 'material element') with a concept or idea.

Saussure's Kantian background is evident – words do not name things out there, only concepts. Two important principles follow – principles waiting in fact in the margins of Humboldt's work and later Cassirer's. First, 'the link between the signal and signification as arbitrary' – there is no natural connection between the two elements of the sign for language is socially instituted. Secondly, and more importantly for Levinas, the signal has a linear character, 'a temporal aspect and hence certain temporal characteristics' (*CGL*, p. 69).[2] A chain of signifiers emerges where each signifying unit becomes significant through its position in a web of identities and differences with other signifiers. With each new act of communication, the web is continually broken (by differences) and recreated (by identities)

Derrida's critique of Saussure, particularly Saussure's idealism, is found in one of his earliest books, *Of Grammatology*. See here also Thomas Pavel's brief but penetrating critique of the way both structuralists and poststructuralists have used linguistic models as paradigms for their philosophical systems: *The Feud of Language* (Oxford: Blackwell, 1989).

[2] Levinas relates this specifically to Husserl's analysis of pro-tension and re-tention which 'reduce[d] the time of consciousness understood as the consciousness of time to the re-presentation of the living present – that is ... the re-presentation of presence' (*TO*, p. 102).

and so 'a language alters, or rather evolves' (*CGL*, p. 76), and signification is in a state of flux.

This is the briefest of sketches of Saussure's 'science', but it introduces the elements important for Levinas's work. Two observations here will enable us to understand how Levinas employs and changes the Saussurean model for the operation of discourse. First, Saussure's system, like all systems, is fundamentally metaphysical: that is, it is founded upon classical metaphysical distinctions between body/soul, temporal/eternal, sign/ idea bipolarities. Furthermore, Saussure wishes to privilege synchrony above diachrony, general laws above accidental violences which create local modifications: 'a synchronic fact is always significant' (*CGL*, p. 85). There is, then, a strong idealism which grounds this 'science' with its explicit aim to relate 'all relevant phenomena in its domain to one first principle' (*CGL*, p. 109). We will have to examine the effect of this implicit idealism in the model upon Levinas's own thinking. Secondly, the model presents time as a parade of instants which is related to the immediacy and spontaneity of speech and the identification of isolatable values (whether the values arise from phonetic or conceptual contrasts) in a chain of signifiers.[3] We will have to examine how Levinas takes up this emphasis in terms of revelation, the event of the Saying within the said.

For Levinas, 'Being and speech have the same time, are contemporary' (*CP*, p. 61) and exist as part of 'the structure of all thought, which is correlation' or the 'chain of signification, which constitutes the world' (*CP*, p. 62). 'Once come into a correlation, the divinity of God dissipates', hence the 'impossibility of manifesting itself in an experience', of becoming a phenomenological object. Even so, in a logical move reminiscent of Anselm and Aquinas, 'the extravagance or hyperbole which language can express by the superlative of the supreme being retains a trace of a beyond-being' (ibid.). Beyond time and the constitution of this world, this trace is diachronic: 'transcen-

---

[3]   The importance of this for Levinas can be assessed by the following quotation from his essay 'Diachrony and Representation' (1982): 'Presence or being ... concretely signifies an ex-position of the other of the ego and thus signifies an *offering of itself*, a *giving of itself*, a *Gegebenheit*. It is a donation of alterity within presence' (*TO*, p. 98).

dence is synchronized with speech and reenters ... a totality
which gives it meaning' (*CP*, p. 63). For Levinas, then, the
attempt to trace 'a meaning that is not synchronized with the
speech that captures it ... a signification that would signify in an
irreducible disturbance' takes place within the model for semiotic operations outlined by Saussure.

But for Saussure, the model describes the structure of discourse within the realm of the phenomenal – it has no access to
objects in themselves, no access to the noumenal. Levinas, then,
in working with Saussure wishes to extend the diachronic axis
from the event of speaking (in Saussure) to the event of Saying.
He wishes to extend diachrony into what he terms 'anachrony'.
The extension occurs at the point when the exterior enters,
puncturing the interior – where Saying ruptures speaking. In
seeking to locate, and isolate, the moment when the 'irreducible
disturbance' enters the synchronic process, two directions for
analysis present themselves for Levinas. 'Is transcendence a
thought that ventures beyond being?' (*CP*, p. 62). That is, is
transcendence constituted by and within the structure of discourse itself? Or is transcendence 'an approach beyond thought
which speech ventures to utter?' (ibid.). That is, is it transcendence which constitutes the very structure of discourse? In the
first case transcendence is an effect of language, while in the
second, it is the condition for language.

It is important to appreciate that Levinas does not give equal
weight to these two possible ways of proceeding. Derrida *will*
give equal weight to both these possibilities and thus relate them
to a profound and heterogeneous indetermination. But in a
lengthy footnote by Levinas, explaining his understanding of the
word 'approach', it is evident that a choice has been made. 'This
approach has been made in feeling, whose fundamental tonality
is desire' (ibid.). This desire 'constitutes the intentionality of the
affective order ... The primordial feeling, precisely in its
ambiguity, is this desire for infinity, the relationship with the
Absolute which does not become correlative with it, and consequently in a sense leaves the subject in immanence' (*CP*, p. 63).
But then how does this 'feeling' of relationship with the Absolute
relate to what Levinas has said earlier about 'the impossibility of

manifesting itself [divinity] in an experience'? And what is the
nature of the 'relationship' with the Absolute that is felt and yet
has no correlation? Is such a relationship possible?[4] Levinas
provides no further elucidation – though what is evident is that
for him the Absolute is not considered to be the effect of
language, but rather the condition for language. The Absolute
engenders the feeling and desire for its infinity. It births a
recognition that the subject in its immanence only exists in that
immanence 'in a sense', for the desire ruptures the totality of that
immanence. The Absolutely other provokes the primordial
desire which issues in discourse with the Other person. This
provocation is the character of the primordial Saying.

Language, then, for Levinas is not socially instituted. It may
be socially perpetuated, but it is instituted by the call of the other
which necessitates response. There is, then, a causal relation for
Levinas between Saying and speaking and, unlike Barth, he
propounds one origin for language, not two. A *tertium quid*
mediates the other and the same. This *tertium quid* presents itself
in the face. The 'nakedness of the face that faces ... *is* this
original trace' (*CP*, p. 65 – italics mine). The face is the trace of
the origin in its appearance. The *is* is significant here, for it
suggests again that Levinas's explicit espousal of the analogy of
appresentation masks an implicit appeal to the order of the
analogia entis. Or, to take Derrida's line, the analogy of appresentation forgets that it is both analogy and appresented and begins
to believe it is the thing itself. The one divine origin for language
has the human face as its analogue. The human face is the *tertium
quid* for 'the withdrawal of the indicated' (ibid.), the face of the
absent transcendental signified. Thus, through the 'face', a
negative natural theology is established.

We now begin to deepen the difference between Levinas's
saying incarnate and Barth's Word made flesh. Levinas appeals
to a general revelation in the specific face and this returns him to
the order of *analogia entis*. For Barth, Jesus of Nazareth is not only
unique in Himself as the Christ, He is unique also in his socio-

---

4   Levinas moralizes and ontologizes Saussure's structure. He views 'synchrony as *being* in
     its egological gathering' (*TO*, p. 99) and that which concerns itself particularly with
     representation as the said.

historical location. This double particularity prevents a simple return to the analogy of Being, because the socio-historical appearance of Jesus Christ is in the past and no longer appears in the present (unlike Levinas's face of the Other person). Of course, Levinas's 'face' points beyond being towards that which cannot be named or presented, but it points in the manner of a negative theology. As Derrida writes, concerning Meister Eckhart's method, the 'negative movement of the discourse on God is only a phase of positive ontotheology' (*WD*, p. 337/398). Scepticism ceases in Levinas's thinking – giving way to an affirmation of the Good beyond Being.

The 'face' mediates the immediacy of the trace. And the economy of this mediation is structured in accordance with Saussure's model for the operation of discourse. But it is, in fact, Saussure reversed, in that for Saussure it is the synchronic which is privileged, and it is in relation to this synchronic that he believes linguistics moves towards a first principle. For Levinas, it is the diachronic which is privileged – for him the synchronic is aligned with a totalizing immanence. The synchronic chain of signifiers covers 'over the trace of the *saying* that left them' (*CP*, p. 69). Nevertheless, the idealism implicit in Saussure structure, the pursuit of an arche, remains. That Levinas will name his first principle an an-archia only reinforces the fact that he is turning Saussure upside down.

Levinas's account of the Saying and the said seems then to run up against a logical inconsistency arising from an implicit idealism, an implicit theology, in the model for the operation of discourse he is employing. It stumbles into a (negative) natural theology it would wish to deny. It is this that Derrida points towards at the end of his essay 'At this very moment in this work'. There he draws attention to how 'In *Totality and Infinity*, the analogy is kept, though not quite in a classical sense, between the face of God and the face of man ... [But] in his commentary on the Talmudic texts, a whole movement is sketched in order to mark the necessity of interrupting that analogy ... Yet the analogy once interrupted is again resumed as an analogy between absolute heterogeneities by means of the enigma, the ambiguity of uncertain and precarious epiphanies' (*DR*, p. 436/

P, p. 200). Levinas's development of the trace makes the positivism of revelation described in his earlier work 'more uncertain and precarious', but it nevertheless establishes an analogy, a correspondence: 'Man, therefore, can be linked with this retreat, despite the infinite distance of the nonthematizable, with the precariousness and uncertainty of this revelation' (ibid.).

BARTH'S DIFFERENCE AND *DIFFÉRANCE*

It has been the argument throughout this book that Barth, unlike Levinas, maintained the double origin of language. In handling the theological problem of needing to speak of that which cannot be spoken about, he always returns to the disparity between 'absolute heterogeneities'. For Levinas 'it is not a question of the meeting of two series of signification that each, with equal rights, lay claim to the same phenomenon' (*CP*, p. 68). But for Barth, whose consideration of 'sin' and 'free will' is more developed, it is precisely the question of 'the meeting of two series of significations' both of which 'lay claim to the same phenomenon' that institutes the problem of speaking about and having knowledge of God. Different interpretations are not only possible, they are inevitable. There is no possibility of theology 'assuring itself that the circle in which this knowledge moved was identical with the life cycle of the absolute spirit' (II.1, p. 249/ 281). 'God is always God and man is always man in this relationship' (II.1., p. 234/265), and so, in the advent of the Word, 'the sinfulness of [human] thinking and speaking no longer have the power of their own, any definitive power' (II.1., p. 213/239). There is no direct communication, no direct saying, for the Word stands in utter contradiction to words, and this contradiction is not simply woven into the text, it is allowed to stop the text, by repeatedly putting the text into crisis (the crisis of its own impossibility). Furthermore, Barth's Kantianism insists that human words are conventional and arbitrary – that human thinking and speaking has only exchange value in a market of representations. Thinking and speaking is 'not imme-diate knowledge but the mediate knowledge which passes into viewing and conceiving' (II.1., p. 186/209). Thinking and speaking, then, is a knowing that is mediated by viewing and conceiving which is a 'mediate knowledge' itself. There is a twofold mediation. This is what we traced in our first chapter. '[T]here is not ... a pure conceptual language which leaves the inadequate language of images [*Sprache der Vorstellungen*] behind, and which ... is, as such, the language of truth' (II.1., p. 195/ 219). There is then no immediate grasp upon the Word, no immediate access to the metalanguage. And so revelation is caught in what Derrida would term a 'double-bind': that is, it is always past (not in the immediate, the now of its realization, its conceptualization and imaging); it is always future (because imaging and representation are teleologically governed by the revelation they are attempting to grasp: 'the revelation of God and its veracity are always future to us' (II.1., p. 214). Revelation, and therefore knowledge of God, is always either in the past or being deferred; it is never now. Its representation, then, is caught up in the logic of supplementarity, for we are always only 'on the way' [*auf dem Wege*].[5]

The righteous judgement of God is, and always remains, absolutely heteronomous to the sinfulness of humankind. The two states stand, each paralyzing the saying of the other, in a Kantian antinomy from the human point of view. For Barth, this sinfulness, always remaining, means disparity, means double origin, and it also means that, unlike Levinas, privileging a metalanguage above language – presupposing one has access to and understands this metalanguage – is not simple. In the closing pages of chapter 5 of *Church Dogmatics*, having spoken of the three-fold 'participation' of the Word in words, having redefined his use of 'analogy' (rendered distinct from both *analogia entis* and even Quenstedt's Protestant *analogia attributionis intrinseca*), Barth makes an utterly astonishing and courageous intellectual move. He recognizes and admits that 'the concept of revelation, too, is obviously a general human concept,

---

[5] Here once more are echoes of themes found in Heidegger; not necessarily an indication of influence, but con-fluence. See here Richard Roberts' essay 'Barth and the Eschatology of Weimar: A Theology on its Way?' in *Theology on the Way: Essays on Karl Barth*.

as it is also that of grace' (II.1., p. 245/277). He asks whether he has not been 'chasing a shadow', for 'we may certainly have represented and understood the veracity of cognition, but not the veracity of cognition of *God*' (ibid.). He asks 'Were we really moving in the *circulus veritatis Dei*?' (II.1., p. 246/279). '[I]t is not sufficient simply to maintain that we have thought and said all this in faith', but 'we cannot in fact protect ourselves from this question' (ibid.). Therefore, 'the final consolation and security ... must definitely consist [*bestehen*] in a simultaneous insecurity and destruction [*Aufhebung*]' (ibid.). The most significant word in this last statement is 'simultaneous', for this distinguishes what Barth, speaking of theological thinking, had earlier in the chapter termed '*die Kraft seiner Bewegung*' (II.1, p. 201/226) from any Hegelian understanding of *Aufhebung* as a dialectic process towards an overriding synthesis. 'Simultaneous' denies synthesis. It also denies the positive movement of denial in negative theology.[6] As we shall see, Barth's appreciation of '*die Kraft seiner Bewegung*' anticipates Derrida's economy of *différance*.

To see this more clearly, to recognize the economy of *différance* as it governs Barth's understanding of the Word in words and gives rise to much that seems only contradictory when read prescriptively, we need to trace this '*die Kraft seiner Bewegung*'. Such an analysis would necessarily differ from how we handled the text of chapter 5 in our own chapter 1, for it is not the content as much as the rhetorical strategy and organization employed by Barth that we need to uncover – we need to consider 'not only the articulation of the signifieds' (*MP*, 293: Derrida is commenting, after Valery, on how to study a philosophical text), but its very literariness. We need to trace the 'destruction' as it operates within Barth's writing and how it embraces that operation as part of the very point he is making. But before we do this we need to clarify the economy of *différance* as Derrida develops it and its own relation to a constellation of concepts and operations: *Aufhebung*, eschatology, teleology, representation, crisis and the quasi-transcendental trace.

[6] See chapter 11 for a discussion of Barth and negative theology.

CHAPTER 10

Derrida's supplement

In examining some of the basic themes of Derrida's work, the intention of this chapter is to focus upon how these themes closely relate to the problematic examined in Barth's work in the first part of this study.[1] Throughout chapter 5 of *Church Dogmatics*, Barth is attempting to clarify the grounds upon which true knowledge of God is possible within human thinking and language. In fact, the examination of the relationship between a primary Logos or Saying and the logocentric was also the concern of Barth's contemporaries Buber and Heidegger, and through them the concern was bequeathed to Levinas. It is Derrida's concern too: 'Such is the question: the marriage between speech and Being in the unique word, in the finally proper name. Such is the question that enters into the affirmation put into play by *différance*' (*SP*, p. 160). His work focuses

---

[1] I am aware throughout this chapter in particlar, but also in others, that so much of my own discourse requires putting between inverted commas. Derrida's examination of the shifting sands of the discursive puts into question my own use of 'themes' and 'intention' in this opening sentence. It puts into question, but it does not annul the possibility and even the necessity of writing *as if* we could extract 'themes' from the text without any difficulty, *as if* we could know and have governance over our intentions. What Derrida's work draws our attention to is the impossibility of beginning to write, the impossibility of beginning in the face of that fact that pragmatically we do write and we do begin. His work draws attention to the pragmatics of discourse – the pragmatic, but otherwise groundless, choice we make in beginning here and with this word. It is groundless because we are already within a con-text, our beginning has always already begun. But there are occasions when even Derrida, to clarify and defend himself from deliberate misrepresentation, speaks plainly. Occasions when he reduces 'just a little the violence and the ambiguity' and '[i]n addressing myself to you [Gerald Graff, who edited the 1988 edition of *Limited Inc.*, in which Derrida wrote an 'Afterword' in the form of an open letter] in the most direct manner possible, I return to a very classical, 'straightforward' form of discussion' (*LI*, pp. 113–14).

209

upon the question of 'the end [*fin*] of metalanguage in the subject of eschatological language' (TA, p. 60). Where '*la fin*' is not necessarily 'the end' but also 'the goal', 'the purpose' and 'the limit'.[2]

Derrida will always emphasize that his concern lies with the 'question' (his admiration for and debt to Heidegger is well charted).[3] The importance of this emphasis will be increasingly evident. There are postmodern thinkers who have made this question concerning the end of any metalanguage into a statement – the post 1970s work of Roland Barthes, for example. But for Derrida the question is central: 'Isn't the apocalyptic the transcendental condition for all discourse, even for all experience, for every mark or trace?' (TA, pp. 77–8). It is the interrogative character of Derrida's explicitly theological question which becomes important for theology, as we shall see.

'UNE TRANSCENDENTALE CONDITION ... DE TOUTE TRACE?'

Into the dichotomy between metalanguage and language, between a transcendental communication (*Rede*) and the immanence of discourse (*Sprache*), Derrida interposes a discussion on the problems of re-production, iterability, citation and translation (*LI*, p. 38). More specifically, his concern with analysing the dichotomy, its constitution and significance, is the 'essentially *interminable* character of such an analysis'. Analysis of the problem will necessarily be a '*prise de partie*, that is: *partial*' (*LI*, p. 39). The analysis is also inevitable [*forcement*]. There is not, therefore, a denial of philosophical teleology or eschatology, two

---

[2] Derrida, in this essay, distinguishes between the eschatology of 'the end' and the limitations of the metaphysical and theological implied by *différance*, for which he uses the word '*la clôture*'. See Critchley's book for a detailed study of this word in Derrida's work.

[3] In *Of Spirit*, whose subtitle is precisely 'Heidegger and the Question', Derrida draws attention to the centrality of *Fragen* as it dominates Heidegger's thinking and relates to Derrida's own. In particular, Derrida, pointing to a relationship (a supplementing one) between *Fragen* and *différance*, suggests 'that the question does no more than *defer* ... the quest and the inquiry' (*OS*, p. 119). He suggests this as a consequence of the deconstruction of the 'humanist teleology' which governs the operation of Heidegger's questioning-theme.

economies which, for Derrida, are indistinguishable in so far as both pursue a final, unveiled truth. But where there is deferral through the inability to foreclose the analysis, the possibility is opened for a multiplicity of approaches and interpretations. Only dogmatic assertion can close the analysis. Derrida points out that within the very language announcing such a closure a deconstruction is in operation undermining the very grounds upon which that assertion can be made. The analysis can only be closed by either divine fiat or death. Meaning is partial and provisional.

Derrida investigates this flaw in meaning's ability to be fully present through the problem of iterability – that any word or phrase can be repeated elsewhere in another context. Not only *can* be repeated, but *must* be. Without the capacity to be repeated, the conventions which underpin the exchange and value of signs, making signs meaningful, cannot become established.[4] But, and this is the very crux for Derrida, in being repeatable and in being repeated, the value and significance of signs are never stable. Meaning shifts and slides in recontextualization. '[I]terability makes possible idealization – and thus a certain identity in repetition that is independent of the multiplicity of factual events – while at the same time limiting the idealization it makes possible: *broaching* and *breaching* it at once [*elle l'entâme*]' (*LI*, p. 61). It is the structure of this economy of representation, this 'general economy' and its inevitability, that Derrida outlines in the development of his examination of *différance*, in his appropriation (via Heidegger and Levinas) of the 'trace' and his notion of the logic of supplementarity.

Several recent philosophers and semioticians have expounded the meaning (which is also the non-meaning) of *différance*.[5] I wish only to draw out those aspects of *différance* which are important

---

[4] Derrida develops his ideas on the economy of exchange, the sign and the gift in his most recent book *Given Time: I. Counterfeit Money*, tr. Peggy Kamuf (Chicago: Chicago University Press, 1992). See particularly, chapter 2.

[5] There are two in particular: Rodolphe Gasché's *The Tain of the Mirror: Derrida and the Philosophy of Reflection* (Cambridge, Mass.: Harvard University Press, 1986) and Irene E. Harvey's *Derrida and the Economy of Différance* (Bloomington: Indiana University Press, 1986). These have both outlined the genealogy and axiomatics of the operation. There is also *Derrida and Différance*, eds. David Wood and Robert Bernasconi (Evanston, Ill.: Northwestern University Press, 1988).

for the theological concerns with language outlined in Barth's work. I begin with Derrida's highly important delineation of the term. 'We provisionally give the name *différance* to this *sameness* which is not *identical*: by the silent writing of an *a*, it has the desired advantage of referring to differing, *both* as spacing/temporalization and as the movement that structures every dissociation' (*SP*, pp. 129–30). Furthermore, in indicating 'the middle voice, it precedes and sets up the opposition between passivity and activity. With its *a*, differance more properly refers to what in classical language would be called the origin or production of differences and the differences between differences, the play [*jeu*] of differences' (*SP*, p. 130).

From these two statements, and with reference to others, I will proceed to draw out three important 'theological' observations about the economy of *différance*.

First, it is both a phenomenon and the transcendental condition for phenomenality. It is a description both of the rupturing and the movement, the dynamic, which organizes the rupturing. It is both an immanent characteristic of textuality – where, following Saussure, it is the difference between words, their spacing, which constitutes their meaning – and an external operation which structures, and structures interminably, textuality. The point where Saussure's model for the economy of discourse is changed[6]

---

[6] Derrida's modification of Saussure's model for discourse closely follows modifications made to Saussure by Roman Jakobson (modifications important for the work of Jacques Lacan also). We can represent Saussure's model by the following diagram:

$$\frac{\text{parole}}{\text{langue}}$$

In his influential book *The Fundamentals of Language* (written in collaboration with Morris Halle, Le Hague: Mouton, 1956) Jakobson proposes the following model:

$$\frac{\text{metaphor}}{\text{metonymy}}$$

is the point where the differences are also simultaneously deferrals. The meaning of a word issuing from its range of differences – differences which are both syntagmatic and connotative – is consequently always slipping, and its final definition is deferred. It is deferred because the signifier in order to be significant is part of a chain of signifiers which supplement the word and yet differ from it (adding only more words), but, in being supplemented, its ability to mean has been replaced and displaced by the other supplementing signifiers in the chain. The signifier is caught up in a never-ending chain of substitutions and so the presentation of what is signified remains locked within an economy of representation, of what is classically understood as secondariness. Derrida challenges the hierarchy, the metaphysical implications, of this secondariness.

The theological consequence of this development of Saussure's model is that there can be no direct revelation of God's Word or philosophy's Saying. The Word cannot appear in words directly. There is only mediation and mimesis; which means there is only interpretation and hermeneutics; which means any belief in an event taking place prior to its communication in language cannot be proved to be more than a belief

He explains that 'the development of any discourse may take place along two different semantic lines' (p. 90). These 'semantic lines' are characterized by similarity and contiguity, respectively, and 'find their most condensed expression in metaphor and metonymy' (ibid.). Metaphor and metonymy are tropes which manifest the operation of two contrary currents within discourse. Metaphors create links with other words through similarity. This is a modification of Saussure's 'associative relations'. Metaphors create systems of correspondence. Metonymy is the movement which necessarily contextualizes one word by another, spatially differentiating one word from another, in order for meaning to emerge. This is a modification of Saussure's 'syntagmatic relations'. Metonymy creates distinctions.

In *Of Grammatology*, Derrida outlines Jakobson's debt to Saussure, but he also points out how, though it is questionable in Saussure's work, Jakobson (and Halle) 'recall the imperfection of graphic representation' (p. 54) and, not surprisingly, 'bind linguistics to semantics' like 'all European linguists from Saussure to Hjemslev' (p. 50). It is, nevertheless, within this model for the operation of discourse that Derrida sketches his understanding of *différance*. *Différance* is that which operates between metaphor and metonymy, that which governs their play, the play of similarities and differences, presences and absences, meanings and their displacement. *Différance* equalizes metaphor and metonymy and so prevents linguistics being subsumed by semantics. It reminds the metaphoric that the metonymic functions as a semiotic system, as '*la langue*'. Derrida asks Jakobson to read Saussure again.

(the privileging, on a basis such as faith, of one interpretation). There are no grounds for constructing a transcendental argument (as Levinas is doing, for example), since the deconstruction of such an argument is immanent to the discourse of origins and grounds itself. Derrida need only point to the rhetoric (the mediating mark) employed to make claims for immediacy of knowledge in order to bring out, not the impossibility of the immediate, but its openness to being questioned. And yet, as we will see more clearly later, Derrida is aware that he himself necessarily constructs a transcendental argument and requires the possibility of immediacy in order for mediacy to have any meaning at all. His attention to our con-textuality can only take place on the assumption there is one Text (or one Book). A self-contained, self-referring text stands in the margins of his own deconstructive work. There remains, therefore (and 'remains' [*restes*] is a significant Derridean word, positively indicating surplus and negatively indicating superfluousness), a haunting: 'The trace is not a presence but is rather the simulacrum of a presence that dislocates, displaces and refers beyond itself' (*SP*, p. 156). As simulacrum the trace 'does not appear in the text as the trace "itself"' (*SP*, p. 158), but it haunts the chain of substitutions, the series which is continually effacing the presence of the trace.

Derrida proposes that Western metaphysics has been dominated by the desire to reappropriate the sign's deferred presence, and so 'the characteristics of origin, beginning, *telos*, *eschaton*, etc., have always denoted presence – *ousia, parousia*' (*SP*, p. 138). It is within this teleology (or, theologically, eschatology) that Derrida locates *différance* as 'the movement by which language ... becomes "historically" constituted as a fabric of differences' (*SP*, p. 141). But since these differences never become dissolved by an ultimate synthesis, the negativity of difference can never be vanquished. It is always kept in play; it always keeps in play a certain indeterminacy. This is where Derrida's economy differs from Hegel's dialectic. *Aufhebung* 'remains in control of the play, limiting it and elaborating it by giving it form and meaning ... this economy of life restricts itself to conservation, to circulation and self-reproduction as the reproduction of meaning' (*WD*, pp.

255–6/376). Derrida affirms, then, the movement, the temporalizing and spatializing which constitutes supplementarity – but he wishes to forestall giving any teleological value to this movement.

The theological consequences of this position are spelled out by Derrida himself at the end of his lecture 'The Apocalyptic Tone Recently Adopted in Philosophy'. Here he writes: 'Our *apocalypse now*: that there is no longer any likelihood [of an apocalypse] other than the likelihood of a thought of good and evil whose notification would *gather together* in order to be itself a word of revelation . . . The catastrophe here perhaps would be *of* the apocalypse itself, its folding [*pli*] and its end [*fin*], a closure [*clôture*] without end, an end without end' (TA, pp. 95–7). Eschatology, it would appear from this, can neither be realized nor future – and that, perhaps, is our contemporary catastrophe. Perhaps. But if we accept the logic of supplementarity outlined above (and, more importantly, if Derrida accepts it), then his own work cannot avoid the economy of *différance* either. Having demonstrated the inability to make definitive statements, he cannot now proceed to make such statements himself. Particularly when this concerns a future eschatology. A realized eschatology is continually postponed, but Derrida cannot make the claim that it will always be postponed, only that the chain of substituting signifiers will, as far as one can judge, continue indefinitely. The economy of *différance*, therefore, questions but can never erase eschatology. Hence the irony and textual ambivalence of Derrida's closing indefinite question:[7] 'The end approaches. Now there is no more time to speak the truth about the apocalypse. But what are you [*tu*] doing, you [*vous*] will insist, to what end do you wish to come when you come to say to us, here now, let's go, come, the apocalypse, it's finished, I tell you, that's what happens' (TA, p. 98). Deferral opens the question 'to what end do you wish to come?' and keeps the question unanswered, it is merely 'what happens'. Hegel's 'restricted economy' becomes Derrida's 'general economy'.

---

[7] The final sentence is both a question and a statement. Its structure, intonation and syntax all indicate a projected question levelled at Derrida [*tu*] by those at the seminar [*vous*]. But the question issues into a statement and is not punctuated interrogatively.

My first observation about the economy of *différance*, then, is that it seems to deny the theological categories of revelation and the eschaton, on the one hand, and yet require them, on the other. We pursue this further in a second observation about the economy of *différance*, which returns us to the orbit of Hegel's *Aufhebung*.

For, secondly, in so far as differences are both required and all differences are equal in importance within the economy of signification, then *différance* pleads for the equal rights of the subordinated and repressed signifiers. The role of the signified over the signifier, immediacy over mediation, speech over writing is not inverted, but democratized. It is important to stress this because some critics of Derrida's work have rested their case for the nihilism of Derrida's perspective on a belief that he wishes to invert the orders of signified over signifier, immediacy over mediation, speech over writing. In his 'Afterword' to the *Limited Inc.* debate with John Searle, Derrida emphasizes that this 'way of thinking context does not, as such, amount to a relativism, with everything that is sometimes associated with it (skepticism, empiricism, even nihilism) ... [T]his 'deconstructive' way of thinking ... to the extent to which it ... is itself rooted in a given context ... does not renounce ... the 'values' that are dominant in this context (for example, that of truth, etc.)' (*LI*, p. 137). This dependency upon (and infestation of) otherness in the same, non-presence within presence, in the chain of substitutions, necessarily leads us back to Hegel's notion of *Aufhebung* (Derrida's *relève*). And this teleological notion, like the economy of negative theology, remains a determinative presence in all Derrida's discussions of both *différance* and the 'trace'.[8]

Derrida presents two antithetical strategies for discussing *Aufhebung*. First, he defines his own position *in contrast* to Hegel's. We can see this in his distinction between restricted and general economies. It is a position clarified further by his essay 'The Pit and the Pyramid: Introduction to Hegel's Semiology', where the economy of the sign in Hegel is determined as 'an agency or

---

[8] See Kevin Hart's *The Trespass of the Sign*, chapter 6 'The Economy of Mysticism', for a discussion on the relationship between Hegel's economy and negative theology.

essential structure of the Idea's return to self-presence' (*MP*, p. 74). By means of, and within the operation of, the spirit 'the sign is understood according to the structure and movement of the *Aufhebung*' (*MP*, p. 76). Here representation is the remembered and interiorized intuition which intelligence recalls to itself in an objectifying process. Intelligence interiorizes sensible immediacy by 'negating the sensory spatiality of intuition' (*MP*, p. 89). Memory [*Erinnerung*] turns this interiorization into an image or sign which intelligence will draw forth as a concept, an idea. The process is a movement towards the ideality of signs or 'the ideality of language' (*MP*, p. 90). The 'sign, as the unity of the signifying body and the signified ideality, becomes a kind of incarnation' (*MP*, p. 82). This is the teleological development of the sign which *différance* questions.

Secondly, Derrida defines his own position *within* Hegel's *Aufhebung* as a modification of Hegel's economy. 'Despite the very profound affinities that *différance* thus written has with Hegelian speech . . . it can, at a certain point, not exactly break with it, but rather work a sort of displacement with regard to it. A definite rupture with Hegelian language would make no sense, nor would it be at all likely' (*SP*, p. 145). And therefore Derrida rewrites or, in placing Hegel within the context of his own work, reinscribes Hegel in terms of *différance*. 'The Pit and the Pyramid' is such a deconstruction of *Aufhebung*, revealing within Hegel's thinking the subtle operation of *différance*. Hegel says much more than he wants to say. Derrida draws attention to two lines of thought in Hegel's semiology. The first is the separation of the signified from the signifier (*MP*, p. 86), where the sign is understood as monument, the body, the pyramid, for a foreign soul or meaning. This material body cannot be done away with, for it is the monument announcing the presence of the meaning within it. The second line of thought is how this body/soul, sign/meaning discontinuity is linked to 'the entire Hegelian system, with its archeology, its teleology, its eschatology'. This is the economy of the sign as an *Aufhebung*. In this *Aufhebung* 'the content of the sensory intuition (the signifier) must erase itself, must vanish before *Bedeutung*, the signified ideality' (*MP*, p. 89). Derrida draws attention to this 'idealizing and *relevant* negativity which works within the sign' (*MP*, pp. 90–1), for it is the sign 'which "relifts" [*relève*] sensory intuition into the ideality of language' (ibid.).

It is the sign which negates the real in favour of the ideal, although the sign itself 'must be hewn from a sensory matter which is in some way given to it' (ibid.). It is also the sign which enables there to be an idea. The need for and impossibility of erasing the materiality of the sign itself, then, leads to 'the equivalence of . . . two readings . . . of the Hegelian circle. The first is a 'sensualist or material reduction', the second 'the idealist teleology'. They proceed 'in opposite directions, along the same line' (*MP*, p. 91). This line Derrida names 'as a provisional convenience, "metaphor"' (ibid.), but elsewhere it is this movement between the materiality and the ideality of the sign which he terms *différance*. Hegel wishes to master the metaphoricity of language, but as Derrida noted in his essay 'White Mythology' 'philosophy is incapable of dominating its general tropology and metaphorics' (*MP*, p. 228). And so the '*Aufhebung – la relève –* is constrained into writing itself otherwise. Or perhaps simply into writing itself. Or, better, into taking account of its consumption of writing' (*MP*, p. 19).[9]

For Derrida, these two different strategies for discussing Hegelian *Aufhebung* mean that 'the very project of philosophy, under the privileged heading of Hegelianism, is displaced and reinscribed' (ibid.). The theological consequences of this position now need to be closely examined. Deconstruction, the task of tracing the economy of *différance* as it pertains to any text, operates *within* a transcendental argument, while also being a critique of that argument. But it cannot operate outside a

---

9 John Llewelyn argues for the closeness of Hegel and Derrida in his article 'Thresholds' in *Derrida and Différance*. See also his essay 'A Point of Almost Absolute Proximity to Hegel' in *Deconstruction and Philosophy*, ed. John Sallis (Chicago: Chicago University Press, 1987). Here Llewelyn succinctly points out what we have seen to be the case, that '*différance* and dialectical difference are not diametrically opposed' (p. 87). He distinguishes between 'the conflict of forces that goes by the pseudonym *différance*, as opposed to the conflict of positions in dialectical contradiction' (p. 87). I am far from sure that such a distinction can be made – Hegel's dialectic moves within the operation of the absolute spirit, after all. It is a position but within an economy and *différance* is also within an economy, although more a phenomenon and effect than a position.

transcendental argument because it *is* a transcendental argument under erasure. It is inevitable, then, that Derrida's own discourse privileges and thus marginalizes. The movement from Hegel's 'restricted' economy to Bataille's and his own 'general' economy, the movement from restriction to generality, itself implies a teleology. Derrida has recently stressed, in the face of misunderstanding, that ' "deconstruction" is firstly this destablization on the move in … "things in themselves"; but it is not negative. Destabilization is required for "progress" as well' (*LI*, p. 147).[10] The quotation marks flanking 'progress' mark the slipping or erasure of meaning, but erasure itself is double-bound – for to be *sous rature* is *both* to be cancelled and to have one's presence in the text emphasized.

In other words, what I am suggesting[11] is that Derrida's deconstruction of Hegel's power-game serves only to elevate deconstruction itself as a more powerful mode of play. For it offers itself as a more adequate description of the forces of textuality. Derrida demonstrates (in Plato, in Rousseau, in Hegel, in Saussure, in western metaphysics) that the desire which privileges, which hierarchizes, is already split, already heterogeneous. But to what extent is *différance* itself an economy of Derrida's desire? Derrida is already aware of the question – witness the question he places in the mouths of his audience in ' The Apocalyptic Tone Recently Adopted in Philosophy': 'what goals do you wish to arrive at? [*à quelles fins veux-tu en venir?*]'. While questioning the move beyond *différance*, he recognizes that 'the question arises as to the other side of nostalgia, which I will call a Heideggerian *hope*' (*SP*, p. 159). The question of the other side remains: 'the fact that this form, this structure, has been deconstructed doesn't mean that after (if there is such a thing as "after deconstruction") we will have nothing, or chaos. We are

---

10 This definition is repeated, more succinctly, in 'Letter to a Japanese Friend', where Derrida writes that 'I have had to … put aside all the traditional philosophical concepts, while affirming the necessity of returning to them, at least under erasure' (*WD*, p.3/*P*, p. 390).

11 See David Wood's articles 'Following Derrida' in *Deconstruction and Philosophy* and '*Différance* and the Problem of Strategy' in *Derrida and Différance*. In both essays he outlines the complexity of following Derrida's strategy where the language of causation is being employed while its metaphysical implications are being refuted.

in the process of deconstruction and there are new things and things which fall apart and new forms – we can perceive many things which survive, not survive but *live through* deconstruction'.[12] There are new things *living through* deconstruction and even when hope is in italics 'there is no word less deconstructible'.[13] Is progress in quotation marks, is hope in italics, any less progress or hope unmarked? They are certainly made less innocent, certainly more guilty for having made any attempt to transgress metaphoricity. Even so, these statements are neither those of an atheist nor a nihilist. Rather they express the need for a certain agnosticism which must be open to the possibility of an impossible answer. Furthermore – and again this is a question Derrida wishes to keep in play – to what does this interminable openness bear witness? To what Other is it open onto? Derrida has spoken recently of a quasi-transcendence, of the not yet of the transcendental, of the 'promise'. He has spoken of the 'Yes' in discourse which is always a 'yes, yes' because it is caught up in representation, the repetition of an origin (see *'Ulysse gramophone: Öui-dire de Joyce'* (1987)). But Barth's own emphasis upon mediation advocates that all transcendence is quasi-transcendence. 'We know that human language can never break through to the absolute' (*2R*, p. 530/94), that 'He encounters us in the dialectic of the supreme categories of our thought' (*2R*, p. 513/497) and therefore is this not a 'pseudo-transcendence of an altogether immanent order?' (*2R*, p. 479/463)? All discourse inscribing a knowledge of transcendence has one foot firmly in the sub-soil of language and one finger pointing towards the moon.

It is at this point that Derrida's repeated return to Hegel has been matched by a similar, and related, return to the question of negative theology. Here we reach the heart of the matter for any discussion of the importance of Derrida's work for theological thinking. I quote from another recent statement and, as Derrida recognizes, a far deeper discussion of the issues involved in *différance* than that available in his earlier work.[14] In '*Comment ne pas parler*' (1987), he writes:

[T]herefore it is in thinking about this movement towards hyperessentiality that I thought I must forbid myself from writing in the register of 'negative theology'. What is 'meant' by '*différance*', 'trace', etc . . . no longer arises from being . . . But the onto-theological reappropriation always remains possible and no doubt 'inevitable' to the extent that one speaks precisely in the element of logic and ontological grammar . . . But this question remains, I concede it, at the heart of thinking about *différance* or writing about writing. It remains a question. (*P*, p. 542)

What I wish to raise at this point (for we will return to this essay and its philosophical/theological implications in a re-negotiation with Barth's work) is the change in tone it announces compared with Derrida's earlier remarks concerning the economy of *différance* and the movement involved in negative theology. I raise this because it seems to me to relate to Derrida's deeper negotiation with Levinas's work evident throughout *Psyché* (1987) and *Of Spirit* (1987).[15] Derrida seems to become

---

[14] Theology, either in its positive form – the God of Neoplatonic or Enlightenment thinking – or its negative form – the mysticism of pseudo-Dionysius and Meister Eckhart – has been a dominant and determinative theme from the earliest essays in *Writing and Difference* to his more recent essays in *Psyché*, with essays like '*La différance*', *Positions* and '*Comment ne pas parler: dénégations*' as decisive expressions of it. This no doubt stems from, first, his questioning of the logocentric and, secondly, his recognition that in tracing the deconstructive strategy that gives rise to such questioning 'the detours, phrases and syntax that I shall often have to resort to will resemble – will be *practically* indiscernible from – those of negative theology' (*SP*, p. 134, my italics). The question of a text's appearance being distinct from what it wishes to say, the form of negative theology running contrary to its contents, being separable from its contents, sits uneasily alongside Derrida's denunciation of such polarities. The question involved here is put succinctly by John Dominic Crossan: 'Why, then, are the syntactics so similar if the semantics are so different?' (*Semeia* 23, p. 39). Furthermore, is Derrida not privileging meaning in the way his philosophy would forbid? The questions remain unanswered (either by Derrida or Crossan), and can only remain unanswered. Derrida's object is to create 'A community of the question . . . a threatened community, in which the question has not found the language it has decided to seek' (*WD*, p. 80/119).

[15] See Critchley, *Re-reading Levinas*, pp. 107–87. Herman Rapaport, in his recent study *Heidegger and Derrida: Reflections on Time and Language* (Lincoln: University of Nebraska Press, 1989), commenting upon Derrida's 'The Apocalyptic Tone Recently Adopted in Philosophy', writes: it 'amounts to an important turn in Derrida's own writing . . . This "turn" in Derrida is accompanied by an even stranger one, perhaps, which is a

aware in these texts of his own power-games, aware that he too cannot make dogmatic claims and so must avoid doing so, aware that he too is not completely the master of his own discourse and its presuppositions. We can detect sliding or evasion in phrases like 'I think I must defend myself' – an evasion that deepens with reference to 'the register'. For what does he mean here, when he has written so much about the impossibility of a metatext, beyond and circumscribing all textuality and the unavoidability of the apocalyptic? 'Register' slides here. For surely, to some extent he does write employing the tones and rhetorical turns of negative theology – and that is why he feels the need to defend himself against it. He has no more control than any other writer over his tropology. Furthermore, there is the sliding involved in erasure itself: 'to mean [*veut-dire*]' in inverted commas and the evasive move in the phrase 'it is always possible and no doubt "inevitable"'. Is 'inevitable' being emphasized, ironized, or both? And finally there is the liturgical act of confession – 'I concede that' – the humbling which follows an implied sin (of pride?), an implied guilt that before now has remained unconfessed. And since it remains [*demeure*] a question [*comme question*], can a final distinction ever be made between negative theology and the economy of *différance*? Is this not the very nature of Derrida's problem? In drawing our attention to the ontotheological nature of all discourse – however secular its intentions it appeals continually to a metaphysics of presence – Derrida increasingly makes it difficult for himself to locate the possibility for a purely non-theological discourse.

Developing this line of thought further leads to the third of my observations about the economy of *différance* – an observation associated with negative theology. In the economy of the mediation there necessarily arises a question concerning the nature of the mediation itself as it upsets, yet requires and to some extent relates antimonies. '*Différance* ... indicates the

turn from ontology to theology ... by way of a re-examination of the philosophy of Emmanuel Levinas' (pp. 16–17). It is an interesting comment, but it would be a mistake to read this 'turn' in Derrida's work as comparable with Heidegger's *Kehre*. The 'turn' to theology is required for any investigation into the nature of discourse. Derrida's turn is a necessary development in his own investigation.

middle voice, it precedes and sets up the opposition between passivity and activity' (*SP*, p. 130), Derrida writes. But *différance* is not a thing in itself, it carries no ontological charge – despite the metaphors of causation used to describe its operation. It is not an origin but the play of heterogeneous origins. It is not, then, simply a *tertium quid*, but functions as an undecidable between passivity and activity.[16] It does not strictly relate the two sides of the antinomy; in fact, it questions such relationships and correspondences. *Différance* stands, then, opposed to the mediation of *analogia entis* which constitutes the very metaphysics of presence and is the clearest expression of logocentrism. '[T]ime is continuous by analogy', Derrida writes, for analogy and correspondence 'lead back, by other names ... to the *enigma* of the "at the same time"' (*MP*, p. 58). It follows from this that all forms of interventionist revelation – 'nows analogous to points' (*MP*, p. 61) – must rest upon an implicit *analogia entis*. What *différance* describes is how analogies and correspondences function 'by other names', and constitute the very dynamics of representation. This 'brings the problematic of the analogy of Being, its equivocalness or unequivocalness, into communication with the problematic of the metaphor in general' (*MP*, p. 184).

It is the problem of metaphor (summed up in the untranslatable *plus de metaphor*[17]) that occupies Derrida in 'White Mythology' (1971) and its supplement '*Le retraite de la metaphor*' (1978). The problem is simply that metaphor always promises more than it can give. It creates the possibility for the ideal while simultaneously undermining it. Philosophical idealism 'is produced in the separation ... between philosophy ... and rhetoric

---

[16] Derrida writes that *différance*, along with 'supplement', 'trace' and 'pharmakon' 'destroy the trinitarian horizon. They destroy it *textually* (*D*, p. 25)'. That is, they destroy the possibility of a third, common ground of meaning. They prevent antinomies being 'dialectically sublated into a third term'. One of the disappointments of Kevin Hart's book is that he does not engage with Trinitarian theology, nor with the question of the *tertium quid*.

[17] A phrase meaning both 'more metaphor' (or possibly 'the more of metaphor' or 'more than metaphor') and 'no more metaphor' (or possibly 'no more by metaphor' or 'no more than metaphor'). The ambiguity is partly one of the nature of the 'de' – whether it is instrumental, partitive or genitive – and partly the colloquialism of the negative 'plus de'.

... [I]t is this separation and this hierarchy that we must question' (*MP*, p. 224). For propositions are composed of 'signs (words/concepts) ... [which] already have their own metaphorical charge. They are metaphorical resisting every meta-metaphorics' (ibid.). The movement of idealization – the movement of philosophical dialectics or the *Aufhebung* or the movement of negative theology towards the transcendental signified – is the attempt to master and overturn this metaphoricity. In the conquest of mediation lies the possibility of directly gazing upon the unveiled truth. Hence metaphor's relation to mimesis, on the one hand, and the analogy of being, on the other; representation and the real presence. An unconquerable metaphoricity is the character of the mark, the character of mediation. Furthermore, it is metaphoricity which perpetuates mediation, for its ever-promised presence calls forth the chain of signifers, the syntax of supplementation, which attempts to dissolve the metaphors. Metaphors are always attempting to overreach themselves.[18]

In a sense, then, Derrida's concentration upon mediation, on the *re* of representation, is sceptical of the analogy which always requires a 'transcategorical condition of the categories' (*MP*, p. 195). This is why he is sceptical of Levinas's use of the analogy of appresentation – because Levinas (unlike Husserl) allows it to function in the sphere of the transcategorical (as an analogy of illeity). In the next chapter we will consider the extent to which this scepticism also throws its mantle over Barth's *analogia fidei*. For the moment, we need to re-emphasize the quasi-transcendence that this leads to for Derrida. Concept is not reduced to metaphor, reference does not disappear – but the rhetorical nature of the concept and the ineradicable sign that constitutes the name, cloud any clear and direct perspective. Words are not windows of transparent but coloured, bubbled glass.

What remains important for theology is that Derrida explores, like Wittgenstein before him,[19] the very limits of language. Derrida is not denying an outside to language – words refer and concepts conceive: 'The outside penetrates and thus

---

[18] It is metaphoricity which is struck through by metonymy – by the syntagmatic chain of words for word substitutions. See note 5.
[19] See Henry Straten's *Wittgenstein and Derrida*.

determines the inside' (*LI*, pp. 152–3). But actually to determine
the character of this outside – to give it a theological reading (*à la*
Eckhart) or an atheological reading (*à la* Mark C. Taylor) –
would be *hâtive* (with its positive connotations of 'too early',
'premature' as well as its more negative one, 'ill-considered').
This is precisely the boundary between philosophy (which keeps
the question in play) and theology (which has decided this
'outside' is plenitude or God). Derrida writes that 'what indeed I
try to "deconstruct" seems to me, insofar as it is desire or need, to
be indestructible, or, I would even venture to say, "immortal"
... Indestructible desire or need, then, but of what, precisely?'
(*LI*, p. 116). Derrida's economy of *différance* is an indestructible
economy of desire. But that desire is neither simple nor single: it
is both a desire for – for self-presence, for completion, for
salvation (speaking theologically) – and a desire of – the
economy of *différance* itself, the play that continually puts into
play and keeps in play. Derrida never answers his own question.
It remains open-ended – for the desire is the operation of this
question. It is in investigating the depths of questioning, in
tracing the quest as it adheres to the very structure of language
and desire, that Derrida self-consciously draws alongside the
theological.

THE ECONOMY OF DESIRE

There remains the 'trace', for 'that which gives us to think
beyond the closure cannot simply be absent' (*MP*, p. 65).
Levinas reads it as the trace of the wholly other, and Derrida
reads the 'archi-trace as erasure: erasure of the present and thus
of the subject' (*WD*, p. 229/339). The 'trace' for Levinas is
origin; for Derrida it is non-origin, or rather difference itself – the
difference between two antithetical origins. And, in that sense,
the origin of origins. Commenting clearly upon Levinas, Derrida writes, 'An unerasable trace is not a trace, it is a full presence
... a son of God, a sign of parousia' (*WD*, p. 230/339). The
'trace' is present only as it is being erased by another signifier in
the ever-continuing chain of signifiers where meaning is always
being supplemented and deferred. '[I]ts force of production

stands in necessary relation to the energy of its erasure' (*D*, p. 331). The very deferral and promise of presence is the site for the operation of the trace. The trace is that which exceeds both presence and absence. It 'elude[s] that which might maintain its presence' (*MP*, p. 65).

Once again, this form of thinking is a speculative transcendental argument which continually forestalls and questions a final synthesis, a unity of apperception. In itself it makes apparent that neither 'trace' nor *différance* can be understood theologically as names for God. This does not prevent the archi-trace being 'read' theologically as the unnameable one, as the one who calls for (and forth) separation and differences. Such a reading would be a reinscription of Derrida which Derrida himself sees as all too possible (if not inevitable). But such a reading would involve a commitment of faith beyond Derrida's philosophical thinking – it would involve the foreclosure of philosophical thinking. In itself, the economy of *différance* is not a negative theology, and it is arguable whether negative theology does operate deconstructively.[20] Those, then, who would wish to see a *rapprochement* between Derrida and theology, whilst limiting the hermeneutical violence of reinscribing him in a theological discourse, must look elsewhere. They must look, it seems to me, at the economy of *différance* as an economy of conflicting desires. If metaphoricity engenders questioning then we must examine closely the dynamics of this questioning, the theology of this questioning and the 'spirituality' of mediation. Derrida appears to be doing exactly

---

[20] This is Hart's thesis. *Pace* Hart, I would submit that there is an important distinction between the openness of *différance* and the openness of negative theology. There is a difference between the necessity of leaving open the question as question and the necessity of leaving open the question of identifying a transcendent Being. Negative theology, on Derrida's terms, must operate within a 'restricted economy'. This is the very point being made in '*Comment ne pas parler*', an essay which is not examined in Hart's thesis. The economy of *différance* is 'radically inhuman and atheological' (*P*, p. 570). Hart wishes to see negative theology as a 'form of deconstruction' (p. 186) or as 'a deconstructive discourse' (p. 189). But for Derrida there is no single form of deconstruction or a deconstructive discourse as such. There is discourse, and Derrida examines the elisions of meaning caused by the economy of *différance* as it manifests itself in this discourse. There is no isolatable deconstructive form that negative theology can compare itself to. Negative theology is a language-use. *Différance* is a language-condition.

this in his most recent work *Psyché* and *Of Spirit*.[21] It is a work that is characterized by a return to Heidegger, a sharpening of the debate with negative theology, a re-reading of Levinas's work and a re-examination of the older metaphysical terms 'soul' and 'spirit'.[22]

There are three characteristics or themes in this recent work that I wish to draw out, each bearing upon the examination of desire within the economy of *différance*.

First, the texts explicitly treating Heidegger's thinking – '*Geschlect I*' (1983), '*Geschlect II*' (1985) and *Of Spirit* (1987) – all consider the difficulty of translation.[23] *Différance* has always implied, and demonstrates within itself, the difficulty of translation. Translation implies, as Walter Benjamin[24] and George Steiner have shown, a universal language in order that meaning can become convertible and transferable. *Différance* calls into question the metaphysics of such a meaning. It draws attention to a certain autism, or solipsism about language. But Derrida is

---

[21] Hart's book does not do this. He concentrates upon Derrida's earlier work and does not see how Derrida's work has developed. Derrida has moved from the discursive style of his essays in *Writing and Difference*, through the mix of genres in *Glas*, to the essays in *Psyché* which deepen the questions of his earlier work both in terms of form and theme.

[22] Of course, in Greek, French and German these words have a wide range of connotations. They are complex, polysemic words and that is why Derrida examines how they are being employed, how their meanings slip and slide, how they evade accurate translation. But that these words remain metaphysical and theological is not without significance for Derrida. In fact, it is the metaphysical and theological elements in their polysemy which attracts him to them.

[23] In '*Geschlecht I*', we have 'the thought of *Geschlecht* and that of translation are essentially the same' (*DR*, p. 391/*P*, p. 405). In '*Geschlecht II*' we have Derrida's admission 'I am already settled in the untranslatable idiom of my language [French], for I certainly intend to speak to you about translation' (*DR*, p. 166/*P*, p. 421). In the opening chapter of *Of Spirit*, Derrida states that one of his intentions in what follows is to put the Germanness of *Geist* 'to the test of translation, or rather if we put to the test its resistence to translation' (*OS*, p. 4).

Derrida has always been aware of the significance of 'translation' for his economy of *différance* (see 'Freud and the Scene of Writing' in *Writing and Difference*, particularly, pp. 213–14). But there is a greater interest in the topic of translation more recently, which perhaps arises from the 1979 Colloquium at the University of Montreal and its roundtable discussions with Derrida on translation. These discussions later appear as *The Ear of the Other*, in 1985. It was in 1979 that Derrida published his essay 'Living On: Borderlines' in which he first talks extensively about translation.

[24] See Derrida's examination of Benjamin's theological understanding of translation in his essay '*Des Tours de Babel*' (1980), in *Psyché* (translated in part in *DR*, pp. 243–54).

aware that translation is possible – his own work has reached a wide audience on the basis of translation. Translation, then, like *différance*, moves between the poles of universalism and particularity. 'A text lives only if it lives *on*, and it lives *on* only if it is *at once* translatable *and* untranslatable ... The same thing will be said of what I call writing, mark, trace and so on' (*EO*, p. 128). In his recent essays on Heidegger, the critical incisions he makes into Heidegger's work are both at places where translating is difficult and at places where the meaning of words such as '*Geschlect*', '*Ört*', '*geistlich*' and '*geistig*' slide and vary in use. Derrida points to how these places are blindspots in Heidegger's thinking. Despite the range and play of meaning, Heidegger privileges 'gathering', the site of origin. But these blindspots are also places where often Heidegger digs deeply into his own language and returns to the old, High German idiom. They are identified in the text by the density of their idiom. For Derrida they are places where deconstruction is already in operation, undermining Heidegger's intention to gather and find the site of origin.

Secondly, and not unrelated, these more recent essays by Derrida explore a recognition that it is an 'analogical continuity [between Being and that which is beyond Being which] permits translation' (*P*, p. 564). This return to the possibility of analogy arises from his negotiation with Levinas's work, and Levinasian themes echo throughout his work on Heidegger.[25] But his exploration is not always done through Levinas's *oeuvre*. For now Derrida begins a specifically theological investigation into analogical correspondence and negative theology – summed up in his highly important essay '*Comment ne pas parler*'. We will look at this exploration in more detail in the next chapter when we examine Barth's *analogia fidei* in terms of Derrida's recognition of the need for, the use, and yet the impossibility of, analogical predication.

Thirdly, there is a movement in this more recent work

---

[25] Derrida claims both Heidegger and Levinas subordinate sexual difference to the sexual neutrality of that which is beyond and dessiminates difference: Dasein, on the one hand, and illeity, on the other (although illeity is, as we have seen, provocatively masculine as a term).

towards 'spiritualizing' the economy of representation – that is, redescribing the economy through distinctively theological categories. *Différance*, 'trace', 'dessimination', 'deconstruction' and 'supplement' weave in and out of these texts, but there is a new note sounding. Towards the end of '*Geschlect I*' Derrida concludes that beyond sexual difference in Heidegger's work we 'accede once again to an ontological or "transcendental" dispersion' (*DR*, p. 397/*P*, p. 410). A 'hierarchical accentuation . . . comes to mark the neutral and dispersion' in such a way that Heidegger 'avoids religious, ethical, indeed even dialectical schemes, claiming to go back further or "higher" than they' (*DR*, p. 399/*P*, p. 412). In '*Geschlect II*' Derrida traces the changes in understanding the word '*Geschlect*' in Heidegger's later work, and concludes that 'the primordial sexual difference is tender, gentle, peaceful' (*DR*, p. 193/*P*, p. 451). 'The primordiality (pre-Platonic, pre-metaphysical, or pre-Christian) to which Heidegger recalls us . . . *has no other content and even no other language* than that of Platonism and Christianity. This primordiality is simply that starting from which things like metaphysics and Christianity are possible and thinkable' (ibid.). The concluding chapter of *Of Spirit* takes up the same theme. Here, in a complex book which traces the changes and dissemination of *Geist* in Heidegger's work, Derrida unveils in the depths of the question the '*Versprechen*', 'the promise which, opening every speaking, makes possible the very question . . . Language always, *before any question*, and in every question, comes down to [*revient à*][26] the promise. This would also be a promise *of spirit*' (*OS*, p. 94). The emphasis (which is Derrida's) draws attention to the ambiguity of the genitive – it can be either the promise belonging to the spirit (already given/being given) or the promise of the spirit (yet to be given). This is, *in nuce*, what the spirit has been seen to be doing through Derrida's book on Heidegger, for it is 'divided by an internal difference' (*OS*, p. 95) and this 'is the spirit in which it inscribes itself, traces itself, retires, or retracts. It

---

[26] The French is important for two reasons. First, one of the words echoing throughout many of these recent essays is the apocalyptic or quasi-apocalyptic '*Viens*'. Secondly, there is a play through *Of Spirit* on '*revenant*', 'ghost', woven into a text concerned with *Geist*, its movement and operation.

belongs to the flame it divides' (*OS*, p. 106). 'Spirit-in-flames' is Derrida's third affirmative determination of 'spirit' in Heidegger's work (*OS*, p. 97).

It is not simply that Derrida is beginning to relocate Heidegger within a theological context in this more recent work. Spirit is beginning to redescribe the double-bind of *différance*, or perhaps we could say *différance* itself is being related to a theological context. The spirit promises, and so in the final chapter of Derrida's book on Heidegger there is an imaginary dialogue between Heidegger and Christian theologians, a dialogue in which Heideggerian thinking negotiates with themes in Levinas's work and Christian negative theology. Here the economy of *différance* is traced in terms of the spirit which keeps open the question in 'the internal logic of this discourse' (*OS*, p. 99), which 'cannot not promise as soon as it speaks, it is promise, but it cannot fail to break its promise' (*OS*, p. 94). Derrida explicitly asks: 'can it not be demonstrated that the question does no more than *defer* ... (through difference and *différance* of difference) the quest and the inquiry?' (*OS*, p. 119). *Différance* is now described in terms of the question and the interminable quest. The dynamic of this quest, giving rise to supplementarity, is the spirit in whom 'the eternal possibility of the worst is already lodged ... the conflagration of the flame which burns itself up' (*OS*, p. 97). The spirit both consumes and perpetuates. And it is 'because *Geist* is flame that there is *pneuma* or *spiritus*' (ibid.). Levinas would call this dynamic in-spiration.

Derrida is negotiating his own work with and through Heidegger's and Levinas's. It is a negotiation which opens up their differences and returns to their similarities. At the end of 'At this very moment in this work', we have already noted that Derrida posits the female voice in order to introduce a radical difference into Levinas's work – the female as the other of the wholly other. But she, '*elle*', is also associated with Levinas, referred to as E.L. many times in the essay, and associated too with Derrida (whose Hebrew name, Elijah, is, in French, '*Elie*'). The final comment in the essay is a masculine one which says: 'I no longer know if you are saying what his work says. Perhaps it comes back to the same. I no longer know if you are saying contrary, or if you have already written something wholly other. I no longer hear your voice, I have difficulty distinguishing it from mine, from any other, your fault suddenly becomes illegible to me. Interrupt me' (*DR*, p. 438/*P*, p. 201). The floating personal pronouns means that 'you' [*tu*] could either be '*la lectrice*' or E.L..

The essay 'At this very moment in this work' issues into a funeral liturgy in which the 'body of our interlaced voices' (voices laced together with 'el' [*entre(el)acées*]) is buried. The body is given to Levinas with the words – returning us to Jewish and Christian metaphors and quotations from Levinas's own work – 'look here I am eat – approach – in order to give to him [*lui*] – drink' (*P*, p. 202). The liturgy is both a funeral and a eucharist – a ritual of absence and departure and a ritual of presence and incorporation. *Différance* issues into a liturgical movement celebrating repetition and the conflict of opposites. The liturgy is, finally, written by Derrida in a dense and cadenced prose, but it also suggests (as does the whole essay) that it is authored elsewhere, that its origin is hieratic and its movement theological. *Écriture* ('writing' or 'Scripture'), has been a favoured word by Derrida since his early essays.

In an interview given in 1990, Derrida explains why 'I have been most cautious with the word "desire", though of course I consider that everything has to be explained by desire ... My concern was to develop a *différance* whereby desire was not seen as a matter of consciousness. If there is desire, it is *because* there is *différance*. This psychologism, this anthropologism bothered me.'[27] Desire as the economy of the spirit is a move beyond the psyche. It is a move within words and beyond them, without explicitly embracing the Word. The economy of *différance* is the operation whereby an author 'authors'. To ally the economy of desire with the economy of the spirit in the way Derrida has been doing in his most recent work is to emphasize that *différance* operates beyond phenomenology and ontology and yet within them both. *Différance* becomes the structure of lived experience

[27] Interview with Raoul Mortley in *French Philosophers in Conversation* (London: Routledge, 1991), p. 101.

('Deconstruction is life to me'[28]), but experience open, to some extent, to the outside. To live the question is to live on the threshold. To live the question is to live the sign, the mediation and the suggestion of promise. It is to live aware of one's finitude, for death as erasure, is inscribed in every sign: 'the *overabundance* of the signifier, its *supplementary* character, is thus the result of a finitude, that is to say, the result of a lack which must be *supplemented*' (*WD*, p. 290/425). To live with this question is not paralysing, it is to participate in a dynamic which is both exterior and interior to language. It is to live also with a quest and the quest as somehow a response to a sending, the trace of a past that cannot be avoided.[29]

Différance calls the theological into play, lends weight to the ineradicable nature of the theological question in and of language. As Derrida wrote in 1967, at the opening of *Of Grammatology*, 'the intelligible face of the sign remains turned towards the Word and the face of God' (*OG*, p. 13). *Différance* sharpens the presence of the Word while trying to maintain itself as beyond the sacred/secular dichotomy, as a metadiscourse internal to discourse. It can only be seen to function through an analysis which continually traverses the theological and draws attention to the necessity of faith or dogmatism for determinative meaning and reference. As the structure of experience ('history as *différance*'), *différance* inscribes anthrolopogy. But it is a theological anthropology because it suggests that although we cannot talk about God, and have no direct knowledge of Him, neither can we cease talking about God, and having the promise of knowledge about Him. *Différance*, examined theologically, becomes the play between the presence and the impossibility of God.[30]

[28] *Postmodernism: ICA Documents*, p. 223.

[29] Sending has been another important theme in Derrida's work since *The Post Card* and his essay '*Envois*' (both 1980). Missives form a textual space in which the play of 'traces' and representations are inscribed. The theme of 'sending' owes much to a demythologized account of Heidegger's call of Being and the givenness of Being (*es gibt*). This responding to the other again recalls Levinas and raises the question Critchley explores so admirably of the ethics of deconstruction. Derrida explored the structure of responding, the desire, the 'yes' and the 'promise' throughout the eighties.

[30] See Richard Sugarman's distinction between the absence and the non-existence of God in Levinas in *Judaism* 28, (1979). Absence is important for Levinas because it does not imply non-existence, but 'the phenomenon of absence positively informs our

It underscores, for theology, the necessity of what Donald MacKinnon once termed 'a very healthy agnosticism'.[31] The word 'God' plays between the Yes in the No of our world. This is the possibility for the impossibility of the Word in our words – the possibility not that God himself appears, but in the economy of theological representation that Jesus Christ is the scene for the impossible made possible; the text for the Word made words. As Derrida has said, *différance* is not the name of the unnameable God. But Christianity's God became a name in Jesus of Nazareth. In terms, then, of a Trinitarian theology, can *différance* operate as a description for what takes place in Jesus Christ as the mediating Word, the mark and the trace?

Derrida does not retract his famous statement that there is nothing outside the text. We all remain caught up in pastiche, in quotation marks, in the iterability of the sign which defers meaning and unmediated knowledge. Nevertheless, *différance* can only define itself within the theological, or, put another way, it cannot define itself with-out the theological. The position is summed up in a few lines from '*Ulysse Gramophone: Deux Mots pour Joyce*' (1987). Here is the pastiche, the quotations, the verbal play, the trace of the Yes which is the dynamic both for the movement of the chain of signifiers and for their displacement. 'In the beginning, there must have been some phone call . . . we hear it resonate unceasingly. And it sets off within itself this *yes* towards which we slowly, moving in circles around it, return' (*DR*, p. 572). Here too is a theology of the Spirit and the Word.

In wishing now to develop the importance of a theological reading of *différance*, the economy (even the spirituality) of the sign, we now need to re-engage Barth in a negotiation with Derrida. We will do this by returning again to chapter 5 of *Church Dogmatics* and examining it in relation to Derrida's essay on negative theology '*Comment ne pas parler*'. For Barth too upbraided those 'theologians who fail to perceive that its

understanding of everyday events' (p. 221). For Derrida no such distinction is made – the absence of God could well imply the non-existence as the hiddenness of God. There is no way, philosophically, of determining which is correct. It is the play of possibilities which is significant.

[31] *The Problem of Metaphysics* (Cambridge: Cambridge University Press, 1974), p. 118.

[Christendom's] truth must be sought not merely beyond all negation ... but beyond even the possibility of contrasting 'Yes' and 'No' ... or of ranging them in a casual sequence, and so playing them off one against another' (*2R*, p. 204/185). What will occupy us in our final chapter is the extent to which Derrida's description of the economy of representation can be read Christologically, and whether this is not exactly what Barth is attempting to do in the closing pages of chapter 5.

CHAPTER 11

Barth and the economy of différance

In a famous attack on Barth, Richard Roberts concludes: 'Wherever the content of revelation and its time draws close to the reality common to humanity, ambiguity results, because the "reality" of revelation must both affirm and deny, recreate and annihilate at the same moment. This ambiguity is consistent with the double-edged quality of much of Barth's talk of man ... and is based upon the fundamental theological developments which led to the adoption of the "analogy of faith".'[1] For Roberts, this 'ambiguity' is the great logical flaw whereby the *Church Dogmatics* rides above us like a Cathedral on a vast cloud. What I wish to argue is that this 'ambiguity', which develops and adopts the analogy of faith, is a precursor for Derrida's *différance*.

MEDIATION, METAPHOR AND THE SPIRIT WHICH QUESTIONS

Throughout chapter 5 of *Church Dogmatics* Barth wishes to stress concurrently two antithetical positions: first, that truth is not immediate, but mediated; secondly, that with this mediation appropriate to us 'we do have to do with the truth of the truth itself' (ii.1, p. 68/73). The first position is related to the second through a Trinitarian openness, but it is antithetical to the second because Barth insists there is no third term between ourselves and the truth. There is a mediating person, Jesus Christ as Son and Word. But since this person is the perfected human nature, not human nature as we know it, the question

[1] 'The Doctrine of Time in Karl Barth', *Theology on the Way*, p. 144.

remains concerning the nature of this mediation or the logic of Christ's representation.

The forms of representation in chapter 5 are multiple. They focus around the employment of different verbs with the sense of 'to represent' and different nouns with the sense of 'representation'. Mediation has three distinct and not always complementary forms: a form associated with the verbs *eintreten* and *vertreten*, a form associated with the verbs *darstellen* and *vorstellen* and a form associated with the verb *repraesentieren*. Within the dialectic structure of chapter 5[2] it is the first two counterpoising forms which are more in evidence. What we need to examine are the distinct epistemologies implied by these forms of presentation, representation and performance.[3]

---

[2] 'Dialectical thinking' in Barth is a complex issue. See chapter 4. There are two interrelated forms of dialectic in operation. Barth speaks of them both when he describes revelation rupturing the 'dialectic which still remains on our part; yet not in such a way that we are still in the grip of that dialectic; rather in such a way that the dialectic is directed and controlled from the side of the event which is God's part' (II.1, p. 75/81). This entry of an 'undialectical certainty', then, establishes 'the dialectic of certainty and uncertainty which is our part of the event' (II.1, p. 74/81). The first dialectic is a positive and immanent dialectic of reasoning; a transcendental dialectic. The second is a negative dialectic which demands that the idealism of the transcendental radically questions itself. This dialectical complexity is one of the cruxes of the modern/postmodern debate. Two questions emerge. The first question concerns the location for the operation of these two antithetical forms of dialectic. Barth would say 'proclamation', 'Scripture' and 'preaching'. Derrida would embrace each of these within his more general economy of mediation, or what he terms the *scène d'écriture*. The second question concerns the consequences of this ongoing dialectical antagonism. That question is neither easily nor quickly answered. In fact, it cannot be answered without returning to one form of the dialectics in negotiation. That question has to remain, then, a question. We are pushed into finally asking what are the consequences of this unanswerable question for theology? The consequences, surely, would be a theology of the question itself and a theological method which would oscillate between statement and interrogation. As Barth explains (for this is one of the axes of Barth's theology and theological method), 'We can only repeat ourselves . . . in the last resort infinitely . . . [O]ur . . . line of thought reveals a vacuum within us which is decisive for the whole' (II.1, pp. 250–2). A theology of the question would concern itself with a fundamental openness. Not simply an anthropological openness (*à la* Gadamer, Ricoeur and Pannenberg), but a more originary and transcendent openness. It would negotiate these opennesses as they inhere to that which constructs reality for us: modes of representation or discourse. That is why Derrida remains fundamental for a re-thinking of contemporary theology. See Derrida's *Aporias*, trans. Thomas Dutoit (Stanford: Stanford University Press, 1993) where this 'openness' is related to the possibility of one's death.

[3] By 'presentation' I am suggesting an ontological repetition of *what* is presented in *the means by which* it is presented. The latter fully participates in the reality of the former. 'Presentation' as such has the syntax of tautology or a Kantian analytical judgement.

First, there is the knowledge of God presented in [*eintreten*] any
creaturely reality encountered by the particularity of the revelatory event [*Ereignis*]. This creaturely reality becomes God's
'clothing, temple or sign'. There is no ontological correspondence for the creaturely reality does not become identical with
God, but God enters it. The form of representation here is closely
related to the immediacy of revelation. It is the immediacy
which signifies. The medium is an object familiar to us, but
Barth leaves unclear in his concept of 'entering in' how we would
recognize that this creaturely reality has been 'invested'. This
form of representation describes God's relation to the object, but
not ours. The creaturely reality becomes a medium from God's
point of view, but it is unclear how His presence is presented to
us. The revelation has no content as such, for we could not know
whether it had indeed taken place. If we are to believe it has
taken place, if we are to take this creaturely reality as an analogy
of faith, then upon what grounds does 'this piece of his [man's]
environment [*einem Stück der ihn umgebenden*]' (II.1, p. 17/17)
rather than any other piece become an object which calls for our
faith?

Related to representation as *eintreten* is a form of representation specifically defining the work of Jesus Christ. We are not
identical with Him, but salvation is effected because he 'represents [*vertritt*] us at the right hand of the Father in our flesh' (II.1,
p. 156/175). Here representation is understood as substitution,
standing in the place of, acting on behalf of. What is emphasized
is the absence of the real object, its inability to be there. We
remain enemies, adopted or annexed, unprepared for Him
(ibid.). Once again, there is no ontological correspondence
between the object and its substitution. But while Barth points
this out, his discourse points up, by constant repetition, that God
is 'for us'. The eternal mode of His being, His eternal capacity to
present Himself (which the Trinity enacts), becomes the ground

By 'representation' I am suggesting an absence of any direct relation or correspondence between *what* is presented and *the means by which* it is represented. Such
representation emerges from the operation of transcendental reasoning and has the
syntax of a Kantian synthetic judgement.

for our 'genuinely participating'.[4] The word 'our' slides. For
Jesus (with whom we are not identical) is 'in our flesh'. The 'is'
slides too, for Christ 'is consubstantial [*gleichen Wesens*] with the
Father' (ibid.). Though the language remains the same, the
words 'our' and 'is' cannot mean the same in both contexts –
otherwise an *analogia entis* would constitute the *tertium quid* Barth
wishes to avoid. It is precisely the nature of that 'our' and that 'is'
in relation to Jesus that is not explicated. It is not only not
explicated, it is concealed by a positivist rhetoric – 'effectually
represented [*wirksam vertreten*]' and 'genuinely participating
[*wirklich teilhaftig*]'. In other words, the logic of the representation only proceeds because of a blindness to the rhetoric that
allows the representation to go ahead. The moment Barth
becomes conscious of the nature of his description of Jesus Christ
as our representation before God, then we must begin again. For
the explication will require another forgetting of the language in
order to describe again a form of representation that cannot be
represented.

We are caught up here in the logic of supplementarity. Barth
is aware 'what follows can only be a sequel [*Folge*] and explanation of this proper and original truth' (ibid.). There is no end to
this supplementarity [*Folge*] because we only ever have to do
with the aftermath of a truth. We handle not revelation but the
memory of revelation. Furthermore, because we are always in
the trail of that which has already passed, our explanation can
never catch up with and present the actual and primary
character of this truth. This can only be done in the ideality of
the Trinity. The explanation is an articulation of the secondary
[*Folge*]. It is a *re*presentation of the presentation; the trace of a
trace. In the logic of this endless supplementation what is never
resolved, what can never be resolved, is the question of who
represents whom, who is the author. The logic of *vertretten* is
caught in a double-bind. Barth represents Jesus Christ who,
before God, represents Barth. But who appoints whom to be that

---

[4] What is suggested here is that 'presentation' is the essential mode of being of the
Trinity, the ground of its perichoresis whereby there is relation in and through
difference. The Trinity is a circle of self-presentation, self-giving; it constitutes the
eternal and ideal dialogue of *Redephilosophie*.

representative? That question can only be kept in play throughout. Keeping the question in play is central both to Barth's and Derrida's method. What Richard Roberts describes as a logical flaw is the appearance of a question whose final answer can only be forestalled. Theological discourse, for Barth, in fact theology for Barth, takes place as a continual negotiation and renegotiation of a problematic that cannot be, cannot be allowed to be, resolved. The fact it remains unsolved, unanswered and illogical is the very point.

Barth employs '*eintreten*' and '*vertreten*', then, as descriptions of Christ's legislative status – '*eintreten*' for his status *vis-à-vis* creaturely reality and '*vertreten*' for his status *vis-à-vis* the Godhead. We saw with the first of these that Christ's mode of presentation is not necessarily represented to us. He could enter creaturely reality without our necessarily being aware of it. The description of Christ's ontological relationship with humankind lacks an epistemological account of how the knowledge, and hence, subsequently, the description, is possible at all. These questions multiply when Christ's mode of representation as '*vertreten*' is added. Here we noted that though this representation (Christ's ontological relationship before God), is again described by Barth, once more an explanation of how this can be known is absent. What are the epistemological grounds for Barth's knowledge and description of this representation when there exists a radical ontological difference between God and creaturely reality? Some form of mediation needs to be outlined.

Barth will employ another set of terms – '*darstellen / Darstellung*' and '*vorstellen/Vorstellung*' – to complicate this picture of the representational process. In the revelation of Jesus Christ, Jesus is the creature who is to take God's place [*vertreten*] and represent [*darzustellen*] Him (II.1, p. 199/223). Here one form of representation is viewed in terms of a second. The relationship between them is neither explicated nor examined. Both infinitives are only related through Barth's own description of Christ's activity. '*Darstellung*' and the verb '*darstellen*' are employed in the sense of an 'account' or 'to give an account', a narrated description. Summing up the way in which the Word relates to words, in chapter 5, Barth speaks of looking 'back at our presentation

[*Darstellung*] of the limits of the knowledge of God' (II.1, p. 246/278). '*Darstellen/Darstellung*' are associated with the human and limited Kantian epistemology. '*Vorstellung*' is employed in the sense of 'points of view' or 'images' that make up such an account or description. For example, commenting upon Augustine's account [*Darstellung*] of his mystical experience at the window in Ostia, Barth writes: 'the knowledge of God is not reached by way of the image [*durch die Vorstellung*] of such timelessness' (II.1, p. 11/10). '*Darstellungen*' and '*Vorstellungen*' stand as human, discursive modes of representation linked to the Kantian transcendental economy of 'viewing, conceiving, speaking' and contradistinctive to '*eintreten*' and '*vertreten*' as divine modes of representation and knowing. The question arises and remains throughout, 'How do we come to say, by means of our language, that which we cannot say at all by this means?' (II.1, p. 220/248). Even this 'how' is caught in a double-bind – for it is both 'by what theological means can we account for the possibility' (i.e. the doctrine of analogy) and 'by what kind of description can we understand the operation of this theological account'. The first treats God's representation and the second Barth's representation. Each form is related to a distinct epistemology – and yet each is caught in the nets of the other. This is the nexus of the problem of knowledge of God and also the problem of understanding Barth's epistemological and positivist representation of it: 'we may certainly have represented [*dagestellt*] and understood the veracity of a cognition [*Erkennen*], but not the veracity of a cognition of *God*, or perhaps a cognition of God, but not the *veracity* of it' (II.1, p. 245/278).

Barth's appreciation that this is the crux of the problematic in chapter 5 leads us to ask what he is doing in insisting the problem should be presented in this way. Put another way, what status is Barth claiming for his own discourse as it mediates these two dialectically opposed epistemologies? Barth insists that God gives Himself to be considered [*anschauen*] and conceived, but 'in this very certainty [*ja vielmehr gerade in ihrer Gewissheit*] it is mediated [*mittelbare*] knowledge' (II.1, p. 9/8). But '*vielmehr gerade*' [rather direct] stands in paradoxical tension to 'mediated'. Furthermore, '*anschauen*' [to perceive, consider or look at], adds a positivist note particularly when contextualized by words like *'wirklich'* [actual, real], *'eigentlich'* [actual, proper, essential] and God's *'Gegenstandlichkeit'* [ability to be an object or concrete]. But it is a positivism contextualized also by the language of mediation. How is *'anschauen'* (and other epistemological words like *'wahrnehmen'* and *'schauen'*) to be read? As a metaphor? As a technical word for a moment in the psychology of cognition? If it is a metaphor, then in what relation does the figure stand to divine reality? If an empirical perception is intended, then God is not Other, for He would be implicated within the noema-noesis structure of intentionality. Barth's discourse moves between two epistemological frameworks – an empirical epistemology in which sense data receives its meaning through a transcendental operation of consciousness and a theological epistemology which hints at, but cannot articulate, an alternative, immediate form of knowing. Barth does not clarify metaphorical from non-metaphorical language-use. Furthermore he is aware of the shifting sands upon which he is building his dogmatics. He takes words freighted with epistemological weight and places them within a theological context which displaces or disrupts their common meaning without his actually redefining their new theological sense. Their theological sense cannot be defined, that is the point. They take on a new sense by means of context. This sense is analogical, but only accessible as such by faith. By faith, we read this epistemological vocabulary as properly and originally belonging to a divine and not a human epistemology.

The doctrine of *analogia fidei* emerges from Barth's engagement with *doing* theology. It is a reflection upon Barth's own mode of discourse, upon what he is already practising. It is an articulation which only emerges from praxis or performance. It is a mode of discourse which negotiates between antinomies *as a process*. It handles, details and weaves a relationship between these antinomies whilst insisting upon the radical difference which makes them distinct. Barth, then, can speak of God's objective presence 'in a double sense' (II.1, p. 10/9). The heart of this double sense is a transcendental relationship established in difference [*Unterschied*] which discourse expresses. In such a discourse, God's revelation is posited while simultaneously calling into question human representation, 'ideas', 'points of view' and 'accounts'. It is a discourse with a self-ironizing alertness to its own language or textuality.[5] The 'undialectical certainty' is the 'other side' of the 'dialectic of certainty and uncertainty which is our part [*unser Teil*] in this event [*Geschehen*]' (II.1, p. 74/81). For our part and from our part this 'undialectical certainty' can only be a trace of the truth, a hint of transcendence, and therefore, to us, a quasi-transcendence. And this is the economy of Derrida's *différance*: 'Our discourse irreducibly belongs to the system of metaphysical oppositions. The break with this structure of belonging can be announced only through a certain organisation, a certain *strategic* arrangement which, within the field of metaphysical opposition, uses the strengths of the field to turn its own stratagems against it, producing a dislocation that spreads itself throughout the entire system, fissuring it in every direction and thoroughly delimiting it' (*WD*, p. 20/34).

Representation as '*repraesentieren*' lies behind Barth's mediating economy and textual strategy. This is a much more general word.[6] It is a term he does not discuss in chapter 5, though he rigorously discusses it throughout chapter 1, 'The Word of God as the Criterion for Dogmatics'. For a general word it is employed quite specifically with reference to proclamation as the Word of God. Proclamation is the announcement and repetition of His promise that 'I am with you always' (I.1, pp. 58–9/59). It is a re-presentation then of what was given in the past and remains promised for the future. Proclamation moves between memory and fulfilment and consists of one's own words repeating God's Yes for humankind. Such a proclamation is 'a

[5] Cf. three interesting studies of the textuality of Barth's theology: George Lindbeck's 'Barth and Textuality' in *Theology Today*, 43 (1988); Stephen H. Webb's *Re-Figuring Theology: The Rhetoric of Karl Barth* (Albany: State University of New York Press, 1991); David Klemm's 'Towards a Rhetoric of Postmodern Theology through Barth and Heidegger', *Journal of the American Academy of Religion*, 55/3. The last two scholars are particularly interested in Barth's metaphor of 'Crisis' in his early theology.

[6] *Duden* and *Brockhaus* associate *repraesentieren* both to its Latin root as *vergegenwartigen*, *darstellen* and *vorstellen* (forms of description and depiction) and to *vertreten* or standing in for a general type or specific value (a form of role). *Repraesentieren* is a general word able to refer to both.

representation [*Repraesentation*] of God's Word' (ibid.). Theology (as dogmatics) is not proclamation, it reflects upon proclamation and presents [*darstellt*] 'investigation and polemic, criticism and correction' (1.1, p. 82/84).

'*Repraesentation*' is linked specifically to a discourse's ability to repeat and present the eschatological promise of full and immediate self-presence, 'I am with you always.' That promise resounds within preaching and the sacraments (discourse and symbols), speaking of the power of God's Word (1.1, p. 60/61). It is always 'only a strictly representative action [*Handung*]'. In order 'to represent this basis of promise it must not consist in further words; it has to be action' (1.1, pp. 60–1/61). '*Repraesentieren*' is the movement of the promise in and in spite of words. It is neither direct presentation [*eintreten*], nor equivocating mediation [*darstellen*], but the tracing of a repeated promise (Derrida's 'Yes, Yes'), a promise moving between its past announcement and its future fulfilment. '*Repraesentieren*' is the movement of discourse itself – discourse aware of its nature as circulating the repetition and memory of a promise that was its origin.

Barth as a writer, and we as readers, are caught in the webs of different forms of representation in which rhetoric chases the immediacy of truth. Barth's appreciation of this necessitates his flawed logic. For the system of salvation cannot be fully outlined and doctrines cannot be tidily expounded.[7] Where the logic of explanation falters there emerges a logic of the movement of Barth's theological discourse itself. And this, I would argue, is more fundamental to Barth and proceeds along lines very similar to Derrida's *différance*, for Derrida too is placing 'the chain of discursive knowledge in relation to an unknowledge which is not a moment of knowledge'. This unknowledge 'will be the absolute excess of every *episteme*, of every philosophy and every science. Only a *double position* can account for this unique relation' (*WD*, p. 268–9/394). Barth's *analogia fidei*, issuing itself

---

[7] In fact, Barth warns us against reading his work in terms of constructed arguments for timeless, unambivalent doctrinal positions, throughout the Introduction to *Church Dogmatics*. The task of dogmatics 'consists in the "conflict against the self-assurance of the modern spirit"' (1.1, p. 27/26). Furthermore, there is no progress 'made towards the answering of its own specific question of knowledge nor towards the establishment of its own body of knowledge' (1.1, p. 29/28).

from a 'double position', anticipates Derrida's own 'unique relation'. Derrida speaks of this 'double law' as 'the double law of Mnemosyne' (*MPM*, p. 51), because memory [*Erinnerung*] recalls the presence of a promise once given and as yet unfulfiled (*MPM*, p. 57). As Barth has it, ' "God with us" ... becomes the truth for us as recollection [*Erinnerung*] and also as promise' (1.1, p. 120/123).

DOUBLING AND THE LOGIC OF MYSTERY

For Barth, the truth of theology lies in this necessity yet impossibility of rendering an account. Caught between divine and human representation, 'the movement of faith or rather the movement of God's Word which only faith can follow, is described [*beschrieben*] ... as twofold' (1.1, p. 176/183–4). Its twofoldedness cannot be dissolved because there can be no synthesis. 'Faith means recognising that synthesis cannot be attained' (1.1, p. 175/182). As a dialectic, then, it has its back firmly turned upon Hegelian idealism. In fact, the 'twofold indirectness' (1.1, p. 169/175) is a prerequisite, for not only is faith thereby invoked, it is also maintained. To have knowledge of 'how far the veiled Word now means unveiling or the unveiled Word means veiling' would be to destroy the very mystery of the Word of God and turn it into 'a paradox like others' (1.1, p. 174/181). The very lack of explanation and clarity constitutes the mystery.[8] The weaving of these two epistemologies (related to the two models of language, '*Redephilosophie*' and '*Sprachphiloso-phie*', outlined in the first part of this book) cannot be foreclosed.[9] There is an inability to complete the logic of the 'unique

[8] This 'mystery' of the Word in human words is akin to Levinas's concept of 'enigma'. In his essay 'Phenomenon and Enigma', Levinas states that 'All speaking is an enigma' (*CP*, p. 69), just as Barth, writes that 'there is no genuinely profane speech. In the last resort, there is only talk about God' (1.1, p. 47/47). For Levinas, the enigma is the recognition on our side of the presence of the other (*CP*, p. 66).

[9] In '*Comment ne pas parler: dénégrations*', Derrida writes that 'the theologian is forced to practise ... the double inscription of his knowledge ... At the crossing of two languages, each of which "bears" the silence of the other, a secret must and must not be divulged' (*P*, pp. 556–7). This crossing is also the site of *différance*. Theological discourse must function then within and by means of the economy of *différance* where two languages meet.

relation'; and this is essential and constitutive. What remains on our side is the *movement* of faith in its engagement with this mystery, this incommensurable aporia. Faith describes what cannot be described, represents a representation which cannot be represented. The movement of faith is the movement of Barth's own discourse 'as it seeks to reproduce [*nachzusprechen*] the actuality of this relation' (1.1, p. 168/175). The logic, then, of Barth's theological discourse lies not in the analysis of concepts and the explication of their relation to each other, but in tracing [*beschreiben*] the deferral of any final explication which adheres to the very act of attempting such an explication. Barth's theological discourse traces how the mystery of otherness evades domestication, how this evasion prevents foreclosure, and generates supplementary attempts to argue for or to this otherness.[10]

Derrida, in noting a similar process in Nietzsche's work, speaks of a 'regular, rhythmic blindness' which takes place in the text and with which one can never have done (*Sp.*, p. 101/100). But the 'regular, rhythmic blindness' is, like Barth's hiddenness [*Vorborgenheit*] of God, constitutive. It is the 'relation of metaphysics to its other' (*Sp.*, p. 118/119). It is constitutive of discourse itself. It is the process of discourse, the logic of its referring and deferring in which the hermeneutical project is both disrupted and returned to, which is the focal interest of both Barth and Derrida. Discourse weaves a way of faith between the Spirit that questions, disrupts and promises and human attempts at representing this action. Discourse is the presentation of otherness *and* human representations of it; the Saying *and* the said, the Word *and* the words. For Barth, it mediates the 'twofold movement of the Word of God' (1.1, p. 179/186) as it hovers between memory and hope, giving and denying, a *theologia gloriae* and a *theologia crucis*, gospel and law,

---

10 Steven Smith, in his book *Argument to the Other*, claims that both Levinas and Barth argue *to* the Other. Argument is not based upon the presupposition of the Other, but upon 'the ultimate presupposition of responsibility to the Other . . . Whatever else we argue *for*, we argue *to* the Other, as a proposal for justice' (p. 6). In this form of argument there is a performing or ongoing practicalization of reason. 'The principle object of the Argument is to call attention to itself as a performing distinct from a thematizing' (p. 212). Nevertheless, a thematizing remains. Smith would concur, both Barth's and Levinas's texts function mimetically *and* prescriptively, as rhetorical strategies *and* sets of related propositions.

promise and demand. This Word does not proceed in a straight line (ibid.) and the indirect knowledge it gives rise to 'can only be thought of as in process [*im Vollzug begriffen zu denkende Aufhebung*] and never as completed' (1.1, p. 173/180). Theological discourse-as-process listens to what 'remains unsaid' (1.1, p. 181/188) and it awaits the coming of the Word, the eschatological promise. It constitutes the time between, relating the no longer to the not yet. It is inspired and promoted by the Holy Spirit and human faith. It takes, like faith, a temporal form (II.1, p. 158/177); it has, like the Spirit, a temporal presence (ibid.). Discourse itself – "we are not concerned with words as such' (II.1, p. 226/255) – is the interminable process of *analogia fidei*.

The textual strategy which permits the saying of what is unsaid, without its sense becoming equivocal, is allegory. Discourse, for Derrida, is 'allegorical metonymy' (*MPM*, p. 37). 'Metonymy' refers here to the unending chain of signifiers, each differing from another, each displacing the meaning of the other.[11] Allegorical metonymy both 'speaks of the other and makes the other speak'. It can make the other speak only because 'the other will have spoken first'. Because of the prior speaking of the other, then this speaking has no choice but to let the other speak. But this means that 'speech is always something other than what it says: it says the other who speaks "before" and "outside" it; it lets the other speak in the allegory' (*MPM*, pp. 37–8). Allegorical metonymy is, therefore, another description of the economy of *différance*. Barth's theology of the Word as a theological reading of *différance* is, then, *allegoria fidei* rather than *analogia fidei*.

Theological discourse as an abiding process of *allegoria fidei* distinguishes what Barth is doing from more traditional appreciations of analogy. In recognizing this distinction, the mistaken line of thinking pursued by those critics presupposing that Barth is working with traditional notions of analogy is made plain. Barth's analogy is not a comparison between two objects in which the nature of one is inferred from the nature of the other. A is not to B what P is to Q. 'This static, instead of dynamic, understanding of the analogy between our word and God's [*und*

---

[11] See note 6 pp. 212–13.

dem, was Gott ist] must, therefore, be expressly repudiated if we
are to adopt the term' (II.1, p. 231/261). Analogy is the process of
discourse expressing the fact that it is caught between past,
realized and future eschatology. As process, it repeats the
remembered presence of a promised hope. *Analogia fidei is* a
mimetic process, performing and presenting Derrida's 'double
law of Mnemosyne', where memory *both* points back to promise
and looks forward to its future realization. Derrida's economy of
différance describes the operation of this 'double law' and the
economy of *différance* read theologically – 'This will always be
possible. Who could forbid it? And in whose name?' (*P*, p. 539) –
is Barth's *analogia fidei*. We are always only on the way. The
'[u]nveiling and veiling thus designate the way which God goes
with us' and from first to last along this way there is 'a question of
the partial agreement and correspondence of our words with
God's being' (II.1, p. 236/266–7).

Derrida's economy of *différance*, therefore, offers Barth's theology
of the Word a coherence for what otherwise has been seen as a
contradiction which logically flaws his Christology and the
soteriological operation of the Trinity. As Derrida has written,
'Since it can no longer be subsumed by the generality of *logical*
contradiction, *différance* (the process of differentiation) permits a
differentiated account for the heterogeneous modes of conflic-
tuality, or, if you will, contradiction' (*Pos.*, p. 101). In the light of
such an economy, Barth's theological discourse is understood as
a rhetorical strategy presenting both the need to do and the
impossibility of doing theology. This is exactly the form, method
and content of Derrida's philosophical discourse, which presents
the inability and the inescapable burden of doing philosophy.
For both thinkers, the central problematic is the ineradicable
otherness which haunts discourse and yet the impossibility of
transcending metaphoricity and positing a real presence: 'There
is not ... a pure conceptual language which leaves the inadequate language of images [*Vorstellungen*] behind, which ... is, as
such, the language of truth' (II.1, p. 195/219).
    Christian theology as a rhetorical strategy examines the move
of language away from and toward meaning. It examines the

inner limitation of all human language in terms of the external limitation, that is the hiddenness of God revealed 'as the source and norm of our knowledge and speech' (II.1, p. 195/219). It examines the economy of *différance* and the experience of a quasi-transcendentalism which haunts its production and promotion. It then reads its findings in terms of what the church preaches, on the basis of the Scriptures, about the life and work of Jesus Christ. Its concern lies with the problematic nature of significance (and therefore signs) as this relates to Jesus Christ, the 'first, original and controlling sign of all signs' (II.1, p. 199/223). It is only in relation to this sign that any sign becomes theologically meaningful. Meaningful, that is, as a testimony to, not a correlate of, this controlling sign. Jesus Christ is the name of the remembered promise of a future presence, which circulates within the economy of *différance*. He is the promised Word, inaugurating and endlessly promoting the chain of signifiers which defer its final, realized presence. He, like *différance*, transcends difference and metaphysical polarities and 'makes the movement of signification possible' (*SP*, p. 142). He, like *différance*, is also immanent to the economy of the sign which erases his presence and endlessly defers his truth. Caught between two heterogeneous origins, the transcendent and the immanent, the divine and the human, *Rede* and *Sprache*, theological discourse is always an *analogia Christi*. The nature of theological discourse is, therefore, inseparable from the doctrine of Christ.

CHRISTOLOGY AND THE MIMETIC PROCESS

'It is impossible to listen at one and the same time to the two statements that Jesus of Nazareth is the Son of God and that the Son of God is Jesus of Nazareth. One hears either the one or the other or one hears nothing' (I.1, p. 180/188). This is the very crux of the logical contradiction which *différance* both negotiates and is implemented by. Jesus Christ becomes the question mark set against us. We stumble upon this question-mark when 'we suppose that we can treat of Him, speak and hear of Him – WITHOUT BEING SCANDALIZED' (*2R*, p. 280/263). In what seems an anticipation of Wittgenstein's investigations into 'aspect-blindness',[12] the movement of Barth's discourse attempts to convey the experience of a twofold 'continuous seeing' as distinct from 'seeing as'. Only Jesus as the incarnation relates representation as *'eintreten'* and *'vertreten'* to representation as *'darstellen'* and *'vorstellen'*. Jesus as the Word in words is, then, testified to in Barth's own theological discourse as *'repraesentieren'*, the movement of which exemplifies Derrida's economy of *différance*. Like his theological discourse, then, Barth's Christology must remain open both to a future fulfilment and a critical scepticism. It must always appear as a contradiction, but a contradiction in process – a movement towards synthesis and a deferral of it. The dynamic behind this process is desire conceived negatively as the project of human intentionality and positively as the work of the Holy Spirit. This dialectical process of human representations called into question by the revealedness of the Spirit, Barth analyses in the final paragraphs of chapter 5 in terms of the economy of Temptation.

Temptation is the recognition of being questioned by God, and it constitutes our participation in the economy of the Trinity. The questioning constitutes the relationship between humankind and the Godhead, human words and the divine Word. It is a moment of self-criticism and doubt which both requires and engenders faith. The moment is, then, both a de-constructive and a re-constructive process. 'By temptation faith is completely destroyed, and in that way completely established' (II.1, p. 248/280). All our knowing, thinking and writing partakes of this ontological insecurity. Our human desire and the project of our intentionality is for an embracing system. This desire is continually crossed by an alternative transcending desire which frustrates foreclosure: 'The confirmation which our systematic needs cannot itself be systematic under any name' (II.1, p. 249/282). And so the nature of Jesus Christ cannot be formulated in 'a Christological article [*Satz*] which we can now utilise as a key' (II.1, p. 250/285). The stasis of definition has to

---

[12] See *Philosophical Investigations*, part II, xi, and S. Mulhall's illuminating book which relates Wittgenstein to Heidegger on this matter, *On Being in the World* (Oxford: Oxford University Press, 1990).

give way to the process of writing itself: 'We can, therefore, only describe [*beschreiben*] Him again, and often, and in the last resort infinitely often' (II.1, p. 250/288). God's word made flesh can only be traced [*beschreiben*] within the infinite process of description itself. Christology can only be narratology.[13] The sphere of questioning, its de-construction and re-construction, is the sphere of Jesus Christ within which we, as the Church, move (II.1, p. 251/285). The Church becomes the community of both the question and the promise, the temptation and the comfort, the Cross and the Resurrection, which 'are the form [*Form*] of the grace of the incarnation applied to this man' (II.1, p. 253/286). Outlining the form of this incarnation by claiming a true knowledge of God and entering the sphere of temptation (ibid.) has been the burden of Barth's presentation itself. This is the movement within his theological discourse, an economy of *différance* which constitutes and inhabits the process of representing Christ's representation. It is the tracing in discourse of the veiling and unveiling of the Trinitarian God, inseparable from this economy of *différance* which forms the household rule for the community of the Church (II.1, p. 254/287).

The revelation of the Word does not occur and cannot occur in Barth's theology, and so its meaning is maintained in mystery. His discourse, as it meditates theologically upon its own possibility, repeats the promise of meaning [*repraesentieren*], mimetically. Derrida calls this 'the performative structure of the text in general *as* promise' (*MPM*, p. 93). Barth's text performs the process that crosses, cancels and recrosses the ontological disparity between the transcendent Word and the immanence of human words. In doing this it 'says' what cannot be said. This saying, the Word of God, resounds in the space opened up by disparity. It is a textual space 'where all the "sonorities" (echoes of meaning) ... penetrate each other and multiply in rapid, discontinuous motions'.[14] Only the writing, the theological discourse itself, presents this space within which the revelatory event has already occurred. The text remembers 'a past and a future yet unpresentable' (*P*, p. 544).

---

[13] See David Ford's *Barth and God's Story* (New York: Peter Lang, 1981).
[14] Preface to *Spurs: Nietzsche's Styles* by Stephano Agosti, p. 11.

As such, theological discourse typifies the nature of all discourse, for all discourse pursues and promotes 'at least the trace of a prior word', a word which is 'this primordial [*archi-originaire*] promise' (*P*, pp. 548–9). Derrida writes that without 'this divine promise which is also an injunction' there 'will only be conventional rhetoric . . . It will suffice to doubt this promise . . . in order to see unfold [*s'ouvrir*] . . . the field of rhetoricity' (*P*, p. 556). Theological discourse articulates the theology of discourse itself. The economy of signification *is* this economy of faith. Faith is not understood as a leap in the dark. It is not simply a matter for human choice. There is a quasi-transcendental promise that is given. Faith is, then, *both* gift and personal commitment. But there is no principle of faith evident prior to and outside the act of faith itself in Christian utterance/testimony. Faith is *both* Christian praxis and its condition. An irreducible openness to the trace of a promise realized in the past and to be realized in the future is not faith. As such, *différance*, as a law of textuality, cannot provide grounds for a natural theology. Faith is a commitment to reading this law theologically, in terms of the Christian Word and its proclamation in the Church. The ambivalent hope of *différance* articulates the infringement of the immanent by the quasi-transcendent, which makes faith a coherent response. Theological discourse, as a discourse of faith, mimes the experience of a time past and a time postponed; the experience of an ineluctable hope. It generates signs that await a truth to come (1.1, p. 14/13). Textuality itself incarnates theology's realism; it is a realism in which God's passing resonates in a language which has learnt how not to say.

CHAPTER 12

Conclusion: Comment ne pas parler[1]

Delivered in Jerusalem in 1986, '*Comment ne pas parler: dénég-rations*' is Derrida's most thorough examination of theological discourse to date. His concern is to clarify the difference between the economy of *différance* and the discourse of negative theology, but the essay is a sustained meditation upon how the difference cannot be clarified. We cannot identify the difference without also putting into play a deferral which forbids such a clinical division. There is neither a purely sacred nor a purely secular discourse.

Within the essay, Derrida sketches three paradigms for 'negative theology and its phantoms in a tradition of thought' (*P*, p. 562). These paradigms 'will surround a resonant space' (*P*, p. 562) within which *différance* and the trace are sited. It is within this space that, finally, we can situate Barth's theology of the Word and gather together the various models for a transcendent Saying in an immanent said which have been the burden of this book.

The first paradigm Derrida designates as Greek. But immediately two radically different movements are located in this tradition. The first movement is associated with the Good beyond Being in Plato's *Republic* and the second associated with descriptions of the *khora* in Plato's *Timaeus*. The first subscribes to

---

[1] I have left the title of this essay, along with two or three others, in French because no English translation can capture the ambivalence of the original. It can translate as 'How to Avoid Saying: Denials' (literally, 'how *not* to say: denials'). But it can also translate as 'How to Speak of the Negative: Concerning Negation' (literally, how not to *say:* a discourse on representations of the negative). The ambivalence is linked to Derrida's third paradigm for negative speech.

an *analogia entis* – a correlation between Being and what is beyond Being (*P*, p. 564). Here we can situate Rosenzweig's and Buber's work. Derrida partly locates Levinas's work here, without naming him: 'One might discern the effects of this analogical continuity in the rhetoric, the grammar and the logic of all discourses on the Good and the beyond Being' (*P*, p. 365). The second movement is characterized by *khora*,[2] which is characterized as beyond limits, placing and the *tertium quid* (*P*, p. 566). Derrida describes this *khora* as not belonging to the realm of the intelligible though 'participating' in some enigmatic way in the intelligible. It is an anchronie promoting further anchronie, for 'the spacing of *khora* introduces a disassociation and a *différance*' (*P*, p. 568). It is inhuman, atheological and ahistorical because it is an absolute singularity beyond the opposition of being and non-being (*P*, p. 569). In its uniqueness it is wholly other. Nevertheless, it leaves an unparalleled trace in language which bears an equivocal promise (ibid.). It can only be spoken about by a negative discourse [*la négativitié du discours*]. There are features of Derrida's understanding of *khora* which would apply both to his analysis of *archi-différance* and Barth's Word.

But Derrida distinguishes this negative discourse from his second paradigm, the Christian *via negativa* (as exemplified in the writings of Denys the Areopagite and Meister Eckhart). This is the apophatic route. Its characteristics are a teleology and a performative dimension which moves increasingly towards the origin or validation for such a performance (*P*, p. 572). This is a movement towards a grand unveiling of a single, generative principle. The textual strategy of Eckhart's sermons sets to work a 'multiplicity of voices and veils which he superimposes or removes like rinds or pelts, thematizing and exploring ... until there is that extreme despoliation' (*P*, p. 576). Here there is light and truth and 'an irreducible relation'. Nevertheless, this 'irreducible relation' must be communicated, and this involves explaining divine truths to mundane minds, so in order to teach the nature of the vision analogy is unavoidable (*P*, p. 580 – Derrida is quoting, at this point, from the writings of Denys the

---

[2] Derrida discusses the character of *khora* in a major article entitled '*Chora*', in *Poilikia: Etudes offertes à Jean-Pierre Vernant* (Paris, 1987), pp. 265–96.

the Areopagite). The logic of such an apophatic discourse is a logos of 'without' (*P*, p. 575), but an analogical correspondence exists in which the 'text of creation would be like the typographical inscription of the non-participable in the participable' (*P*, p. 582). Thus Derrida views apophatic discourse as essentially Greek: it combines the positive theology of *analogia entis* with the negativity of *khora*. The only difference is that here the apophasis triggers the process – the revelation commands its expression by provoking a desire to repeat the apophatic moment – whereas *khora* is passive. Apophatic discourse strives to conquer itself and arrive at ' "a Non-God, a Non-Intellect, a Non-Person, a Non-image" ' (*P*, p. 583 – Derrida is quoting Eckhart). This is Levinas's form of negative theology as Derrida commented upon it in 'Violence and Metaphysics'.

As we saw in chapter 8, a deconstruction operates within such a discourse. The immediacy is caught within the webs of language, and so, with Denys the Areopagite and with Eckhart, negative theology is ineluctably drawn into supplementation and commentary after the event. The economy of *différance* haunts negative theology; it constitutes the very text of negative theology. But for *différance* there is no moment of 'extreme despoliation'; there is no place from which to observe 'the nakedness of God'. There is a trace of the transcendent horizon, a threshold, but there is no crossing of 'the threshold of Being towards non-Being in order to see what is not presented' (*P*, p. 584). *Différance* always returns us to de-negation or how not to say [*comment ne pas parler*].

We cannot locate Barth's work, as we can locate Levinas's, within this paradigm for negative theology. His is not an apophatic discourse, for the apophasis is always qualified: 'we can certainly say what God's Word is, but we must say it indirectly. We must remember the forms in which it is real [*wirklich*] for us and we must learn [*entnehmen* – literally, to take away or remove] from these forms *how* it is' (1.1, p. 132/136). Here is Derrida's logic of how not to say, a logic emphasizing that revelation is in the past and we re-member the forms of the Word of God. Similar to the discourse of negative theology, these forms must be 'removed' from *how* God is, but this process of removing will only leave in 'the attainable human reflection

[*Spiegelbild*] of the unattainable divine What' (ibid.). Barth does not transcend language and gaze upon the 'nakedness of God'; he remains staring into a '*menschliche Spiegelbild*'. This human reflection displays [*repraesentiert*] the faith which 'recollects the past revelation of God and in this faith expects the future revelation that has yet to come' (1.1, p. 108/110). This is a theological affirmation of what still remains in question according to Derrida's law of textuality. For Derrida, this law can only be the 'condition for the possibility and impossibility of eschatology, the ironic allegory of messianism' (*MPM*, p. 145).

Derrida's third paradigm returns us to the work of Heidegger. Heidegger, as we saw, divides onto-theology from theology as the science of faith. Derrida recalls Heidegger's two examples of avoiding the word 'Being': the famous comment made in 1951 at a seminar in Zurich, when Heidegger remarked that 'If I were to write a theology, as I am sometimes tempted to do, then the word "Being" ought not to appear there [*vorkommen*]'; and the equally famous crossing out [*Durchstreichung*] of *Zur Seinsfrage* in 1952. Derrida's interest lies mainly with the first example. He draws attention to how, in making the statement, Heidegger has in some sense written 'a theology "without" the word "Being", a theology with and without God. He has done that which he said it would be necessary to avoid doing' (*P*, p. 592). He has therefore left 'a trace which is, perhaps, no longer his own, but which remains "quasi-owned" [*qui rests "quasiment" la sienne*]' (ibid.) We can note the hesitant 'perhaps', but it is this quasi-transcendence which concerns Derrida in this third paradigm of how to avoid saying. In disclosing the economy of *différance* in Heidegger's remarks, Derrida raises again the spectre of this quasi-transcendence and admits 'I am not sure that it is only a matter of rhetoric' (*P*, p. 593). The case remains open, the question of the theological remains very much in play in the '*scène d'écriture*'. Derrida concludes his lecture in an avalanche of questions which come to rest on 'Will a theology be possible?' (*P*, p. 595) – which is his own version of Heidegger's comment. For the tone and tense suggest a hope. But the possibility for a theology, if there is one, lies in the future. It haunts the margins of every text. It makes questioning significant.

Here we can locate Karl Barth, who, from 1916 when he

recognized that 'our dialectic has reached a dead end',[3] understood theology was a necessary but impossible task. He makes explicit from the opening section of his *Church Dogmatics* that the 'concept of truths of revelation in the sense of Latin propositions given and sealed once for all with divine authority in both wording and meaning is theologically impossible ... [I]t is a fact that revelation ... is thus strictly future for us' (1.1, p. 15/14). The Church's proclamation, and theology's examination of it, must mean repetition, representation and textuality. Karl Barth's theology of the Word in words, his Christology and the whole edifice of his incarnational theology are theological readings of a law of repetition, representation and textuality described by Jacques Derrida as the economy of *différance*. Or, put another way, Barth has shown how the unerasable theological question inherent to all discourse can become the basis for a dogmatics. Either way, Derrida has provided Barth's theology of language in chapter 5 of *Church Dogmatics* with a philosophical supplement. Barth provides Derrida's economy of *différance* with a theological supplement.

Such a conclusion does not theologize Derrida's work. Derrida remains 'on the threshold'. His is a metaphysics of liminality. He, like Heidegger, keeps the question of theology open. He, unlike Barth, makes no prior commitment of faith. His trace of a gift, a promise, a yes, a hope bears none of the specifics of Christian proclamation or Jewish eschatology. Such a conclusion allows us to see how the coherence of Barth's theology of the Word only emerges clearly in the crisis of logocentrism, the crisis of representation, fostered by postmodernism. Rather than encouraging theology to pin its tattered hopes on a post-Christian materialism, this crisis has been seen as the very crux of theological discourse. The postmodern critique of logocentrism actually generates theological investigation; an investigation particularly into the nature of incarnation.

What the consequences of these observations are must now become the basis for a postmodern theology of the Word.

---

[3] Quoted by Busch, *Karl Barth: His Life*, from a newspaper article written by Barth in 1916, p. 92.

Index